Bloomberg Visual Guide to

Municipal Bonds

Robert Doty

BLOOMBERG PRESS
An Imprint of
WILEY

How to Use This Book

The Bloomberg Visual series is meant to serve as the all-encompassing, yet easy-to-follow, guide on today's most relevant finance and trading topics. The content truly lives up to the series name by being highly visual; all charts are in color and presented in a large format for ease of use and readability. Other strong visual attributes include consistent elements that function as additional learning aids for the reader:

- Key Points: Primary ideas and takeaways, designed to help the reader skim through definitions and text.

- Definitions: Terminology and technical concepts that arise in the discussion.

- Step-by-Step: Tutorials designed to ensure that readers understand and can execute each section of a multi-phase process.

- Do It Yourself: Worksheets, formulas, and calculations.

- Bloomberg Functionality Cheat Sheet: For Bloomberg terminal users, a back-of-the-book summary of relevant functions for the topics and tools discussed.

For e-reader users, The Bloomberg Visual series is available as an enhanced e-book and offers special features, like an interactive Test Yourself section where readers can test their newly honed knowledge and skills. The enhanced e-book version also includes video tutorials and special pop-up features. It can be purchased wherever e-books are sold.

Bloomberg Visual Guide to

Municipal Bonds

Robert Doty

BLOOMBERG PRESS
An Imprint of

Published by John Wiley & Sons, Inc., Hoboken, New Jersey.

Published simultaneously in Canada.

For general information on our other products and services or for technical support, please contact our Customer Care Department within the United States at (800) 762-2974, outside the United States at (317) 572-3993 or fax (317) 572-4002.

Wiley also publishes its books in a variety of electronic formats. Some content that appears in print may not be available in electronic books. For more information about Wiley products, visit our web site at www.wiley.com.

NOTICE

Notices and other materials and information published by the Municipal Securities Rulemaking Board (MSRB) are subject to change and revocation. They are included in this book as they exist at a specific time. For additional and updated information, you should consult the Board's website at *http://www.msrb.org*.

"EMMA" is a registered trademark of the Municipal Securities Rulemaking Board, and is used in this book with permission of the Board.

NOTICE

Standard & Poor's Financial Services LLC (S&P) does not guarantee the accuracy, completeness, timeliness or availability of any information, including ratings, and is not responsible for any errors or omissions (negligent or otherwise), regardless of the cause, or for the results obtained from the use of ratings. S&P GIVES NO EXPRESS OR IMPLIED WARRANTIES, INCLUDING, BUT NOT LIMITED TO, ANY WARRANTIES OF MERCHANTABILITY OR FITNESS FOR A PARTICULAR PURPOSE OR USE. S&P SHALL NOT BE LIABLE FOR ANY DIRECT, INDIRECT, INCIDENTAL, EXEMPLARY, COMPENSATORY, PUNITIVE, SPECIAL OR CONSEQUENTIAL DAMAGES, COSTS, EXPENSES, LEGAL FEES, or LOSSES (INCLUDING LOST INCOME OR PROFITS AND OPPORTUNITY COSTS) IN CONNECTION WITH ANY USE OF RATINGS. S&P's ratings are statements of opinions and are not statements of fact or recommendations to purchase, hold or sell securities. They do not address the market value of securities or the suitability of securities for investment purposes, and should not be relied on as investment advice

---

Library of Congress Cataloging-in-Publication Data:

Doty, Robert, 1942-
 Bloomberg visual guide to municipal bonds / Robert Doty.
  p. cm. — (Bloomberg visual ; 136)
 Includes index.
  ISBN 978-1-118-15255-3 (pbk.); ISBN 978-1-118-20900-4 (ebk); ISBN 978-1-118-21697-2 (ebk); ISBN 978-1-118-21709-2 (ebk); ISBN 978-1-1183-4187-2 (ebk);
ISBN 978-1-1183-4188-9 (ebk)
  1. Municipal bonds. I. Title.
 HG4726.D68 2012
 332.63'233—dc23
                    2011038807

Printed in the United States of America

10 9 8 7 6 5 4 3 2 1

MIX
Paper from
responsible sources
FSC® C101537
www.fsc.org

To Deborah

Contents

Acknowledgments

I wish to acknowledge the especially generous and extremely valuable contributions made to this book by a number of especially helpful individuals and organizations from the municipal securities market's professional, issuer, and investor sectors.

I am grateful to Bloomberg Press and John Wiley & Sons for having confidence in me to work on this application of Bloomberg's concept for an imaginative book bridging both the old print tradition and still-emerging electronic technology, with all of its exciting new forms of textual, graphic, and electronic communication. This book is a genuine team product involving outstanding professionals from both Bloomberg and John Wiley & Sons. Although I do not know, and have never met, some of those professionals, I am aware of important contributions made by Judy Howarth, as editor, Evan Burton, Bill Falloon, and Chris Gage of John Wiley & Sons, and by Stephen Isaacs and Joe Mysak of Bloomberg. Without their significant participation, creativity, and guidance, this book would not have been possible. In particular,

Sowjana Sivaloganathan of Bloomberg was invaluable and truly impressive with her abilities to generate data and creative ideas regarding useful information. She added substantially to the value of the book.

I benefited greatly from comments and generous cooperation by many market participants who allowed me to cite or quote them, or who readily provided their views and insights on specific subjects. That content was substantial and invaluable for examination and presentation of issues associated with municipal securities.

For substantial insights, assistance, and criticisms that added immensely to the content and subject matter in this book I extend special thanks to James Spiotto of Chapman and Cutler, the most knowledgeable lawyer in the nation regarding municipal bankruptcies pursuant to Chapter 9 of the Bankruptcy Code; John Petersen of George Mason University, long recognized as the leading economist studying defaults and other economic aspects of the municipal securities market, a leading contributor over the past 35-plus years to efforts to improve municipal disclosure to investors, and currently a member of the Municipal Securities Rulemaking Board; Joe Mysak of Bloomberg, for decades an especially articulate and well-informed journalist and observer and, when warranted, critic of the municipal securities market and its constituents; Matt Fabian of Municipal Market Advisors, a leading and oft-quoted spokesperson from a truly outstanding firm serving investors, issuers, and bankers in the market with publication of a daily wealth of data, information and insightful analysis regarding market activity; Tim Schaefer of Magis Advisors, a respected financial advisor to issuers of municipal securities, an adviser to investors, and a former bond trader who provided especially helpful comments framed for the benefit of investors; Richard Ciccarone of Merritt Research Services LLC, a widely respected municipal securities analyst who provided helpful data on continuing disclosure compliance; Michael Bartolotta of First Southwest, a brilliant banker and technician, and in 2010–2011 the chair of the Municipal Securities Rulemaking Board, who emphasized especially, based upon his long experience, information that investors need in making their investment and trading decisions; and

Chuck Youtz, a successful investment banker of George K. Baum & Co., who provided both helpful comments and significant technological access.

Other individuals cheerfully provided important insights, information, encouragement, and criticisms that I took to heart. They include John Murphy, bond counsel, of Stradling Yocca Carlson & Rauth; Gary Pope, also bond counsel, of Pope Zeigler; Alan Hoban, comptroller of the Massachusetts Housing Finance Agency; Michael Hillyard, an experienced individual investor; and Todd Meierhenry, bond counsel, of Meierhenry Sargent LLP. Among organizations that allowed me to cite or quote them are the Municipal Securities Rulemaking Board, Standard & Poor's, Moody's Investors Service, Fitch Ratings, and the California Municipal Bond Advisor.

Nevertheless, the views expressed in this book are solely my own. I stress that cooperation by various parties, as identified herein, does not signify that those parties necessarily agree with me on any or all issues discussed in this book. Indeed, some may disagree strongly on particular topics. They certainly do not share in my errors or mistakes.

Preface

Experts Forecast: Municipal Bonds in Serious Danger!

Widespread Defaults Predicted!

Hundreds of Billions in Municipal Bonds at Risk of Default!

Municipal Bankruptcies Loom!

In 2010 and 2011, a relentless drumbeat of dramatic, and at times irresponsible, headlines—such as those paraphrased above—alarmed municipal securities investors with serious, and unwarranted, exaggerations of market risks. Pundits—talking heads—predicted large-scale defaults of hundreds of billions of dollars of municipal securities, and even bankruptcies. Certain news media presented variations on the theme. News stories frequently highlighted valid criticisms of sometimes significant governmental pension fund liabilities and excessive spending in unbalanced budgets. In gigantic leaps of logic, however, some (but not all) stories were accompanied by assertions of purported disastrous consequences overhanging the municipal market portending a municipal securities version of the financial crisis.

While state and local governments certainly have experienced financial stress, some self-induced, the predictions of collapse and doom were not fulfilled. This book explains why.

A massive volume of truly frightening information confronted investors. In response to unduly pessimistic statements, large numbers of investors sold municipal securities at disadvantageous prices or withdrew their monies from municipal bond funds under conditions of stress. Many investors were harmed needlessly.

Given the real potential for serious financial harm to so many people, the headline sound bites were akin to screaming "fire" in a crowded theater. If people do that, they had better have solid grounds to believe there really is a fire. Those who did so failed to have a genuine basis for excessively dire predictions.

There is no cause for panic. Much media hype stemmed from self-anointed experts, some of whom

> **KEY POINT:**
>
> While state and local governments certainly have experienced financial stress, some self-induced, the predictions of collapse and doom were not fulfilled. This book explains why.

> **KEY POINT:**
>
> If people scream "fire" in a crowded theater, they had better have solid grounds to believe there really is a fire. They lacked that foundation in making dire predictions for municipal securities.

were conflicted and self-promotional. Some were expert in other financial sectors, but not in municipal securities. Many news analyses were written by well-meaning journalists who were unfamiliar with the nature of municipal credit structures and who made inaccurate and ill-informed assumptions regarding structures prevailing in the market.

As I discuss in this book, these analyses evidence fundamental misconceptions regarding the strength and enforceability of key municipal general obligation and traditional revenue securities credits. For other less secure lease-purchase (lease certificate of participation) credits of general governments (cities, counties, etc.), there seems to be an assumption that those governments would choose to serve their constituencies by defaulting. That certainly has not been the case historically, however—both over the long-term and also during the financial crisis and afterward.

Moreover, I do not see evidence that the pattern will change even in the face of fiscal stress, as it would result in substantial future difficulties in terms of providing services.

For certain other types of municipal securities, there are indeed risks that I discuss, but interestingly, these are not the types of credits upon which the pundits and media reports are focusing.

So, those analyses constitute a serious disservice to investors. Municipal securities investors are often retirees who benefit from owning tax-exempt municipal securities for stability and preservation of income. Other investors may be parents saving for their children's college educations, at times, but not always, through state-sponsored Section 529 Plans.

These and other individual investors are especially vulnerable to hype because they often do not themselves grasp important specifics or the substantial diversity of the municipal securities market. After suffering enormous equity portfolio losses in the financial crisis, they do not need to suffer financial harm again.

Investors, like you, need balanced information. In seeking to provide that balance, I have no intention of papering over or attempting to justify or deny unwise, or at times reckless, governmental employee benefit practices or irresponsible failures to balance governmental budgets, when those occur.

I do not pretend that municipal budgeting or disclosure practices are all they could be. They aren't.

Yet, in the midst of the noise, you should understand that it is taxpayers, rate payers, and the general public served by state and local governments, not their investors, who will suffer from fiscal distress and even mismanagement.

Another significant development in the municipal market is the severe reduction in the use of bond insurance. From its beginning in the early 1970s, bond insurance had evolved into a staple of the market. In the process, what became seven triple-A bond insurers provided credit enhancement by the 2000s for more than half of municipal securities issued annually.

That seeming credit homogeneity was always an illusion, but searching for simplicity, investors acted otherwise. In reality, most bond insurers—all private companies—behaved like many other private companies and, in the process, over-reached. In addition to municipal securities, they began to insure subprime mortgage pools, collateralized debt obligations, and other risky financial products that they understood poorly, and regarding which they all-too-often failed to conduct careful due diligence. Investors did not know this because, as Bloomberg has reported, some companies did not disclose it. Now, today, many investors find themselves holding substantial volumes of municipal securities that are no longer rated triple-A and, therefore, have lost market value.

The perception of bond insurance homogeneity has disappeared. Investors have found that they must review information regarding, and must understand, specific municipal securities the investors are considering.

This book is intended to point you in appropriate directions in terms of resources and concepts that should be helpful to you in your efforts to make careful investments.

It should be of some comfort that, almost without exception, investors in traditional municipal securities, which are those issued for essential governmental purposes (e.g., city halls, streets, key school facilities, water and wastewater systems, and other publicly-owned utility systems) will be paid regardless of governmental fiscal practices. Those traditional securities are sound because they are secured by obligated taxes, or by dedicated revenue streams, that are enforceable under state law.

In addition, state and local governments are predisposed to honor their obligations, and with few exceptions, debt service on municipal securities is generally only a relatively small part of state and local budgets.

Whatever their faults—and those faults exist too often from the perspective of taxpayers, rate payers, and the general public—municipal issuers and municipal securities have a demonstrated historical record that is surpassed in terms of performance only by United States Treasury securities.

Certainly, there are specific municipal securities market sectors with greater risks (and offering potentially greater rewards) than are found in other municipal market sectors. The riskier sectors rely upon private credits or performance or upon revenues anticipated from start-up or rapidly-expanding enterprise projects. This is discussed in more detail under Chapter 6, "Greater Rewards and Greater Risks."

Still, bankruptcy is almost nonexistent among major municipal debt issuers, with most Chapter 9 bankruptcies filed by small special districts. As I explain, the vast majority of state and local governments assiduously avoid default and bankruptcy. Despite the predictions, defaults and bankruptcies actually decreased recently. Even if a few defaults and bankruptcies do occur, they do not fall within, or close to, the numerical range predicted by some. Debunking false prophets is not, however, my sole goal. Taxable municipal securities are drawing into the market new investors who want to know more about the market and its practices.

SMART INVESTOR TIP

The perception of bond insurance homogeneity has disappeared. Investors have found that they must review information regarding, and must understand, specific municipal securities the investors are considering.

SMART INVESTOR TIP

Municipal issuers have a demonstrated historical record that is surpassed only by United States Treasury securities.

SMART INVESTOR TIP

Bankruptcy is virtually nonexistent among major municipal issuers.

So that you and other municipal investors can be better prepared to sort through the confusion, I believe that you and they deserve to receive a balanced and accurate picture.

I intend this book to explain, hopefully in a measured, rational, and understandable tone, the nature and diversity of municipal securities credit structures, to demonstrate the dependability of the overwhelming majority of municipal securities, and to point out particular market sectors that may yield greater rewards, but also present greater risks.

This book also directs you to information sources and useful market tools resulting from recent market enhancements, so as to assist you in making informed investment decisions.

In providing my perspectives, I wish to reassure you, and also when appropriate to caution you, so that you may be able both to preserve your principal and to receive fair returns on your portfolio.

Five States Dominate the $3.7 Trillion Municipal Bond Market

The pie chart (Exhibit P1) shows issuer concentration in the municipal market. Of the $3.71 trillion in total outstanding debt sold, the top 10 states and their municipalities account for $2.15 trillion, or 58 percent. The top five states alone—California, New York, Texas, Illinois, and Florida—account for $1.65 trillion, or almost 46 percent of the entire market. Exhibit P2 shows the amount outstanding that Bloomberg has calculated for each

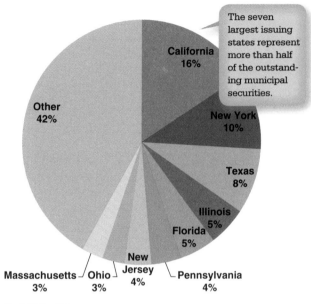

Exhibit P1

Source: "Bloomberg Brief: Municipal Market" (June 21, 2011). Chart and table reprinted with permission. Copyright 2011 Bloomberg L.P. All rights reserved.

state and its various issuers. The amount outstanding includes both long- and short-term issuance (fixed- and variable-rate), prerefunded and escrowed-to-maturity issues and the full accreted value of all capital appreciation bonds sold, as well as bonds marketed on behalf of corporations and not-for-profit organizations. It excludes bonds sold as derivatives, such as tender option bonds sold from a trust.

State	Amount Outstanding for Investors (Billion)	State	Amount Outstanding for Investors (Billion)
California	585.7	Oregon	37.4
New York	373.6	Alabama	36.5
Texas	320.0	Nevada	33.4
Illinois	190.8	DC	30.5
Florida	182.5	Mississippi	26.1
Pennsylvania	148.4	Utah	24.8
New Jersey	135.5	Kansas	24.2
Ohio	113.4	Iowa	21.2
Massachusetts	107.1	Oklahoma	20.5
Puerto Rico	105.1	Nebraska	18.4
Michigan	88.7	New Mexico	17.9
Washington	83.9	Hawaii	16.5
Georgia	79.1	Rhode Island	15.0
Colorado	69.9	Montana	14.2
Virginia	66.5	Arkansas	13.0
Arizona	61.7	New Hampshire	12.2
Indiana	61.1	Alaska	11.8
North Carolina	60.3	West Virginia	11.8
Missouri	58.9	Idaho	11.5
Minnesota	55.8	Delaware	9.3
Tennessee	50.5	Maine	8.8
Maryland	50.3	South Dakota	7.8
Connecticut	47.8	Vermont	6.1
Wisconsin	47.3	North Dakota	4.1
South Carolina	40.9	Wyoming	4.0
Kentucky	38.5	Virgin Islands	2.5
Louisiana	38.3	Guam	2.0
		Total (including other territories)	3712.4

Exhibit P2

*Source: "Bloomberg Brief: Municipal Market" (June 21, 2011).
Chart and table reprinted with permission. Copyright 2011
Bloomberg L.P. All rights reserved.*

CHAPTER 1

Introduction

The municipal securities market is widely misunderstood by commentators, investors, issuers, regulators, legislators, and even many market professionals.

In reality, the market consists of two vastly different markets. One market is traditional municipal securities that are very sound and are secure, with extremely low default risks. The other is a market of readily identifiable, much riskier securities dependent primarily upon private performance (profit and nonprofit) or issued for start-up or rapidly expanding projects. That second municipal securities market deserves significantly greater attention from everyone.

Municipal securities are issued by state and local governments. Despite considerable negative publicity in the media and from certain pundits, traditional municipal securities are safe. That is, they have evidenced extremely low payment default rates historically. Further, despite unarguable fiscal stress resulting from the financial crisis and from pension and other employee benefit costs, a key feature of traditional municipal securities for essential purposes is that the securities structures are strongly protective of investors. The net result is that those state and local government stresses will become burdens on the taxpayers long before they will harm investors. Indeed, it is highly unlikely that investors will suffer in the case of the traditional municipal securities. There are, however, certain municipal securities that warrant a closer look and greater rewards. This book seeks to identify many of those for you.

What Are Municipal Securities?

Municipal securities are debt securities issued by state and local governments primarily to fund governmental projects and programs. Municipal securities are debt securities—effectively, loans—payable from taxes or governmental or other project revenues.

The following screen (Exhibit 1.1) from the Bloomberg Terminal illustrates the volume of municipal securities issued by certain states and nationally from January 1 through August 5, 2010.

YTDM 2010   Muni **YTDM**

	Competitive	Negotiated	Bloomberg Municipal Issuance YTD Total
1) Northeast	YTD Issuance(Mlns)	YTD Issuance(Mlns)	YTD Issuance(Mlns)
6) New York	4584 08/05	13356 08/05	17940 08/05
7) New Jersey	886 08/05	3505 08/05	4390 08/05
8) Massachusetts	1534 08/05	3152 08/05	4686 08/05
2) Midwest			
9) Illinois	418 08/05	7345 08/05	7763 08/05
10) Ohio	89 08/05	3163 08/05	3252 08/05
11) Michigan	465 08/05	2256 08/05	2721 08/05
3) South			
12) Texas	1394 08/05	10632 08/05	12026 08/05
13) Florida	1943 08/05	4284 08/05	6227 08/05
14) Virginia	1767 08/05	1109 08/05	2876 08/05
4) West			
15) California	1954 08/05	12934 08/05	14888 08/05
16) Washington	2264 08/05	2357 08/05	4621 08/05
17) Oregon	263 08/05	1881 08/05	2144 08/05
5) United States			
18) Taxable	2456 08/05	11325 08/05	13781 08/05
19) Bank Qualified	3664 08/05	5628 08/05	9292 08/05
20) US Issuance	33079 08/05	97003 08/05	130083 08/05

Australia 61 2 9777 8600 Brazil 5511 3048 4500 Europe 44 20 7330 7500 Germany 49 69 9204 1210 Hong Kong 852 2977 6000
Japan 81 3 3201 8900   Singapore 65 6212 1000   U.S. 1 212 318 2000   Copyright 2011 Bloomberg Finance L.P.
SN 268301 CDT   GMT-5:00 G515-401-2 10-Aug-2011 09:36:05

Exhibit 1.1
Reprinted with permission from Bloomberg. Copyright 2011 Bloomberg L.P. All rights reserved.

The following table (Exhibit 1.2) and graph (Exhibit 1.3), based upon Bloomberg data, provide the annual volumes of long-term, fixed-rate municipal securities issued nationally from 2003 through 2010. The issuance in 2009 and 2010 reflects the issuance of Build America Bonds (BABs) and other taxable municipal securities subsidized under the American Recovery and Reinvestment Act of 2009 (ARRA). In the first half of 2011, however, issuance declined following the expiration of the BABs and other subsidy programs

Year	Annual LT Fixed-Rate Issuance (Bn)
2003	293
2004	367
2005	312
2006	296
2007	338
2008	281
2009	379
2010	408

Exhibit 1.2

Reprinted with permission from Bloomberg. Copyright 2011 Bloomberg L.P. All rights reserved.

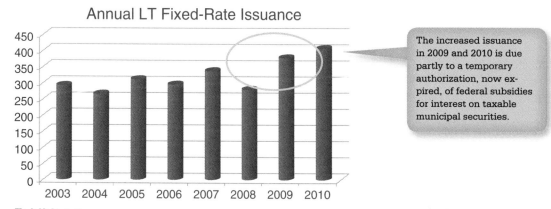

Annual LT Fixed-Rate Issuance

The increased issuance in 2009 and 2010 is due partly to a temporary authorization, now expired, of federal subsidies for interest on taxable municipal securities.

Exhibit 1.3

Reprinted with permission from Bloomberg. Copyright 2011 Bloomberg L.P. All rights reserved.

As discussed throughout this book, some other municipal securities provide funding that benefits private parties.

The two polar categories of uses of municipal securities—governmental and private—lead to vastly different investment considerations.

You should be aware of these, and other, distinctions among the enormous diversity of municipal securities and of their implications for you and your investments.

How Do Municipal Securities Differ from Corporate Securities?

Municipal securities are quite different from corporate securities in many respects discussed throughout this book. Briefly, municipal securities are not equity securities. Investors in municipal securities do not receive ownership interests in the issuing governmental entities (or even in private borrowers that gain access to the market through the governments).

Further, even as debt securities, municipal securities for governmental purposes are very different from corporate debt securities. The governmental issuers of municipal securities borrow for different reasons than do corporations.

For example, unlike corporations, municipal issuers rarely borrow for leverage. That is, they do not borrow funds that the issuers intend to be invested at higher yields. Municipalities do not borrow to increase shareholder value because there are no shareholders. Municipalities rarely go out of existence; corporations often do so. Few municipalities compete directly with other municipalities or with the private sector, but rather, with a few exceptions (e.g., certain toll roads, public educational institutions, and public hospitals) they tend to operate natural monopolies. Except in the case of municipal securities payable by private parties, municipal securities are not payable from private "earnings," but from taxes and governmental user revenues—user fees—imposed for governmental services. Regarding private involvement in some types of municipal securities issues, see Chapter 4, "General Fund and Other Municipal Securities," the section entitled "Private Involvement."

The screen in Exhibit 1.4 from the Bloomberg Terminal illustrates, in a partial listing, some of the diversity of municipal securities.

How Sound Are Municipal Securities?

State and local governments have issued trillions of dollars of municipal securities over many decades with very few defaults and almost no bankruptcies for major municipal issuers.

When defaults occur, they do so almost entirely in transactions with readily-identifiable characteristics—reliance on private credits or performance or upon startup or rapidly-expanding enterprises. See Chapter 6, "Greater Rewards and Greater Risks."

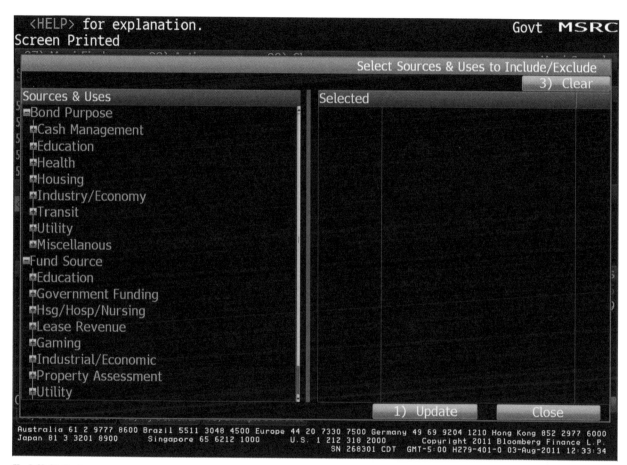

Exhibit 1.4

What Is the Diversity and Size of the Market?

The municipal securities market is a vast market with enormous diversity. According to Bloomberg, approximately $3.7 trillion of municipal securities are outstanding (the Federal Reserve makes a lower estimate of $2.9 trillion). Ernesto A. Lanza, deputy executive director and chief legal officer to the Municipal Securities Rulemaking Board (MSRB), testified that there are about 1.5 million municipal securities outstanding. (See "For Additional Information" at the end of this chapter.)

Exhibits 1.5 and 1.6 from "Bloomberg Brief: Municipal Market" illustrate, as of July 20, 2011, (1) the "Volume" of municipal securities issued from January 1 through that date in 2011 and the then-pending "New Supply;" (2) selected sizeable municipal securities offerings "In the Pipeline" as of that date; and (3) the results of then-recent "Long Term Bond Sales Results."

For many, there also are a surprising number of municipal securities issuers. The Securities and Exchange Commission (SEC) estimates that there are 50,000 municipal securities issuers, while the Municipal Securities Rulemaking Board (MSRB) estimates 80,000. Joe Mysak,

VOLUME

NEW SUPPLY:		SOLD YTD	TRADED		OFFERINGS	
30-day	⬇	$84.4 Bln (Neg Fixed LT)	$7.1 Bln	⬇	$10.9 Bln	⬆
$10.5 Bln	0.5%	$27.6 Bln (Comp Fixed LT)	(MSRB)	14%	(Bloomberg Pick)	23%

IN THE PIPELINE

MUNICIPALITY	AMOUNT
Washington	$741 million GO
Maine Health and Higher Ed	$290 million Rev
San Buenaventura Health CA	$346 million Rev
Maryland	$618 million GO
San Diego Water	$98 million Rev
Montgomery County MD	$579 million GO

Exhibit 1.5

Source: "Bloomberg Brief: Municipal Market" (July 20, 2011). Chart reprinted with permission. Copyright 2011 Bloomberg L.P. All rights reserved.

Results of Sales

Long-Term Bond Sales Results

Selling Date	Issue	State	Tax	Amt (MM)	1 Year	5 Year	10 Year	20 Year	Status	Type	Senior Manager
07/18	Texas pub fin auth-ref	TX	N	344.02	3.000/NRO	5.000/1.330	5.000/2.890	4.000/4.200	Final	Negt	Siebert brandford shank
07/18	Tampa bay water-a-ref	FL	N	140.65	2.000/0.400	5.000/1.690	3.125/3.210	-	Final	Negt	Citigroup global mkts inc.
07/18	Washington-b2	WA	N	89.35	-	5.000/1.360	5.000/2.880	4.000/4.080	Final	Negt	Jp morgan securities inc.
07/18	Mountain view regl pk-a	CA	N	39.03	2.000/1.125	4.000/3.030	5.000/4.600	5.500/5.600	Final	Negt	Stone & youngberg llc
07/18	Florida comm wtr/swr-ref	FL	Q	8.69	2.000/0.700	2.500/2.040	4.000/3.600	4.750/4.780	Final	Negt	Crews & associates inc.
07/19 11:00	Eastport-south manor csd	NY	N	20.65	-	2.000/1.350	3.000/2.880	4.000/NRO	Awarded	Comp	Ubs financial services
07/19 11:00	Dodge cnty	WI	N	16.09	2.000/NRO	3.000/1.450	3.000/2.950	4.200/4.200	Awarded	Comp	Robert w. Baird & co. Inc.
07/19 11:00	Saint paul isd #625-ref	MN	N	16.01	-	4.000/1.280	3.000/2.870	-	Awarded	Comp	Robert w. Baird & co. Inc.

Exhibit 1.6

Source: "Bloomberg Brief: Municipal Market" (July 20, 2011). Chart reprinted with permission. Copyright 2011 Bloomberg L.P. All rights reserved.

a well-regarded long-time market observer with Bloomberg, estimated, based upon Census data, that there are 90,000 state and local governments in the United States. Not all of those governmental entities, however, are securities issuers.

The vast majority of those issuers enter the market only infrequently. They and their officials are not particularly sophisticated regarding municipal finance, disclosure practices, or the informational needs of investors. Instead, as one might expect, they focus strongly on local concerns.

Municipal issuers include states, state agencies, counties, cities, towns, townships, school districts, colleges and universities, public hospitals, water and sewer agencies and other publicly-owned utilities, transit agencies, toll road and other transportation agencies, conservation agencies, fire districts, joint action agencies, housing agencies, stadium authorities, and numerous types of other special purpose agencies, authorities and districts. There also are governmental issuers

of "conduit" securities that provide funding for private borrowers. See Chapter 12, "Investor Questions and Answers (Q&As)," the section entitled "What Are Conduit Financings?"

Municipal securities come in a number of forms, including bonds, notes, lease revenue bonds, and certificates of participation (COPs) in underlying leases or installment purchase contracts.

Municipal securities are payable from many different sources, varying from one securities issue to another. Some are payable from specific obligated taxes. Often, communities are obligated to raise taxes to whatever level is required in order to pay the principal of and interest on the securities. Other municipal securities are payable from highly reliable revenue streams collected from users of water or wastewater systems, or other essential governmental enterprises.

Still other municipal securities are paid from hospital revenues, toll road or bridge tolls, university tuitions and other revenues, nursing home fees, stadium

KEY POINT:

The vast majority of municipal issuers enter the market only infrequently. They and their officials are not particularly sophisticated regarding municipal finance, disclosure practices or the informational needs of investors.

KEY POINT:

In order to continue to serve their citizens, unlike private corporations, state and local governments must remain in existence and in operation and must have ready access to the municipal securities market for cash flow and for essential project and program financing.

and arena rental payments by sports teams, mortgage payments by first-time homeowners or owners of multifamily housing properties, loan payments by private businesses receiving funding in industrial development bond issues, and many other public or private sources permitted under federal tax law and state laws.

What Is the Historical Record of Municipal Securities?

In the midst of such extensive diversity, one basic characteristic of municipal securities market sectors is that, with only a few exceptions, they have been quite sound historically. Debt service on municipal securities is generally only a relatively small part—3% to 6% is a common estimate—of state and local budgets.

Municipal issuers are loathe to default on governmental securities because they must preserve their reputations in order to maintain access to the market. Unlike corporations, state and local governments virtually never go out of business. They must continue to serve their citizens and, to do that, must continue to obtain funding for their projects and programs. Municipal issuers cannot afford to alienate investors.

Historically, data on municipal defaults present issues as to how comprehensive records may be. On one hand, there may be defaults that have not been reported. On the other hand, when an issuer or borrower misses one payment, or a portion of a payment, the entire principal amount of the securities issue may be reported as

"defaulted." Nevertheless, it is possible to draw reasonable conclusions, to detect trends, and to identify those municipal market sectors most prone to defaults. You may wish to keep in mind these data strengths and weaknesses as you read the following information.

From July 1, 2009, to January 28, 2011, there were defaults in terms of payments to investors on 258 municipal securities, according to Municipal Market Advisors (MMA), an independent municipal research firm that serves investors, dealers, and issuers. Only 15 of those were securities that had been rated initially. Given 25,000 rated municipal issues outstanding, according to MMA, that is a default rate of .01%. (See "For Additional Information" at the end of the chapter.)

In this vein, on February 14, 2011, Matt Fabian, Managing Director of MMA, testified as follows—

MMA maintains a database of all ongoing default and impairment filings made to the MSRB's EMMA system since July 1, 2009. These show that current municipal default activity is largely confined to smaller, non-rated transactions with security pledges that skew almost entirely to so-called "risky" sectors, meaning bond types that have been responsible for the large majority of payment defaults over the last four decades. As of January 28, 2011, there were $8.1Bn of municipal bonds outstanding (issued by 258 different entities) where there is an uncured default in either principal or interest. Of those 258 entities, 117 were special districts created to speculate on the development of a real estate property or properties, 47 were bonds *backed by the net income of an apartment building, and 27 were bonds backed by nursing homes. Only 15 of the 258 entities sold bonds that carried any rating at all, implying an effective default rate of less than 0.1% among the 25,000 or so rated municipal entities. Finally, none of these 258 bonds in payment default are "traditional" munis, meaning governmental general obligation bonds.*

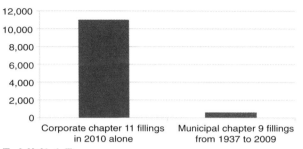

Exhibit 1.7
Source: Data provided by James Spiotto, Chapman and Cutler, Chicago.

(Note: Ratings for this purpose may include ratings based upon credit enhancement regardless of whether the underlying municipal securities were rated.)

Meanwhile, according to James Spiotto, a widely-recognized bankruptcy expert with Chapman and Cutler in Chicago, as of September 30, 2011, there had been only 256 municipal bankruptcies in the prior 30 years, or about 8.5 per year. (These data do not include Chapter 11 filings because those are for private parties, not local governments.) Chapter 9 of the Bankruptcy Code relates solely to municipal bankruptcy filings, subject to state permission. Mr. Spiotto also pointed out that the 627 municipal bankruptcies that have occurred since the enactment of Chapter 9 in 1937 are a small fraction of the over 11,000 corporate Chapter 11 reorganizations filed in 2010 alone. Almost all of the municipal bankruptcies involved very small municipalities and special districts. The significant majority of the bankrupt local governments did not issue municipal securities. (See "For Additional Information" at the end of the chapter.)

Mr. Spiotto's observation is illustrated in Exhibit 1.7.

Despite this comfort, yes, there are certain municipal market sectors that deserve closer examination in the process of making investments. And yes, again. You always should investigate and understand the investments you are making. Yet, the overall performance of rated municipal securities issued for essential governmental purposes is outstanding.

In a January 2008 commentary, MMA published the data shown in Exhibit 1.8, which MMA drew from a Fitch Ratings report on the percentages of total payment defaults represented by various municipal market sectors (total = 100% of defaults).

The following graphs (Exhibits 1.9 and 1.10) illustrate the default relationships among the various market sectors, with green indicating municipal securities as a whole, red indicating market sectors that depend substantially (although not entirely) upon private credits or private performance, and blue indicating sectors that are reliant primarily upon governmental performance. (See "For Additional Information" at the end of the chapter.)

Sector	% of Total Defaults
Corporate-Backed IDBs	31.9
Housing	25.1
Long-Term Care	19.1
Land-Secured	10.2
Hospitals	5.5
Utilities	3.5
GO & Lease*	1.8
Public Facilities	1.2
Transportation	1.0
Education	0.8

Municipal Market Advisors, "Corporate Ratings for Munis" at 1 (Jan. 17, 2008), drawing on a Fitch Ratings report on defaults between 1980 and 2002. The Fitch report from which MMA drew the data is Fitch Ratings, "Municipal Default Risk Revisited" (June 23, 2003).

Although the table groups GO (general obligation) securities and leases together, they are quite different in terms of investor considerations. You should review the separate sections in this book relating to general obligation securities, on one hand, and leases and other general fund securities, on the other.

*The table, as published by MMA, combined general obligation securities and certificates of participation (lease-purchase securities) to reflect the aggregate 1.8% share of total defaults.

Exhibit 1.8
Source: Fitch Ratings data as published by Municipal Market Advisors.

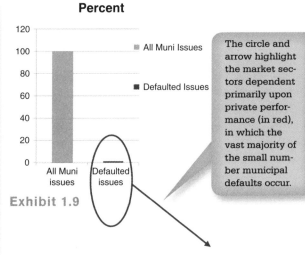

Percent

The circle and arrow highlight the market sectors dependent primarily upon private performance (in red), in which the vast majority of the small number municipal defaults occur.

Exhibit 1.9

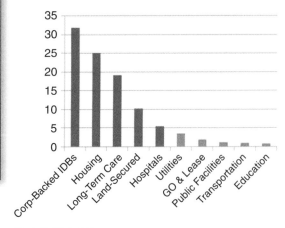

Percent of Total Defaults

Exhibit 1.10
Source: Fitch Ratings data as published by Municipal Market Advisors.

To be clear, the table and graph do not show that 31.9% of corporate-backed IDBs (industrial development bonds) defaulted. Instead, they show, on an historical basis, that of the total number of municipal securities that defaulted in the period from 1980 through 2002 (significantly less than 1% of total municipal securities outstanding), 31.9% of them were IDBs.

As MMA's historical data demonstrate, even within the low level of municipal securities market payment defaults, the bulk of defaults occurred in sectors primarily involving private credits or performance—being 91.8% of the municipal market's defaults. The private sector borrowers include both profit-making and nonprofit entities.

I refer again below to this statistic based upon these data presented by MMA indicating that more than 90% of the defaults in the municipal securities market from 1980 through 2002 occurred in market sectors primarily dependent upon what I describe as private performance. As demonstrated by Bloomberg data discussed below, municipal securities in those riskier sectors represent a distinct minority of the securities outstanding in the municipal market.

Those securities include industrial development bonds, housing securities (which cover both private mortgage financings and multifamily financings in developer apartment projects), long-term care securities (nursing homes and assisted living facilities), land-based securities (which fund special tax, special assessment and tax increment development projects), and hospitals (primarily nonprofit private).

The remaining municipal securities—those that were dependent primarily upon governmental performance—made up, on an historical basis, only 8.3% of the total payment defaults in the municipal market in the 1980 to 2002 period, an already very low number. Some of the governmental purpose defaults involve start-up or rapidly-expanding governmental enterprises owned and usually operated by state and local governments.

The following graph (Exhibit 1.11) indicates the relationship between defaulted municipal securities sectors, dependent primarily upon private performance, and those dependent primarily upon governmental performance.

These data provide significant historical evidence that municipal securities issued for governmental purposes and supported by governmental credits are sound.

More recent default data provided by Bloomberg confirm the trend indicated in MMA's earlier data.

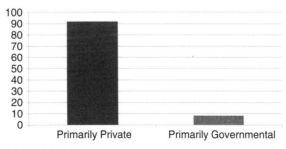

Percent of Total Defaults

Exhibit 1.11
Source: Fitch Ratings data as published by Municipal Market Advisors.

Bloomberg's data show a low number of municipal securities defaults spanning the period from the beginning of the financial crisis in 2007 through 2010. Bloomberg reports that, during the 2007 through 2010 period, 392 issuers or borrowers experienced monetary defaults that involved failures to make payments to investors. Significantly, Bloomberg also reports that, during the period, 737 issuers or borrowers experienced either monetary or "technical" defaults. Bloomberg's data indicate, therefore, that a large number of "technical" defaults, such as draws on reserve funds and various violations of securities documentation, did not result ultimately in failures to make payments to investors. Regarding debt service reserve funds, see Chapter 12, "Investor Questions and Answers (Q&As)," the section and subsection entitled, "What Are Basic Provisions in Securities Structures?, What Are Debt Service Reserve Funds?"

The accompanying table (Exhibit 1.12) presents Bloomberg's data (those market sectors that are primarily private are marked in red, with those that are primarily governmental are shown in green).

The monetary defaults reflected in the table demonstrate that those municipal securities primarily dependent upon private performance represent approximately 80% of the total number of monetary defaults in the 2007 through 2010 period, while those primarily dependent upon governmental performance represent approximately 20%.

That contrast is emphasized further in the second table of Bloomberg data regarding the dollar volumes of outstanding municipal securities, by market sector, as of August 2011 (Exhibit 1.13). Again, those market sectors that are primarily private are marked in red, with those that are primarily governmental are shown in green.

For comparison, the second table also replicates Bloomberg's data regarding the numbers of issuers and borrowers experiencing defaults for some of the market sectors that are primarily private. For example, Bloomberg's data for the "Land-Secured" sector show that sector with a default representation of 33% in the period from 2007 through 2010, but in the second table, that same sector represented only 2% of the outstanding municipal securities by volume in August 2011.

Using Bloomberg's data on an aggregate basis, issuers of approximately 20% of the dollar volume of municipal securities outstanding in August 2011 were dependent primarily upon private performance. However, those private-performance borrowers—both profit-making and nonprofit entities—experienced approximately 80% of the number of defaults by municipal securities issuers with defaults in the period from 2007 through 2010. This behavior was not far from the default results demonstrated in the MMA data presented earlier for the period from 1980 through 2002. I refer further to these data again later.

The future, of course, requires prediction. Officials of two of the major rating services, Moody's Investors Service and Standard and Poor's Financial Services

Number of Borrowers Who Defaulted on Muni Bonds and Their Industry Dispersion (2007–2010)	
All Monetary and Technical Defaults 737	Monetary Defaults 392
Issuer/Borrower Category	% of Total Issuers/ Borrowers with Monetary Defaults
Land-secured	33
Housing	18
Long-term care	15
Economic or corporate-backed industrial development	9
Hospitals	3
Government-backed leases, public facility leases	3
Charter schools	3
Cultural and human service provider charities	2
Universities	2
Local public utilities	2
Private schools	1
Public education	1
Native American	1
GO	1
Public transportation	1
Toll roads/bridges/ tunnels	1
Parking facilities	1
Other	5
Total	100

Exhibit 1.12

* Of the borrowers that had monetary default, this table shows how many fell into the categories listed. These percentages are not based on dollar amount. Primarily Private: 82%; Primarily Public: 17% (not 100% due to rounding). Reprinted with permission from Bloomberg L.P. Copyright 2011 Bloomberg L.P. All rights reserved.

LLC, provided their outlooks for the municipal market in testimony before Congress to the effect that, while there could be some increase in default levels as a result of stress upon municipal credits, any such increase is unlikely to be substantial among rated obligations. (See "For Additional Information" at the end of the chapter.)

What Is the Historical Level of Defaults?

As shown in Exhibit 1.11 the municipal securities market has an historical record of an especially low level of defaults. That is particularly true for traditional investment-grade–rated securities issued for essential governmental purposes in diverse communities—roads, city halls, water and wastewater systems, and the like.

Municipal Bonds Outstanding in August 2011: Where Is the Money Coming From?

Type of Revenue	Amount Outstanding ($ Billions)	% of Outstanding Market	% of Total Monetary Defaults
State General Fund or Ad Valorem property tax (GO)	727	20	
Ad Valorem property tax (school districts)	426	12	
Hospital revenues	270	7	3
Water and sewer revenue	260	7	
Higher education revenues	215	6	
Miscellaneous taxes	204	6	
Housing revenues	187	5	18
Nuclear, public power, solid waste and municipal utility system revenues	185	5	
Economic or corporate-backed industrial development	134	4	9
Government-backed leases, public facility leases	128	3	
Tobacco settlement	106	3	
Toll-backed roads/bridges/tunnels	101	3	
Airport revenues	86	2	
Land-secured	62	2	33
Public transportation revenues	54	1	
Long-term care revenues	46	1	15
Cultural and human service provider charities	22	1	2
Other	455	12	
TOTALS	3668	100	80

The circled columns contrast market share vs. default share of certain municipal market sectors, all primarily representing private credits.

Exhibit 1.13

Although it should be observed that historical experience may not be repeated in the future, there is a long history with favorable results for municipal securities issued for essential governmental purposes.

Even in the Great Depression, when approximately 1.65% of municipal debt service had defaulted as of 1933, according to Dr. John Petersen, an economist at George Mason University specializing in studying the municipal market,

about 40% of the total defaulted amounts were erased within a year and the defaulted principal and interest declined to about 0.5% of all outstanding debt by 1938.

(See "For Additional Information" at the end of the chapter.)

That experience is echoed by the New York City default in the 1970s, when the City eventually paid all the principal amount the City owed investors, with interest for the delay. In the case of Orange County, California, which entered into bankruptcy in 1994, bond investors were paid in full. Investors in Orange County notes received a delayed payment of debt service at a higher interest rate to compensate for the delay.

In the 1980s, the Washington Public Power Supply System (WPPSS) defaulted on billions of bonds issued for new nuclear facilities to provide power in the Northwest. The defaults followed on the heels of state judicial rulings invalidating the bond structures under state law. That transpired after the costly start-up nuclear power projects were unsuccessful, and rate payers, although

not receiving power service from the unfinished projects, would have been liable to pay for the costs that had been incurred. Jefferson County, Alabama, defaulted on securities issued for substantial sewage system improvements to remediate significant environmental difficulties The County's variable rate and auction rate securities were insured, so insurers that had experienced rating downgrades absorbed losses, as did liquidity banks holding variable rate securities that could not be remarketed. Individual and other investors also lost money.

For a discussion of bond insurance, see Chapter 7, "Considerations When Buying," the section entitled "What Is the Significance to Me of the Bond Insurance Industry's Decline?" Regarding variable rate securities, see Chapter 4, "General Fund and Other Municipal Securities," the section entitled "What Are TRANs, BANs, VRDNs, VRDOs and Other Municipal Notes?"

Investors incurred significant losses in the case of the WPPSS defaults. WPPSS and Jefferson County highlight a Key Point for caution—you may have greater risk when municipal securities are issued for start-up or rapidly-expanding revenue-producing enterprises. Further, you are well-advised to pay close attention to and to understand expert work products (such as feasibility studies and appraisals) prepared in connection with municipal securities issues for start-up and rapidly-expanding projects. See Chapter 10, "Understanding Expert Work Products."

In any event, historically, municipal securities as a whole have incurred especially low default rates. This is reflected in Dr. Petersen's economic research for the four decades from 1970 to 2009.

Dr. Petersen concluded that, if WPPSS and Jefferson County—financings for start-up or rapidly-expanding projects—are "netted out" of the equation,

> the overall adjusted percentage of the dollar value of bonds in default fluctuates between 0.10 and 0.24 percent, and shows, if anything, a slight downward trend over the four decades.

Dr. Petersen added with respect to recent experience,

> although the country did enter into a prolonged Great Recession, the recorded defaults by state and local governments did not increase, nor did any states or major cities verge on defaulting on their outstanding debt.

(Harrisburg is an exception.)

Dr. Petersen concluded with respect to current circumstances facing state and local governments in contrast to the period of the Depression,

> State and local governments, while faced with fiscal stress, are not nearly as indebted nor are they faced with heavy annual debt service burdens in a sustained period of declining prices and a shrinking money supply. Adjustments are being made by these governments, but not with the sudden unrestrained downward spiral in income and prices that occurred in the 1930s. Revenue bases are broader and are more stable and the economy and incomes, even when underperforming, are more resilient.

Dr. Petersen provided the "Estimated Defaults and Default Rates by Decade: 1970 through 2009 (Dollars in Millions)" for municipal securities, which are shown on the table in Exhibit 1.14.

At this point, I recall MMA's and Bloomberg's data I discussed previously indicating that somewhere in the range of 80% to more than 90% of defaults in the municipal securities market occurred in municipal securities market sectors that were dependent primarily upon private performance, and Bloomberg's data indicating that approximately 20% of all outstanding municipal securities were attributable to those private borrowers.

One can apply the remaining 10% to 20% of municipal defaults that occur in the approximately 80% of the municipal securities issues that are dependent primarily upon governmental performance to Dr. Petersen's market-wide estimates of less than 0.4% of all municipal securities outstanding that are in default. This requires making certain assumptions about the average size of the bond issues that experience a monetary default. Using SIFMA data regarding the average issue size of new issues in 2010, Dr. Petersen suggests one can estimate that the average size of privately supported debt reporting default was about $30 million and that of government purpose debt was about the same. (See "For Additional Information" at the end of the chapter.) If that is so, then Dr. Petersen suggests it is possible to estimate that municipal securities dependent primarily upon governmental performance are currently responsible for a default rate of only 0.03% to 0.06%, as based upon the total amount of outstanding municipal debt. In other words, those issues that are primarily for governmental purposes are estimated to default at a rate of less than 0.1% (one-tenth of one percent).

Decade Default Rates

Period	Total	Adjusted Total *	Total	Adjusted Total*
1970s	$574	$574	0.24%	0.24%
1980s	3,109	859	0.36%	0.10%
1990s	2,071	2,071	0.16%	0.16%
2000s	6,037	2,567	0.27%	0.12%
Total	$11,791	$6,071		

> Dr. Petersen's data demonstrate that municipal securities total default rates in all decades shown were well under 0.4%.

Exhibit 1.14

* Adjusted for WPPSS default in 1983 (2.25 billion) and Jefferson County, AL default in 2006 (3.47 billion).

Source: Dr. John E. Petersen, George Mason University.

That is an outstanding record! Certainly, outspoken pundits and many media have misunderstood the municipal market, and have missed that story entirely.

With reference to even more recent post-crisis data, research released by J. R. Rieger, vice president of Fixed Income Indices at S&P Indices in March 2011, concluded that the rate of municipal securities defaults in January and February 2011 had declined from 2010. Mr. Rieger stated:

A total of 8 municipal bond deals have entered monetary default this year totaling over $222 million in par value.

One is a zero coupon bond. Compare this to the same period last year where there were 16 municipal bond deals entering monetary default totaling over $329 million in par value. Fewer defaults so far than last year.

Through the end of February the monetary defaults include:

1 industrial development or corporate backed bond
1 multi-family bond
1 civic center
1 G.O. bond

KEY POINT:

It is possible to estimate that municipal securities dependent primarily upon governmental performance are currently responsible for a default rate of only 0.03% to 0.06%, as based upon the total amount of outstanding municipal debt. In other words, those issues that are primarily for governmental purposes are estimated by Dr. Petersen to default at a rate of less than 0.1% (one-tenth of one percent). That is an outstanding record!!

1 tax and revenue bond

1 toll road

2 land backed bond issues

According to Mr. Rieger of S&P Indices, with still more recent data, "High default projections within the municipal bond market simply haven't materialized. The first half of the year the municipal bond market saw 28 monetary defaults totaling over $511 million in par value." S&P Indices provided the following (Exhibit 1.15) comparative data.

	Number of Monetary Defaults	Total Par Value
First half 2011	28	$ 511 million
First half 2010	53	$ 1,546 million
First half 2009	67	$ 1,471 million

Exhibit 1.15
Reprinted by permission of S&P Indices.

The default data, as reported by S&P Indices may be represented graphically, as shown in Exhibit 1.16.

In reality, most defaults in the municipal securities market occur in readily-identifiable securities issued in relatively smaller principal amounts for projects in which private profit-making or nonprofit borrowers have a direct financial interest; for infrastructure to serve private real estate developments; for projects that depend upon the success of private parties (such as parking garages to serve shopping malls, or convention centers or sports arenas in connection with economic development projects); or as noted above with reference to the WPPSS and Jefferson County defaults, for new or rapidly-expanding governmental revenue projects. Many of those securities are not rated at investment-grade levels.

In addition, according to Fitch Ratings, "municipal bonds have an average recovery rate of 68.33% based on the number of defaults and a 66.92% recovery rate based on the dollar weighted average, both of which are higher than public corporate bonds that have a long-term average recovery rate of approximately 40%." Fitch added that municipal securities that are not rated at investment grade levels or rated at all "are approximately 10 times more likely to default" than are investment grade municipal securities.

In other words, for municipal securities issued for essential purposes and payable from obligated taxes, or from dedicated revenue streams of traditional governmental enterprises, in established, diverse communities, you are well-secured.

This is illustrated by the Chapter 9 bankruptcy of the City of Vallejo, California. In Vallejo, although the City made only partial payment of debt service on general fund securities (certificates of participation in lease obligations, as opposed to general obligation securities), investors in other City securities that were not payable from the City's general fund were protected. Those other securities included, according to the California Municipal Bond Advisor, "water revenue bonds; sanitation and flood control district debt; redevelopment agency tax

The graph illustrates data indicating decreasing numbers of municipal securities default rates in 2010 and 2011 following the financial crisis.

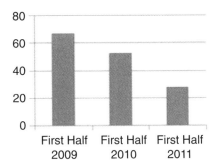

Number of Monetary Defaults

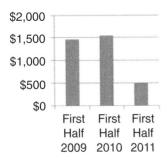

Total Defaulted Par Value (000,000s)

Exhibit 1.16
Source: Data provided by S&P Indices.

allocation bonds; multi-family housing and mortgage revenue debt; and land-secured bonds tied to real estate development." It should be noted, however, that Vallejo's non-defaulting securities were subjected to risks of market volatility and price decreases and of illiquidity. (See "For Additional Information" at the end of the chapter.)

Securities payable from a local general fund, such as Vallejo's COPs, are *not* "general obligation bonds" as that term is widely used by many in the municipal securities market. Nevertheless, there is an excellent historical record even regarding these municipal securities for reasons discussed later in this book under Chapter 4, "General Fund and Other Municipal Securities."

You should understand and pay close attention to the differences in credit support for various municipal securities. Even when municipal securities are insured, you should pay attention to underlying credits and underlying ratings as discussed under Chapter 7, "Considerations When Buying," in the sections entitled "What Are Underlying Ratings and Why Do They Matter?" and "What Is the Significance to Me of the Bond Insurance Industry's Decline?"

What Types of Defaults Occur?

Municipal securities can experience a variety of defaults. The most significant default is a failure to pay principal of or interest on the securities in a timely manner or at all.

In other cases, issuers or borrowers may fail to honor promises they make when the securities are issued. These generally are called technical defaults, but in some cases, these defaults may have serious impacts upon your securities and upon their market value and liquidity. These defaults are discussed in Chapter 12, "Investor Questions and Answers (Q&As), in the section and subsection entitled " What Types of Defaults May Occur?, What Are Technical Defaults?" The most significant technical defaults are invasions of debt service reserve funds for the securities. When a reserve fund is invaded on an unplanned basis, it means the issuer or borrower did not make a payment when due. See Chapter 12 "Investor Questions and Answers (Q&As)," the section and subsection entitled "What Are Basic Provisions in Securities Structures?, What Are Debt Service Reserve Funds?"

In many cases, when reserve fund draws do occur, the issuer or borrower is able to work out its financial issues.

Occasionally, although not commonly, for reasons unique to particular securities issues, municipal securities structures may create intentional uses of reserve fund dollars that do not signal fiscal issues. When such a structure is used, the planned reserve fund draws should be disclosed in official statements at the time the securities are first offered.

What Is the Incidence of Municipal Bankruptcy?

Defaults on municipal securities are not the same as bankruptcies. Municipal securities can, and do, default without the issuer or borrower entering into bankruptcy. Likewise, municipalities can enter bankruptcy without defaulting on their securities.

The relevant chapter of the Bankruptcy Code for municipal securities issuers is Chapter 9. (Private borrowers use Chapter 11 or Chapter 7; individuals use Chapter 13.) Under the legal provisions of Chapter 9, creditors are not able to force a municipal issuer into involuntary bankruptcy. The issuer must file voluntarily on its own, a step that the vast majority of issuers diligently avoid. Chapter 9 limits the power of bankruptcy courts, so that the courts cannot interfere in municipal governmental affairs (which include municipal revenues, property, and local legislative affairs). Municipalities prepare and submit their own remedial plans to bankruptcy courts.

An important aspect of the municipal securities market is that state and local governments almost never experience bankruptcy. Bankruptcies in the municipal securities market are extremely rare. Chapter 9 of the Bankruptcy Code, which applies solely to local governments, has proved to be expensive, uncertain, time-consuming and burdensome to the municipal entities using it.

Of the 90,000 estimated governmental entities in the United States based upon Census data, in 2010, only 6 municipal bankruptcies were filed, all of which were by small municipalities and special districts. That was a decrease from 10 filings in 2009.

Chapter 9 does not permit states to file for bankruptcy. James Spiotto testified that, since the post–Civil War era of the late 1800s, only one state has defaulted on a general obligation security. That state, Arkansas, did so during the Depression, but paid all of its investors on a delayed basis after refinancing its debt.

Moreover, local governments cannot enter into Chapter 9 proceedings unless the laws of their states permit it. According to Mr. Spiotto,

Municipalities have to be specifically authorized by their state to file Chapter 9 municipal bankruptcy. Only the municipalities in 12 states are specifically authorized to file (and in 12 additional states the authorization is conditional on the approval of some state official or commission to file).

The 12 states that Mr. Spiotto identified as permitting municipalities to file for bankruptcy as of October 2011 are:

States Specifically Authorizing Local Governments to File for Bankruptcy

Alabama

Arizona

Arkansas

Idaho

Minnesota

Missouri

Montana

Nebraska

Oklahoma

South Carolina

Texas

Washington

Mr. Spiotto added that:

Another 12 States authorize a filing conditioned on a further act of the State, an Elected Official or State entity (CA, CT, FL, KY, LA, MI, NJ, NC, NY, OH, PA, RI). Three states (CO, OR and IL) grant limited authorization, two states prohibit filing (GA) but one of them (IA) has an exception to the prohibition. The remaining 21 are either unclear or do not have specific authorization.

The map (Exhibit 1.17) was provided by Mr. Spiotto to illustrate those differences among states in terms of their approach to Chapter 9 bankruptcy filings by their municipalities.

One caution is that losses may be realized when the payment of municipal securities is dependent upon the performance of private parties. Bankruptcies or reorganizations of private parties occur generally under Chapters 7 or 11 (but not Chapter 9) of the Bankruptcy Code.

Reliance upon private performance may occur in the form of obligations to make payments that are to be ap-

form of a municipal parking garage to serve a private shopping mall to be developed or refurbished by a private party. Additional examples of private involvement include municipal securities issued for profit-making or nonprofit hospitals or nursing homes, multi-family housing apartment projects, airport financings supported by airline revenues, and stadium and arena financings for professional sports teams. See Chapter 4, "General Fund and Other Municipal Securities," the section entitled "Private Involvement."

It is important for you to understand when private performance is critical to municipal securities credits, and if so, how.

Will Pension Liabilities and Spending Patterns Cause Extensive Bankruptcies or Defaults?

Despite media hype, state and local government pension liabilities, OPEB liabilities (such as retiree health care benefits), and spending patterns should not cause extensive bankruptcies or defaults.

As I discuss earlier, there are substantial legal, economic, and practical barriers to municipal bankruptcy filings.

Security in the form of obligated taxes and dedicated revenues is enforceable under state law. Securities with that protection often require that municipal issuers raise taxes or fees as much as is necessary in order to pay principal of and interest on the securities.

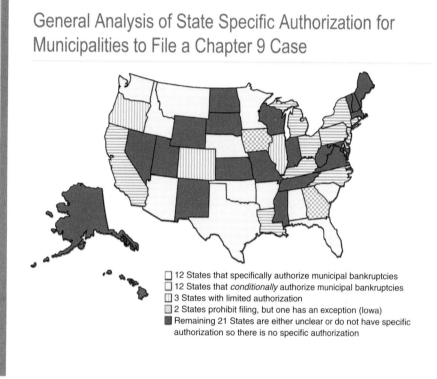

General Analysis of State Specific Authorization for Municipalities to File a Chapter 9 Case

☐ 12 States that specifically authorize municipal bankruptcies
☐ 12 States that *conditionally* authorize municipal bankruptcies
☐ 3 States with limited authorization
▨ 2 States prohibit filing, but one has an exception (Iowa)
■ Remaining 21 States are either unclear or do not have specific authorization so there is no specific authorization

Exhibit 1.17
Source: James E. Spiotto, Partner, Chapman and Cutler LLP, Chicago, IL (October 10, 2011).

DEFINITION:
OPEB
The term "OPEB" means "other post-employment benefits," referring to "other than pensions."

plied to pay municipal securities, such as in an industrial development bond issue. It may also occur in terms of development of property associated with municipal infrastructure, such as infrastructure to serve a future housing development in a land-based district, or in the

James Spiotto adds that bankruptcy courts should not overturn dedicated revenue security and should not overturn a state statute providing that security; that dedicated revenues securing revenue securities are considered to be "special revenues" that are protected in Chapter 9 bankruptcy; and further, that precedent should support similarly strong protection for general obligation securities, if they are secured by obligated taxes supported by statutory liens. The statutory liens should render those securities protected in the event of a Chapter 9 bankruptcy. You may wish to review bond counsel opinions and official statements to verify that bond counsel has opined that any general obligation securities you are considering have the support of a statutory lien.

In other securities issues, while compromising other forms of obligations (e.g., claims of general creditors, suppliers and employees under union contracts), municipalities preparing remedial plans seek to avoid harming their securities investors because of the need for continued market access.

Localities situated in states in which bankruptcy filings are permitted to be pursued legally are well-aware that the proceedings are extremely expensive, cumbersome, and time-consuming, with uncertain outcomes. Those localities are aware that, if they enter bankruptcy, the communities will have severely damaged their reputations with investors and may pay a significant price in the market for years to come.

Those are key reasons why defaults occur so rarely by governmental entities and even more rarely by governmental entities with outstanding municipal securities.

How Can I Obtain More Information?

Regardless of the high level of safety of many municipal securities, prudence dictates that you always understand the securities you are considering. I recommend that you seek out available information, such as identified in Chapter 2, "Basic Information Resources," and in the Appendix to this book. If suitable information is unavailable on a timely basis, you may wish to avoid the issuers and borrowers and their securities.

Fortunately, although there remains room for improvement in the content and timing of municipal securities disclosure, substantial information is available on all newly-issued municipal securities. Further, information in the secondary, or trading, market is improving, even if it is imperfect.

One of my purposes in writing this book is to show you how to obtain available information.

For Additional Information

- Ernesto A. Lanza, deputy executive director and chief legal officer to the Municipal Securities Rulemaking Board (MSRB), written testimony at the Securities and Exchange Commission's Field Hearing in Jefferson County, Alabama, on the State of the Municipal Securities Market, at 6 (July 29, 2011), stating that "The 1.5 million municipal securities compares with 5,700 equities that trade on U.S. exchanges and about 254 Treasury securities."

■ There are other types of failures, of varying degrees of seriousness, to comply with securities requirements. These are known in the market as "technical defaults." They are discussed under Chapter 12, "Investor Q&As—What Are 'Technical Defaults'?"

Historical default data in the municipal market have been difficult to obtain and define, with differing default concepts (such as when credit enhancement pays defaulted payments or when draws are made on reserve funds) and public vs. private purposes.

Among the more serious technical defaults are issuer or borrower payment defaults that require unscheduled draws on reserve funds pending workout efforts. Those occurrences may or may not lead ultimately to payment defaults to investors. See also Chapter 12, "Investor Questions and Answers (Q&As)," in the section and subsection entitled "What Are Basic Provisions in Securities Structures?, What Are Debt Service Reserve Funds?"

Sometimes, parties tracking defaults may include in their default statistics difficulties resulting in draws on reserve funds or may include staged defaults at the behest of federal agencies or bond insurers as part of workout programs. Many of those occurrences do not result, however, in missed payments to investors. For example, when draws on reserves occur in the context of traditional water or wastewater revenues securities, issuers use the time period afforded by the reserve funds to increase user charges in order to comply with rate covenants, as discussed in Chapter 5, "Revenue Securities," in the section and subsections entitled "Traditional Revenue Securities, Why Are Traditional Revenue Securities Extremely Safe?" and "What Are Rate Coverage Requirements?"

Another possibility is that some parties may assume that, when a governmental issuer enters Chapter 9 bankruptcy, all the municipal securities of that issuer are defaulted. Those assumptions are distinctly inaccurate. Indeed, a central point of this book is that traditional revenue securities are protected in Chapter 9 bankruptcies, and that, based upon precedent, general obligation securities secured by obligated taxes supported by statutory liens should be similarly protected.

The default data cited in this book does not include such incidents.

■ Testimony of Matt Fabian, Managing Director, Municipal Market Advisors, Before the House Judiciary Committee, Subcommittee on Courts, Commercial and Administrative Law at 4–5 (February 14, 2011).

These data would not include defaults that are not reported to EMMA.

■ Information provided for this book by James Spiotto. See also Testimony of James E. Spiotto, Partner, Chapman and Cutler LLP, Before the House Judiciary Committee, Subcommittee on Courts, Commercial and Administrative Law at 2 (February 14, 2011).

■ This book points out that general obligation securities are stronger than lease-purchase securities, although both of those sectors have good records on an historical basis. The original data published by Fitch Ratings show that general obligation securities (unlimited and limited tax) provided 0.38% of the total defaults in the municipal market during the 1980 through 2002 period, while certificates of participation, usually lease financings, provided 1.37%.

- Testimony of Robert Kurtter, managing director, U.S. Public Finance, Moody's Investors Service, Before the United States House of Representatives Oversight Committee on TARP, Financial Services and Bailouts of Public and Private Programs at 4, 7 (March 15, 2011) ("There is unprecedented strain on the U.S. public finance sector and this is reflected in the negative outlooks we have on all major sub-sectors in this market."; "[W]e do not expect any states to default on their bond obligations in the next twelve to eighteen months. In the Moody's-rated local government sector, we expect a relatively small increase in defaults from historically low levels, but we do not expect a wave of defaults.... We expect there will likely continue to be selective instances of severe credit stress.")

- Testimony of Robin Prunty, managing director, Ratings Services, Standard & Poor's Financial Services LLC, Before Committee on Oversight and Government Reform, Subcommittee on TARP, Financial Services and Bailouts of Public and Private Programs, United States House of Representatives at 2 (March 15, 2011) ("S&P") ("S&P believes the difficulties faced by states and municipalities will give rise to tough policy decisions, but not defaults for our rated universe in the overwhelming majority of cases. This is because debt obligations are secured either by a specific pledge of the government's full taxing authority or dedicated taxes, user revenues or fees, and there is often a priority status for debt relative to other obligations. We generally have seen a very strong commitment by governments to their debt obligations over time, despite difficult economic cycles.")

- During the Depression, the 1.65% is a percentage of debt service actually in default (e.g., semiannual payments), not total principal amount of defaulted municipal securities for which future payments were not yet due. The percentages are greater for total principal amounts of securities in default.

- Petersen, "Municipal Defaults: Eighty Years Does Make a Big Difference" at 6 (2011), from a book in preparation. Dr. Petersen adds that "The occurrence of default was both swift and short-lived," finding it contemporaneous with widespread closures of local banks that served as paying agents for the municipalities. The paper prepared by Dr. John Petersen of George Mason University concludes at 20:

This paper provides evidence that, in addition to the 80 years of general prosperity that has occurred in the nation, the wave of defaults in the 1930s dramatically overstated the apparent fiscal difficulties. First, the defaults in the 1930s were short-lived and the ultimate losses were small in the aggregate, amounting to 0.5% of principal. The subsequent years saw default rates that were low and driven by two large instances since 1980, the defaults of WPPS [Washington Public Power Supply System] and Jefferson County Alabama. If these two defaults are excluded, the average default rate on municipal securities has been 0.10% to 0.24%, and the defaults that have occurred were concentrated in housing, economic development and medical-care bonds, many of which are small and most, unrated.

Dr. Petersen attributes many municipal defaults during the Depression to bank failures and temporary closures that prevented municipal issuers from accessing their funds in order to make debt service payments to investors. This was remedied, according to Dr. Petersen, when the banking system re-opened.

Dr. Petersen stated:

There may indeed be hundreds of small defaults that occur over the years, but they are unrelated to the operations of governments. These defaults almost invariably involve special development districts, housing projects, and medical facilities that represent small, speculative undertakings that are financed by revenue bonds. The bond issues are typically unrated and small in size. But the woes of this fringe of this market can generate "body counts" that seem impressive, while they are completely misleading as to the sector as a whole. A reprise of the post World War II period shows that a handful of defaults accounted for the great bulk of dollars involved:

just two defaults amounted to 48% of all the principal of defaulted bonds during the last 40 years.

■ SIFMA *Municipal Bond Credit Report. Full Year 2010.* Dr. Petersen notes the average size of issue for general obligation bonds was $17 million. That for revenues bonds was $52 million. It is estimated that the average size of bonds reporting default was $30 million. Thus, Dr. Petersen suggests the Bloomberg defaults on governmental bonds would imply $2.3 billion reporting default in government supported debt and $9.4 billion in private-purpose debt. On the other hand, the MMA results would imply $10.5 billion in defaulting private-purpose bonds and $1.1 billion in government supported bonds at current rates of default.

■ Fitch Ratings "Municipal Default Risk Revisited" (June 23, 2003); Fitch Ratings, "Default Risk and Recovery Rates on U.S. Municipal Bonds" (Jan. 9, 2007).

■ California Municipal Bond Advisor, "Lessons from Vallejo's Bankruptcy for Smaller (and Bigger) Investors" at 3, 8 (Jan. 2011). The Bond Advisor stated "Our point is that a bankruptcy filing by a city shouldn't harm certain 'special revenue' bonds or so-called 'related entity' obligations...."

■ The conditional authorizations require localities to consult first with state authorities. Many states themselves prefer to avoid bankruptcies among their local governments and frequently are inclined first to impose remedial budgetary restrictions and, if necessary, to provide financial assistance.

CHAPTER 2

Basic Information Resources

Y ou have access to information regarding municipal securities through several readily available sources. This chapter identifies some of these sources.

A key resource that is growing in importance is the Municipal Securities Rulemaking Board's EMMA, or Electronic Municipal Market Access, located at www. emma.msrb.org/. Important document resources include official statements and continuing disclosure documents filed with EMMA by issuers or borrowers.

Official statements and continuing disclosure documents are fundamental resources for issuer and borrower information. That information is critical to your understanding of municipal securities you are considering.

The Appendix discusses your resources in greater detail.

What Is EMMA?

At the outset of your decision to invest in municipal securities, you should know about EMMA.

EMMA is an online resource created and maintained by the Municipal Securities Rulemaking Board (MSRB).

"EMMA" is an acronym for "Electronic Municipal Market Access." EMMA's website address is www.emma.msrb.org/.

I refer several times to EMMA is this book, and again in the Appendix, because it is an especially helpful resource, and the MSRB is improving it constantly for investors.

At EMMA, you can obtain municipal securities disclosure documents (official statements and continuing disclosure documents), real-time pricing and trading data for municipal securities, information for investors, and other useful assistance.

EMMA also contains information that municipal issuers and borrowers may file voluntarily, such as budgets and interim financial information, as well as information filed by dealers.

At EMMA, you are able to monitor changes relating to your municipal securities, both in terms of issuer and borrower continuing disclosure filings and new securities issues.

As noted, EMMA is useful in terms of your ability to obtain access to prices and trading activity for your securities. Understanding pricing and trading data is an art, not a science. Regarding use of EMMA's pricing and trading data, which may need interpretation, see Chapter 8, "Municipal Securities Pricing and Trading," in the section entitled "What Pricing Information on EMMA Should I Consider?"

I recommend strongly that you become familiar with EMMA.

What Do Information and Documents on EMMA Cost?

Information and documents on EMMA are free for individual investors.

The MSRB sells subscriptions to institutional investors for large quantities of data and documents.

What Are Official Statements?

Tim Schaefer of Magis Advisors suggests that a "Basic Rule of Investing Is Investigate First, Then Invest."

Official statements are a vital source of information regarding municipal securities. They are the prospectuses (disclosure documents) that municipal securities issuers and private borrowers prepare for investors as a part of the municipal securities issuance process.

Dealers offering the securities upon issuance and shortly after issuance are required by the Securities and Exchange Commission (SEC) in its Rule 15c2-12 and by the Municipal Securities Rulemaking Board (MSRB) in

its Rule G-32 to give investors access to the official statements in most offerings.

In addition, if the issuers or borrowers prepare "preliminary official statements," which almost always occurs, then dealers offering the securities are required to provide those documents to requesting investors. You should request a copy when you are offered municipal securities in an initial offering. Some issuers or borrowers may file their preliminary official statements with the MSRB, although they are not required to do so. If they do, you may obtain a copy there, as well. Preliminary official statements are required to contain all the disclosure information that is material to an offering, except certain information dependent on the offering process (such as prices).

You are able also to obtain final official statements on the MSRB's EMMA website. EMMA contains most official statements published since 1990.

The screen (Exhibit 2.1) is the cover of an Official Statement of the City of Boise, Idaho, for an offering in 2011 of Airport Revenue Refunding Bonds, and illustrates the location of CUSIP numbers. Most official statements make similar presentations.

What Continuing Disclosure Is Available?

SEC Rule 15c2-12 prohibits underwriters from offering most municipal securities in public offerings unless the issuers or private borrowers agree to file with the MSRB certain annual financial and operating information within identified periods following the end of the issuers' or borrowers' fiscal years.

Annual Disclosure

One of the pillars of the continuing disclosure system for municipal securities is annual financial statements and other annual information that issuers and borrowers file with EMMA. The information to be filed regarding an issue of municipal securities is to be identified in issuers' and borrowers' continuing disclosure agreements contained in official statements.

The screen (Exhibit 2.2) from the Bloomberg Terminal illustrates a list of annual reports filed by the City of Chattanooga, Tennessee, for fiscal years from 2006 through 2010.

Once the annual financial statements and information are filed, you can review this useful information. In addition, services, such as the Bloomberg Terminal, may extract and present useful information and analysis for you.

The second screen (Exhibit 2.3) from the Bloomberg Terminal shows revenues and expenses of the State of Indiana for its fiscal years ended June 30, 2006 through 2010.

Information on local governments may be extracted and presented in the same manner.

The third screen (Exhibit 2.4) from the Bloomberg Terminal shows general fund revenues and expenses of the City of Chicago for its fiscal years ended December 31, 2004 through 2010.

Information on state and local governments also may be extracted and presented in summary form.

OFFICIAL STATEMENT DATED FEBRUARY 17, 2011

NEW ISSUE
BOOK ENTRY ONLY

RATINGS (See "RATINGS" herein)

Underlying Ratings	Insured Ratings
Moody's: A1	Moody's: Aa3
Fitch: A+	

In the opinion of Bond Counsel, under existing law, interest on the Series 2011 Bonds is excluded from gross income for purposes of federal income taxation pursuant to Section 103 of the Internal Revenue Code of 1986, as amended (the "Code"), and Idaho income taxes provided that the City complies with all requirements of the Code that must be satisfied subsequent to the issuance of the Series 2011 Bonds. The Series 2011 Bonds are private activity bonds, and interest on the Series 2011 Bonds is a preference item for purposes of computing the federal alternative minimum tax imposed on individuals and corporations. Interest on the Series 2011 Bonds is taken into account in the computation of adjusted current earnings for purposes of the corporate alternative minimum tax under Section 55 of the Code. See "TAX MATTERS."

$32,480,000
City of Boise City, Idaho
Airport Revenue Refunding Bonds, Series 2011
(Air Terminal Facilities Project)

Dated: Date of delivery   **Due: September 1st as shown below**

The City of Boise City, Idaho Airport Revenue Refunding Bonds, Series 2011 (Air Terminal Facilities Project) (the "Series 2011 Bonds") are being issued to refinance the outstanding City of Boise Airport Revenue Certificates of Participation, Series 2000 (Air Terminal Facilities Project), to satisfy the debt service reserve fund requirement for the Series 2011 Bonds and to pay the costs of issuing the Series 2011 Bonds.

Interest on the Series 2011 Bonds accruing from the date of delivery is payable on March 1 and September 1 of each year, commencing September 1, 2011. The Series 2011 Bonds are not subject to optional redemption.

The Series 2011 Bonds will be issued and secured pursuant to a Trust Indenture, dated as of February 1, 2011 (the "Indenture") between the City of Boise City, Idaho (the "City") and The Bank of New York Mellon Trust Company, N.A. (the "Trustee"). **THE BONDS ARE LIMITED OBLIGATIONS OF THE CITY, PAYABLE SOLELY FROM THE NET REVENUES AS DEFINED IN THE INDENTURE. THE CITY'S PAYMENT OBLIGATIONS ARE SECURED BY A SECURITY INTEREST IN (i) THE NET REVENUES DERIVED BY THE CITY FROM ITS AIRPORT FACILITIES AND PROPERTIES, AND (ii) THE FUNDS AND ACCOUNTS CREATED UNDER THE INDENTURE, AS DESCRIBED UNDER "SECURITY AND SOURCES OF PAYMENT FOR THE BONDS." NEITHER THE FULL FAITH AND CREDIT NOR THE TAXING POWER OF THE CITY, STATE OF IDAHO, NOR ANY POLITICAL SUBDIVISION THEREOF, IS PLEDGED FOR PAYMENT OF THE SERIES 2011 BONDS.** See "SECURITY AND SOURCES OF PAYMENT FOR THE BONDS."

The scheduled payment of principal of and interest on the Bonds maturing on September 1 of the years 2017 through 2020 inclusive (the "Insured Bonds"), when due will be guaranteed under an insurance policy to be issued concurrently with the delivery of the Insured Bonds by **ASSURED GUARANTY MUNICIPAL CORP. (FORMERLY KNOWN AS FINANCIAL SECURITY ASSURANCE INC.)**

ASSURED GUARANTY
MUNICIPAL

When issued, the Series 2011 Bonds will be registered in the name of Cede & Co., as nominee of The Depository Trust Company, New York, New York ("DTC"). DTC will act as securities depository for the Series 2011 Bonds. Purchases of beneficial interests in the Series 2011 Bonds will be made in book-entry form, in denominations of $5,000 and integral multiples thereof. Purchasers will not receive bonds representing their interests in the Series 2011 Bonds, except as described herein. So long as DTC or its nominee is the registered owner of the Series 2011 Bonds, payments of principal of and interest on the Series 2011 Bonds will be made directly to DTC or to such nominee. Disbursement of such payments to DTC's Direct Participants is the responsibility of DTC, and disbursement of such payments to the Beneficial Owners is the responsibility of the Direct Participants and the Indirect Participants. See Appendix F "BOOK-ENTRY SYSTEM."

MATURITY SCHEDULE*

Maturity (Sept. 1)	Principal Amount	Interest Rate	Yield	CUSIP Number [1]	Maturity (Sept. 1)	Principal Amount	Interest Rate	Yield	CUSIP Number [1]
2011	$1,400,000	3.00%	0.95%	097428BM7	2017[2]	$1,500,000	4.00%	4.05%	097428BT2
2012	2,860,000	4.00	1.65	097428BN5	2017[2]	2,085,000	5.00	4.05	097428BX3
2013	2,975,000	4.00	2.26	097428BP0	2018[2]	3,750,000	5.50	4.33	097428BU9
2014	3,095,000	5.00	2.80	097428BQ8	2019[2]	3,960,000	5.75	4.55	097428BV7
2015	3,255,000	5.00	3.39	097428BR6	2020[2]	4,185,000	5.75	4.80	097428BW5
2016	3,415,000	5.00	3.75	097428BS4					

[1] CUSIP Base #
[2] Insured

The Series 2011 Bonds are offered when, as and if delivered and received by Morgan Keegan & Company, Inc. (the "Underwriter"), subject to approving legal opinions of Skinner Fawcett LLP, Boise, Idaho, Bond Counsel, and certain other conditions. Certain legal matters will be passed upon for the City by Cary B. Colaianni, Boise City Attorney. Certain legal matters will be passed upon for the Underwriter by its counsel, Hawley Troxell Ennis & Hawley LLP, Boise, Idaho. It is expected that the Series 2011 Bonds will be available for delivery to the Trustee on behalf of DTC by Fast Automated Securities Transfer on or about February 28, 2011.

Morgan Keegan

Exhibit 2.1

The arrows point to CUSIP numbers identifying each maturity of these Bonds. CUSIP numbers assist you in searching for information on these securities.

EquityCF

Enter all fields and press <GO> to continue.

| 1) Search | 2) Settings | 3) Alert | Page 1 Company Filings |

◍ = As Reported Data   * = Amendment   √ = Image   ◍ = Info   ▯ = PDF   ▯ = XBRL   ▯ = RedLine

Company City of Chattanooga TN   Date Range Received ▾   Past 5 Years ▾

Form Type All ▾

■Include Related Company Filings   ☑Include Insider Filings

	Document Type	Received	Period	Reporting Entity/Security	Lang	Size	
23)	Annual Report	01/24/11	06/30/10	7903MF US Equity	English	5894K	
24)	Annual Report	12/09/10	06/30/10	7903MF US Equity	English	1884K	
25) √	Annual Report	04/08/10	06/30/09	7903MF US Equity	English	1571K	
26) √	Annual Report	11/18/09	06/30/09	7903MF US Equity	English	216K	
27) √	Annual Report	03/19/09	06/30/08	7903MF US Equity	English	5731K	
28) √ *	Annual Report	04/08/08	06/30/07	7903MF US Equity	English	5392K	
29) √	Annual Report	03/13/08	06/30/07	7903MF US Equity	English	9701K	
30) √	Annual Report	03/22/07	06/30/06	7903MF US Equity	English	6007K	

Australia 61 2 9777 8600 Brazil 5511 3048 4500 Europe 44 20 7330 7500 Germany 49 69 9204 1210 Hong Kong 852 2977 6000
Japan 81 3 3201 8900   Singapore 65 6212 1000   U.S. 1 212 318 2000   Copyright 2011 Bloomberg Finance L.P.
SN 268301 CDT   GMT-5:00 G515-401-2 10-Aug-2011 10:40:32

Exhibit 2.2

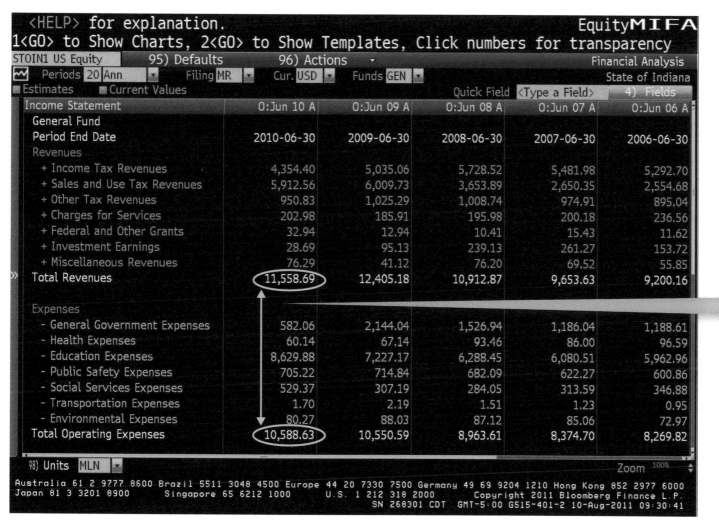

<HELP> for explanation. EquityMIFA
1<GO> to Show Charts, 2<GO> to Show Templates, Click numbers for transparency

STOIN1 US Equity   95) Defaults   96) Actions   ▾   Financial Analysis

Periods 20 Ann ▾   Filing MR ▾   Cur. USD ▾   Funds GEN ▾   State of Indiana
■ Estimates   ■ Current Values   Quick Field <Type a Field>   4) Fields

Income Statement	O:Jun 10 A	O:Jun 09 A	O:Jun 08 A	O:Jun 07 A	O:Jun 06 A
General Fund					
Period End Date	2010-06-30	2009-06-30	2008-06-30	2007-06-30	2006-06-30
Revenues					
+ Income Tax Revenues	4,354.40	5,035.06	5,728.52	5,481.98	5,292.70
+ Sales and Use Tax Revenues	5,912.56	6,009.73	3,653.89	2,650.35	2,554.68
+ Other Tax Revenues	950.83	1,025.29	1,008.74	974.91	895.04
+ Charges for Services	202.98	185.91	195.98	200.18	236.56
+ Federal and Other Grants	32.94	12.94	10.41	15.43	11.62
+ Investment Earnings	28.69	95.13	239.13	261.27	153.72
+ Miscellaneous Revenues	76.29	41.12	76.20	69.52	55.85
Total Revenues	11,558.69	12,405.18	10,912.87	9,653.63	9,200.16
Expenses					
- General Government Expenses	582.06	2,144.04	1,526.94	1,186.04	1,188.61
- Health Expenses	60.14	67.14	93.46	86.00	96.59
- Education Expenses	8,629.88	7,227.17	6,288.45	6,080.51	5,962.96
- Public Safety Expenses	705.22	714.84	682.09	622.27	600.86
- Social Services Expenses	529.37	307.19	284.05	313.59	346.88
- Transportation Expenses	1.70	2.19	1.51	1.23	0.95
- Environmental Expenses	80.27	88.03	87.12	85.06	72.97
Total Operating Expenses	10,588.63	10,550.59	8,963.61	8,374.70	8,269.82

98) Units MLN ▾   Zoom 100%

The circles and arrows identify Indiana's positive revenue vs. expenditure record.

Australia 61 2 9777 8600 Brazil 5511 3048 4500 Europe 44 20 7330 7500 Germany 49 69 9204 1210 Hong Kong 852 2977 6000
Japan 81 3 3201 8900   Singapore 65 6212 1000   U.S. 1 212 318 2000   Copyright 2011 Bloomberg Finance L.P.
SN 268301 CDT GMT-5:00 G515-401-2 10-Aug-2011 09:30:41

Exhibit 2.3
Reprinted with permission from Bloomberg. Copyright 2011 Bloomberg L. P. All rights reserved.

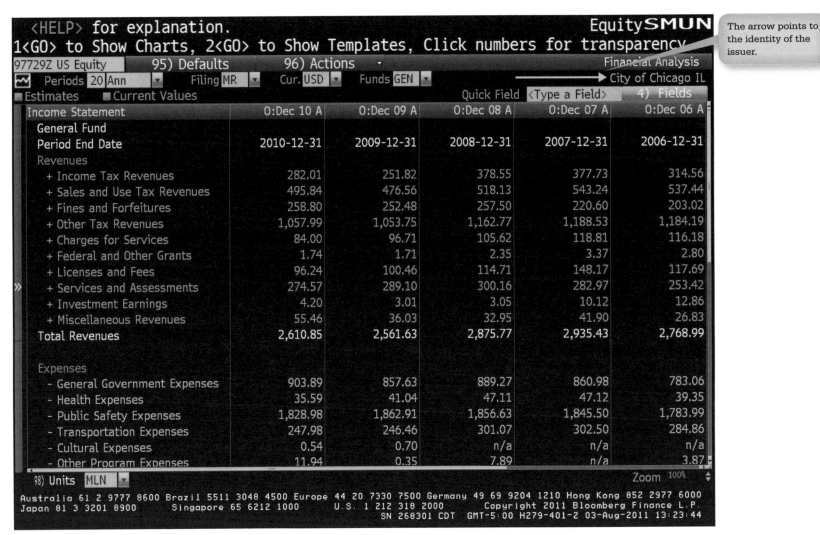

Exhibit 2.4

The screen (Exhibit 2.5) from the Bloomberg Terminal shows summary financial information for certain California local governments. The City of San Diego, which had been affected severely by a Securities and Exchange Commission enforcement action several years ago leading to substantial delays in publishing financial audits, caught up and filed its 2010 audit shortly after this screen was created.

Disclosure of Certain Events

In addition to annual information, issuers or borrowers are to agree to provide disclosure of the occurrence of certain events, such as payment defaults, unscheduled draws on debt service reserves, events affecting taxability of interest, and a list of other events identified by the SEC in its Rule 15c2-12. (See "For Additional Information" at the end of the chapter.) For securities issued on or after December 1, 2010, issuers and borrowers are required to agree to provide notices of additional event occurrences and to file the event notices within 10 days after the events occur.

The following list summarizes the events of which issuers and borrowers are required to file notices.

Required Event Disclosures

- Principal and interest payment delinquencies*
- Material non–payment-related defaults
- Unscheduled draws on debt service reserves reflecting financial difficulties*
- Unscheduled draws on credit enhancements reflecting financial difficulties*

- Substitution of credit or liquidity providers, or their failure to perform*
- Certain adverse tax opinions and certain IRS actions with respect to the tax status of the security‡
- Material modifications to rights of security holders
- Material bond calls
- Tender offers†
- Defeasances*
- Material releases, substitutions, or sales of property securing repayment
- Rating changes*
- Bankruptcy, insolvency, receivership, or similar events of obligated persons†
- Material mergers, consolidations, or acquisitions of issuers or borrowers, or sales of substantially all assets, or entering into or terminating agreements for such transactions†
- Appointment of successor or additional trustees, or material changes of names of trustees†
- Notices of failure to provide required annual financial information as required

*Not subject to issuer or borrower determination of materiality with respect to securities issued on or after December 1, 2010.

†Added with respect to securities issued on or after December 1, 2010.

‡Expanded with respect to securities issued on or after December 1, 2010.

<HELP> for explanation.   EquityMIFA
<MENU> to Return, Edit criteria to start a new search
  96) Output ▾   97) Actions ▾   98) Customize ▾   Page 2/33 Muni Issuer Screening
Add/Edit Criteria   ≫
Sectors GO ▾ Types General   ▾ States California ▾ Issuers All ▾ Fiscal Years All ▾
  Name _____ Field <Select a searchable field> ▾ 9) Displayable Fields
    Selected Screening Criteria   Matches
  3) ◉ Fund Type = General and State = California   420

	Name	Type	Current Fiscal Year	Tot GF Rev	Net Chg Fd Bal	Tot Assets	GF Tot Liab	Total Operating Expenses
21) ①	City of San Diego CA	GEN	2009	1,014.63	-10.39	175.24	60.85	1,106.12
22) ①	County of San Mateo C	GEN	2010	887.32	28.13	676.50	390.89	763.98
23) ①	County of Ventura CA	GEN	2009	869.23	15.37	496.72	291.63	786.83
24) ①	County of San Joaquin	GEN	2010	674.39	-6.83	240.16	151.62	635.26
25) ①	City of San Jose CA	GEN	2010	649.28	-40.31	234.84	63.95	683.48
26) ①	County of Kern CA	GEN	2010	548.73	-4.08	183.37	43.16	511.78
27) ①	County of Monterey C	GEN	2010	528.08	-12.88	151.23	74.73	523.18
28) ①	City of Oakland CA	GEN	2010	519.24	-3.90	379.30	146.25	437.12
29) ①	County of Tulare CA	GEN	2010	512.77	-0.73	184.08	125.55	520.05
30) ①	County of Marin CA	GEN	2010	385.26	17.55	207.28	18.23	354.56
31) ①	County of Sonoma CA	GEN	2010	375.32	-16.40	261.96	157.04	343.47
32) ①	County of San Luis Ob	GEN	2010	362.24	11.92	161.91	45.81	329.84
33) ①	County of Santa Cruz	GEN	2010	356.19	11.24	124.62	95.91	341.36

Although San Diego is shown as late in filing its 2009 annual report, actually it has made substantial progress in catching up following SEC actions relating to the city's reporting on pension liabilities.

1) Table View (SMUN)   2) Map View (SMUN MAP)   Numbers are in Millions
Australia 61 2 9777 8600 Brazil 5511 3048 4500 Europe 44 20 7330 7500 Germany 49 69 9204 1210 Hong Kong 852 2977 6000
Japan 81 3 3201 8900   Singapore 65 6212 1000   U.S. 1 212 318 2000   Copyright 2011 Bloomberg Finance L.P.
                            SN 268301 CDT GMT-5:00 G515-401-2 10-Aug-2011 10:28:24

Exhibit 2.5

You are able to obtain on the MSRB's EMMA website copies of issuer and borrower annual and event disclosures since July 1, 2009.

The screen in Exhibit 2.6 from the Bloomberg Terminal lists both annual information and event reports filed by the Alaska International Airport Authority.

One issue that is debated in the municipal market is the level of compliance by issuers and borrowers with their agreements to provide continuing disclosure information. There is disagreement in the market about how rigorously and how timely some issuers and borrowers comply with their continuing disclosure agreements.

In any event, the information is important. The Financial Industry Regulatory Authority (FINRA) stated: "Investors should treat missing or past-due financial information from a bond issuer as a potential red flag."

Some cautions regarding continuing disclosure:

■ If an issuer or borrower fails to comply fully and timely with a continuing disclosure agreement, it may affect the liquidity (and therefore, the price) of municipal securities you are considering. You may wish to consider patterns of nondisclosure for both annual disclosure and event disclosure.

■ Some issuers and borrowers file their annual financial information well after their fiscal years have ended. That means their information may be stale—out-of-date—even before the filings are made. You may wish to review their continuing disclosure agreements as to how quickly they agree to make their filings.

■ Older continuing disclosure agreements do not require as much information as do those into which issuers or borrowers enter after December 1, 2010, when changes in the regulation became effective for newly-issued securities. Further, in those older agreements, issuers and borrowers are not required to file event notices as quickly as for agreements on or after that date.

How Can I Find Issuers' and Borrowers' Continuing Disclosure Agreements?

The agreements that municipal securities issuers and private borrowers make to provide annual and event disclosures are contained in the official statements for the initial offerings of the securities.

What Have Issuers or Borrowers Promised to Disclose and When?

The agreements that issuers and borrowers make to provide annual and event disclosures are required to identify the types of information that is to be disclosed and the timing of the disclosures.

You may wish to review those agreements to determine what information you can expect to be filed with EMMA and when you should expect the filings to occur. The MSRB now also requires underwriters to provide some of that information directly on the EMMA website.

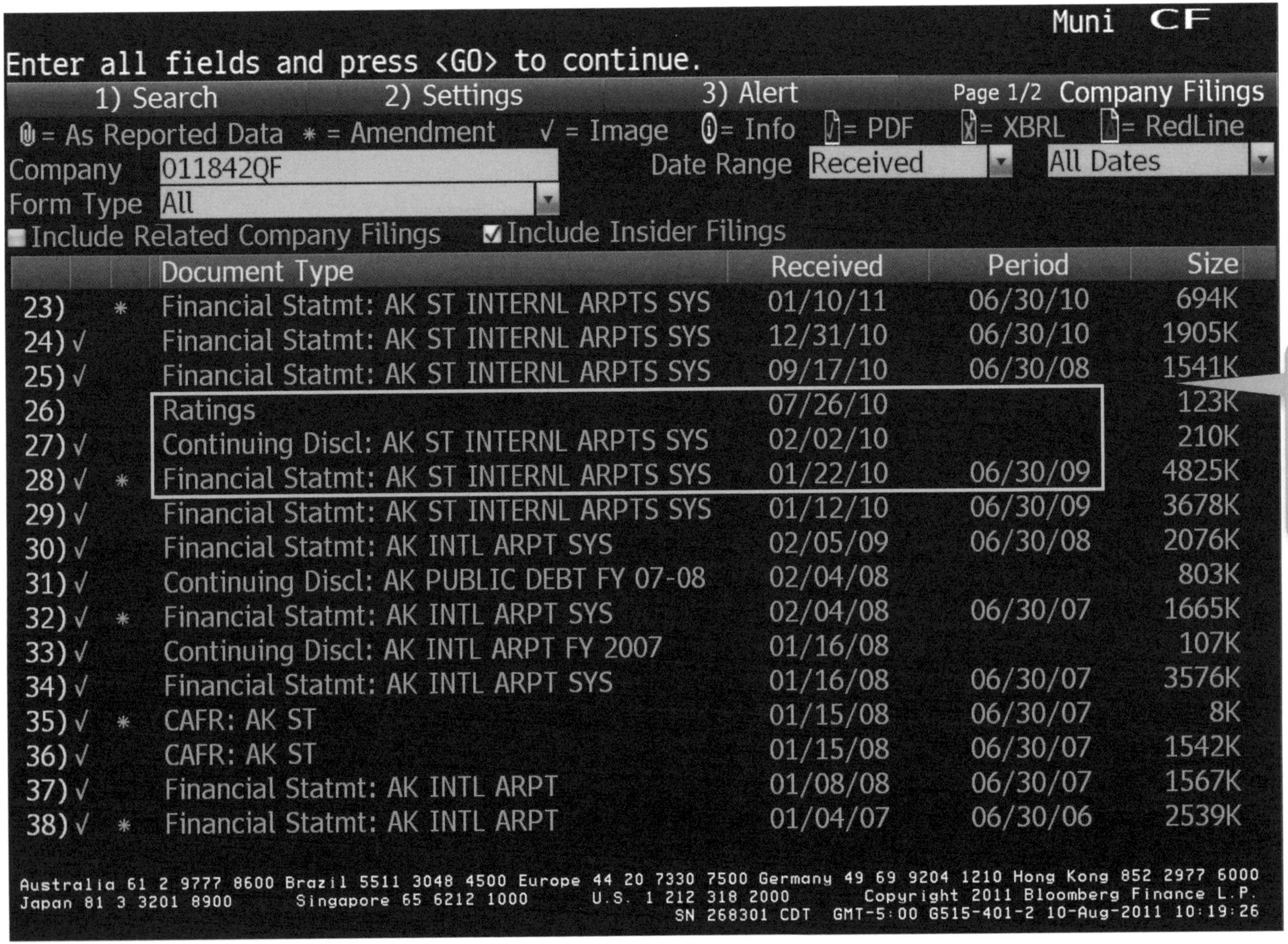

Muni CF

Enter all fields and press <GO> to continue.

1) Search 2) Settings 3) Alert Page 1/2 Company Filings

= As Reported Data * = Amendment √ = Image = Info = PDF = XBRL = RedLine

Company 011842QF Date Range Received All Dates

Form Type All

Include Related Company Filings ☑ Include Insider Filings

			Document Type	Received	Period	Size
23)		*	Financial Statmt: AK ST INTERNL ARPTS SYS	01/10/11	06/30/10	694K
24)	√		Financial Statmt: AK ST INTERNL ARPTS SYS	12/31/10	06/30/10	1905K
25)	√		Financial Statmt: AK ST INTERNL ARPTS SYS	09/17/10	06/30/08	1541K
26)			Ratings	07/26/10		123K
27)	√		Continuing Discl: AK ST INTERNL ARPTS SYS	02/02/10		210K
28)	√	*	Financial Statmt: AK ST INTERNL ARPTS SYS	01/22/10	06/30/09	4825K
29)	√		Financial Statmt: AK ST INTERNL ARPTS SYS	01/12/10	06/30/09	3678K
30)	√		Financial Statmt: AK INTL ARPT SYS	02/05/09	06/30/08	2076K
31)	√		Continuing Discl: AK PUBLIC DEBT FY 07-08	02/04/08		803K
32)	√	*	Financial Statmt: AK INTL ARPT SYS	02/04/08	06/30/07	1665K
33)	√		Continuing Discl: AK INTL ARPT FY 2007	01/16/08		107K
34)	√		Financial Statmt: AK INTL ARPT SYS	01/16/08	06/30/07	3576K
35)	√	*	CAFR: AK ST	01/15/08	06/30/07	8K
36)	√		CAFR: AK ST	01/15/08	06/30/07	1542K
37)	√		Financial Statmt: AK INTL ARPT	01/08/08	06/30/07	1567K
38)	√	*	Financial Statmt: AK INTL ARPT	01/04/07	06/30/06	2539K

Australia 61 2 9777 8600 Brazil 5511 3048 4500 Europe 44 20 7330 7500 Germany 49 69 9204 1210 Hong Kong 852 2977 6000
Japan 81 3 3201 8900 Singapore 65 6212 1000 U.S. 1 212 318 2000 Copyright 2011 Bloomberg Finance L.P.
SN 268301 CDT GMT-5:00 G515-401-2 10-Aug-2011 10:19:26

The boxed filings by the Airport System include both an annual report and two event reports, one of which is for a rating change.

Exhibit 2.6

Reprinted with permission from Bloomberg. Copyright 2011 Bloomberg L.P. All rights reserved.

How Can I Find Identities of Cooperative Issuers/Borrowers?

As in the corporate securities market, some municipal issuers and borrowers evidence a greater willingness to provide information than do others.

The MSRB offers incentives to cooperative issuers or borrowers in the form of special recognition on EMMA when the issuers or borrowers agree voluntarily to file their annual financial statements within 150 days after the ends of the issuers' fiscal years (120 days after December 31, 2013).

Other MSRB incentives (listed below) provide special recognition when issuers or borrowers agree to prepare their financial statements in accordance with applicable generally accepted accounting principles (GAAP) or when the issuers or borrowers post on EMMA their URLs as sources of additional Internet-based information. See also "What Information Is Available on Issuer Websites?" later in this chapter.

MSRB Special Recognition Incentives to Issuers/Borrowers

- Issuer/Borrower Agreement to Provide Annual Financial Statements within 150 Days Following Fiscal Year-Ends (120 Days after December 31, 2013)
- Issuer/Borrower Agreement to Prepare Financial Statements in Accordance with GAAP
- Issuer/Borrower Posting of URL Regarding Additional Internet-Based Disclosure Information on Investor Pages on Issuer/Borrower Websites

How Can I Obtain Information on Variable-Rate Securities?

For short-term municipal securities issues, EMMA contains certain interest rate data and securitization documentation relating to the liquidity of variable-rate securities.

As discussed under "What Information and Documents Are Dealers Required to Submit to EMMA?" later in this chapter, dealers underwriting variable-rate securities are required to submit certain data and documents regarding the securities.

The same is true regarding auction-rate securities. Although those no longer are being issued, some auction-rate securities remain outstanding. If you encounter auction-rate securities, you may wish to be aware of significant problems that many investors have experienced with those securities. See Chapter 6, "Greater Rewards and Greater Risks," in the section entitled, "What Are Auction-Rate Securities?"

Is Rating Information Available on EMMA?

Yes. In addition to issuer and borrower continuing disclosures of rating changes, the MSRB intends that EMMA will begin to provide current municipal securities credit ratings.

A caution: The MSRB plans for EMMA to provide certain ratings, but not necessarily all of them. As of this writing, S&P and Fitch have agreed to cooperate in providing their ratings directly to EMMA.

Can Issuers/Borrowers Provide Additional Information to EMMA?

Yes. The MSRB accepts on EMMA certain additional information and documents that issuers or borrowers may choose to provide voluntarily. The information and documents consist of both primary market documents and continuing disclosure information.

When issuers or borrowers provide additional information voluntarily, you may regard them as more likely to be interested in you than are other issuers or borrowers.

The list below summarizes certain of that information and those documents.

Certain Information and Documents That Issuers/Borrowers May Provide Voluntarily on EMMA

- Budgets
- Quarterly financial statements or information
- Additional event information, such as communications from IRS
- Preliminary official statements and official statements
- Pre-sale offering documents, such as notices of sale
- Section 529 plan documents for state-sponsored college savings programs
- Advance refunding documents
- Documents for securities excluded or exempt from Rule 15c2-12
- Amendments to documents

What Information and Documents Are Dealers Required to Submit to EMMA?

MSRB rules require dealers to provide to EMMA certain information and documents relating to municipal securities that the dealers underwrite. Some of these are summarized in the list below.

Certain Information and Documents That Underwriters Are Required to Submit to EMMA

- Official statements
- Section 529 plan disclosure documents
- Existence of continuing disclosure agreements
- Identities of issuers/borrowers or other obligated persons that are to file continuing reports
- Contractual timeframes for filing issuer/borrower annual financial statements
- Certain data and documents regarding variable-rate securities and auction-rate securities

What Information Is Available on Issuer Websites?

Many municipal securities issuers and private borrowers are proactive in terms of providing useful information for investors. Often, the information appears on issuer or borrower websites.

Information on issuer websites may include financial statements (both audited and unaudited), budgets, other financial information, staff reports, and minutes of meetings of governing bodies and committees.

In many instances, you may find information on issuer or borrower websites that is more current than information in filed documents. In addition, website information may go beyond information in filed documents, such as, for example, budgetary information or interim financial data or statements.

That information may be a valuable resource for you.

Information on issuer or borrower websites will vary. Some issuers or borrowers may not provide any information useful for investors. You may wish to take that into account in deciding to invest in their securities.

What Information Is Available Through Local Press Reports?

Local governments are public entities, and are not able to maintain many secrets. Often, there is an intense local interest in local governmental affairs. More thorough investors may wish to search Internet resources for local press stories regarding the financial and other performance of local governments and their projects. It is relevant to keep in mind that local news media have their own biases, and that local reporters may not have much financial expertise.

Private borrowers are not necessarily subject to the same public coverage, although sometimes there may be local press coverage regarding projects in which private borrowers have interests.

How Can Brokers, Dealers, and Financial Advisors Help?

An important ready source of information regarding municipal securities may be your broker, dealer, or financial advisor. This can be a way to obtain a professional perspective from someone you know.

Dealers that serve as underwriters of particular municipal securities issues generally remain in touch with the issuers and borrowers, and track their filings with EMMA. Dealers trading municipal securities are required to be informed regarding that filed information.

How Can Ratings and Ratings Analyses Help?

Bond ratings provide rating agencies' views regarding credit quality of municipal securities. Rating agencies may also issue analyses that discuss factors they consider useful regarding particular ratings.

SMART INVESTOR TIP

In many instances, you may find information on issuer or borrower websites that is more current than information in filed documents.

SMART INVESTOR TIP

Information on issuer or borrower websites will vary. Some issuers or borrowers may not provide any information useful for investors. You may wish to take that into account in deciding to invest in their securities.

SMART INVESTOR TIP

More thorough investors may wish to search Internet resources for local press stories regarding the financial and other performance of local governments and their projects.

SMART INVESTOR TIP

An important ready source of information regarding municipal securities may be your broker, dealer, or financial advisor.

Should I Rely on Ratings?

Ratings and rating analyses provide one source of potentially useful information about municipal securities. Some investors, however, make a significant mistake when they allow ratings (or credit enhancement) to serve as the sole criterion for their investment judgment. Ratings are best viewed as general guides, not a substitute for your own review and analyses of information available regarding municipal securities. Rating agencies stress that their ratings are *not* recommendations that you buy, sell, or hold any security. As an official of Moody's stated, "If people choose to consider our opinions, we expect them to use those opinions to supplement, and not replace, their own credit analysis." (See "For Additional Information" at the end of the chapter.)

Undue reliance on ratings can lead easily to making investments that you do not understand well and that may not be appropriate for your investment goals. An investment may not satisfy your own investment needs in terms of liquidity, maturity, duration, security, pricing, redemption features, or other parameters. As this book demonstrates, there are significant differences within the diversity of municipal finance structures available in the market.

In addition, rating agencies do not engage in extensive independent due diligence of the nature expected of underwriters. They do receive and rely upon information provided to them by issuers and borrowers, with a degree of supplemental inquiry and review that may vary according to the rating agency and transaction.

For your purposes, the relevant ratings reflect rating agencies' views regarding specific municipal securities *issues*. *Issuers* are distinct in that sense from their *issues*.

Many issuers have multiple municipal securities issues outstanding. Those differing securities issues may have significantly different structures and credit supports, and consequently, different ratings. For example, a general obligation bond may have a far different rating from a general fund security, a sales tax bond or a wastewater enterprise revenue security. Industrial development securities issued by the same issuer will have credit considerations focusing on the private borrowers, and may carry vastly different ratings.

How Do Municipal Ratings Relate to Corporate Ratings?

Muni market professionals have long been aware that rating agencies often rated corporate and municipal securities using the same symbols, but with different criteria. (See "For Additional Information" at the end of the chapter.)

Rating agency analyses of default experiences demonstrated on an historical basis that even a triple-A rated corporate obligation had greater default risks than much lower rated municipal securities. (See "For Additional Information" at the end of the chapter.) Municipal Market Advisors (MMA) noted that "AAA-rated corporate bonds have defaulted almost 10 times more frequently than single-A-rated municipal bonds."

This was demonstrated graphically when bond insurers' credit practices in insuring subprime mortgage pools and other risky obligations came to light and all of the triple-A-rated, private insurers (and municipal securities the insurers insured) were downgraded. Some of the downgrades were substantial.

Some municipal securities that did not have underlying ratings lost their ratings entirely due to bond insurers' actions. Many investors who relied solely upon the corporate triple-A ratings of bond insurers (later downgraded) lost value on their investments and, when they traded insured municipal securities, lost money.

In 2009 and 2010, rating agencies took steps to coordinate ratings of corporate and municipal securities to a greater extent. Those steps made significant progress in reducing the differences, although there still are indications that corporate securities may continue to receive a degree of rating advantage over municipal securities. (Rating agencies, however, maintain that municipal and corporate obligations are rated on comparable scales.)

What Additional Tools Are Available for Investors?

In addition to issuers' or borrowers' disclosure documents—official statements and continuing disclosure documents—and other resources identified above, you are able to take advantage of other valuable information resources.

The Appendix to this book directs your attention to additional valuable resources.

For Additional Information

■ Rule 15c2-12 contains certain exclusions and exemptions for small municipal issues (under $1 million), certain short-term and variable-rate securities, and securities sold in limited placements. Certain issuers or borrowers with small principal amounts of securities outstanding are subject to modified continuing disclosure requirements.

Although variable-rate municipal securities are exempt from the Rule on initial issuance, for securities issued on December 1, 2010, or later (as well as variable-rate securities with certain changed terms), the issuers and borrowers must file continuing disclosure information described by the SEC, as follows:

The information to be provided consists of: (1) certain annual financial and operating information and audited financial statements; (2) notices of the occurrence of any of 15 specific events ("event notices"); and (3) notices of the failure of an issuer or obligated person to make submission required by a continuing disclosure agreement ("failure to file notices").

The amended Rule does not apply to demand securities outstanding as of November 30, 2010, so long as they meet specified requirements. They must continuously remain in authorized denominations of $100,000 or more and may, at the option of the holder thereof, be tendered to an issuer of such securities or its designated agent for redemption or purchase at par value or more at least as frequently as every nine months until maturity, earlier redemption, or purchase by an issuer or its designated agent ("limited grandfather provision").

SEC, "Amendments to Municipal Securities Disclosure—A Small Entity Compliance Guide" (August 8, 2010).

In addition, the MSRB requires certain dealers to submit to EMMA information and documents regarding variable-rate and auction-rate securities. The information and documents relate, among other things, to interest rate resets and reset mechanisms, auction bidding, and procedures, and liquidity terms.

■ Testimony of Robert Kurtter, Managing Director, U.S. Public Finance, Moody's Investors Service, Before the United States House of Representatives Oversight Committee on TARP, Financial Services and Bailouts of Public and Private Programs at 2 (March 15, 2011).

■ In addition to the Fitch Ratings data cited in the Introduction to this book, in 2009 Standard & Poor's (S&P) released reports showing significantly greater levels of corporate defaults than municipal defaults. S&P, "U.S. Municipal Rating Transitions And Defaults, 1986–2009" (March 11, 2009) and "Default, Transition, and Recovery: 2008 Annual Global Corporate Default Study And Rating Transitions" (April 2, 2009). In 2007, Moody's Investors Service (Moody's) published similar results. Moody's, "The U.S. Municipal Bond Rating Scale: Mapping to the Global Rating Scale and Assigning Global Scale Ratings to Municipal Obligations" (March 2007).

■ Testimony of Matt Fabian, Managing Director, Municipal Market Advisors, before the House Judiciary Committee, Subcommittee on Courts, Commercial and Administrative Law at 4 (Feb. 14, 2011).

CHAPTER 3

General Obligation Securities

General obligation securities are payable from dedicated real property (and sometimes, in addition, other) taxes. The securities are extremely strong. The payment of these securities is *not* subject to stresses affecting municipal general funds or budgets. Commonly, municipal issuers are required under state law to levy and collect the taxes without regard to rate or amount in order to pay the securities. At times, there are tax-rate limits that you should understand, but most of those securities incorporate excess tax capacity for protection.

Not all municipal securities are created equal. Some have proved to be extraordinarily sound historically. Others incorporate greater risks (and with the risks, potentially greater rewards).

In this book, I attempt to provide guidance as to certain circumstances when you need to be especially alert and careful in making investment decisions. See, for example, Chapter 6, "Greater Rewards and Greater Risks."

General obligation municipal securities are one type of municipal securities that is especially sound. Pundit assertions and news stories suggesting otherwise are sadly in error.

This chapter discusses certain municipal securities that have proved to be strong and sound over many decades.

Why Are General Obligation Securities Sound?

Many communities have suffered tremendous calamities in the form of floods, earthquakes, fires, and devastating storms without defaulting on their general obligation securities. Similarly, many local governments have experienced disastrous financial adversities without default. Even when those isolated defaults occurred, the experience in the municipal market is that governmental issuers pay their obligations on a delayed basis.

When an issuer's general obligation security is supported by a statutory lien, precedent indicates that the general obligation security is especially strong, even in Chapter 9 bankruptcy.

Perhaps short of a tornado or earthquake that destroys an entire community (this example is given by Todd Meierhenry, Meierhenry Sargent LLP, bond counsel in South Dakota), it is extremely difficult to cause one of these traditional municipal general obligation securities issues to default.

Neither general fund pension obligations nor general fund budgetary issues should prevent the payment of these municipal securities.

This is one of the key reasons that various pundits and certain media have failed to present an accurate portrayal of municipal securities.

What Is a General Obligation Bond?

General obligation bonds are supported by the continued levy and collection of real property taxes—"ad valorem" taxes—upon all taxable property in established communities. The taxes generally are levied upon both improved and unimproved real property (although those may be taxed at different rates) and often, but not in all states, certain personal property (such as automobiles, airplanes, boats, and the like), as well as intangible property. "Ad valorem" taxes are taxes levied upon property based upon the property's governmentally-determined value (which may differ from market value).

Under state law, the obligated taxes must be collected and paid to investors regardless of whether the financed improvements are completed. Many, if not most, general obligation securities have been voter approved.

Standard & Poor's, one of the major rating agencies, describes general obligation bonds in S&P's online rating criteria for general obligation bonds, as follows (see the Appendix regarding S&P's and the MSRB's websites):

When a state or municipal issuer sells a general obligation (G.O.) bond the issuer pledges its full faith and credit to repay the financial obligation. Unless certain tax revenue streams are specifically restricted, the GO issuer frequently pledges all of its tax-raising powers. Typically, local governments secure the obligation with their ability to levy an unlimited ad valorem property tax; state governments, which have different tax structures, usually pledge unrestricted revenue streams.

The strength of ad valorem taxation, which is the property tax that general purpose local governments (*e.g.*, cities and counties) and school districts are able to levy, makes general obligation bonds sound. None of the pundits, and few news media, explain this crucial strength of general obligation bonds.

This is more than a detail. It is the essence of general obligation bonds. It is inexcusable for pundits and some media to frighten investors, especially individual investors who have already suffered greatly in the financial crisis, into selling these municipal securities at disadvantageous prices.

What Are Unlimited Tax Bonds?

Most general obligation bonds are supported by unlimited taxes. Without regard to pension liabilities or unbalanced budgets, the local governments issuing unlimited tax general obligation bonds generally are obligated under state laws or constitutions to pay the bonds first from tax revenues or to raise the taxes to whatever level is required in order to pay the bonds in full.

A common description used in the municipal market is that the issuer of unlimited tax general obligation bonds has "pledged" (i.e., promised) its "full faith and credit" to the payment of the securities. As also described in the municipal market, it is said that the issuer is obligated to levy taxes as necessary for that purpose "without regard to rate or amount."

Bond counsel's opinion included in the official statement when these securities are first offered for sale typically opines that this obligation is enforceable under state law.

As noted, when state law provides a statutory lien, precedent supports the protection of the general obligation security, even in Chapter 9 bankruptcy.

If some property owners are delinquent in paying their taxes, their properties can be foreclosed in tax sales. The remaining property owners must make up the difference in the meantime by paying slightly higher taxes.

Only in the tiniest of communities would the failure of particular property owners to pay their taxes impact other property owners to a meaningful degree. (See "For

Additional Information" at the end of the chapter.) There need be little concern about property owners abandoning their properties to avoid the taxes. Whether they like it or not, they will pay the taxes to preserve the property values they do have. Commonly, mortgage lenders also will pay the taxes to preserve their security.

In such circumstances, which are the rule in the municipal securities market, not the exception, financial issues surrounding local government budgets cannot and do not deter the obligations or abilities of localities to levy and collect the taxes and to use the collected taxes to pay investors.

What Are Limited Tax Bonds?

Some bonds, called general obligation bonds, are supported by limited taxes, rather than unlimited taxes. You need to understand which type of tax secures general obligation bonds you are considering.

In the case of limited tax bonds, there is generally excess capacity in the tax authorization to levy the taxes to pay the bonds despite property owner delinquencies pending tax foreclosure. You may wish to identify a sufficient level of protection between the amounts owing on the bonds and the authorized tax level. That excess coverage provides protection.

Once again, financial issues surrounding local government budgets cannot and do not deter the obligation or ability of localities to levy and collect the taxes up to the authorized level. Again, bond counsel's opinion included in the official statement when these securities

KEY POINT:

General obligation bonds are supported by the continued levy and collection of real property taxes upon all taxable property in established communities—improved and unimproved real property (although those may be taxed at different rates), and, often, certain personal property (such as automobiles, airplanes, boats, and the like), as well as intangible property.

KEY POINT:

Example of Offering Description of General Obligation Security

"In order to provide sufficient funds for repayment of principal and interest when due on the Bonds, the County is empowered and is obligated to levy ad valorem taxes upon all property subject to taxation by the City, without limitation as to rate or amount. Those taxes are in addition to other taxes levied upon property within the City. When collected, the tax revenues are deposited in the City's Debt Service Fund required to be maintained by the County and to be used solely for debt service on bonds of the District."

are first offered for sale typically opines that this obligation is enforceable under state law.

What Enforcement Mechanisms Are Available Under State Law?

Standard and Poor's (S&P) has stated:

> GO bonds generally are regarded as the broadest security among tax-secured debt instruments. GO bonds effectively create a link between public and personal debt: a homeowner unable to pay his property taxes will forfeit his house just as surely as if he could not pay his mortgage, and an unlimited tax GO pledge would enable a trustee to invoke mandamus to force the issuer to raise the tax rate as much as necessary to pay off the bonds.

The first enforcement mechanism, then, for general obligation bonds is foreclosure by issuers upon delinquent property owners through tax sales. This is usually such an effective mechanism that property owners (and their mortgage lenders) rarely allow their properties to go through the foreclosure process. As S&P stated, "a homeowner unable to pay property taxes will forfeit his house."

The second enforcement mechanism for general obligation securities is in state courts to enforce the issuers' obligations to raise, levy, and collect obligated taxes. That generally includes, in the case of unlimited tax general obligation securities, the issuers' obligation either to use taxes first to pay the securities or to raise taxes as

much as necessary in order to pay principal of and interest on the securities.

Official statements also generally describe the enforcement mechanisms available under state law, and should so state when the tax security is supported under state law by a statutory lien.

That obligation may be enforced by the trustee for the securities, as S&P indicated, or in the case of securities that do not have trustees, may be enforced by investors or a designated proportion of investors.

General obligation securities generally are enforceable by a writ of mandamus or other process pursuant to state law requiring that the local government levy the taxes needed to pay the bonds.

Official statements for general obligation securities contain bond counsel opinions to the effect that the securities are valid and enforceable under state law. The preparation and provision of those opinions is a key function of bond counsel in general obligation securities offerings.

What Is the Role of Credit Diversity in Communities?

The credit diversity of established communities effectively spreads the risk for your benefit to all the real property owners, and often personal property owners.

In order to gain perspective, it may help to visualize a community with many thousands, or tens or even hundreds of thousands, of residential properties, commercial businesses and industries paying the real property taxes that are obligated to pay the municipal securities. (In the case of traditional revenue securities, those residences, commercial business, and industries would pay the enterprise user fees.) With that perspective, it becomes easier to understand why a few delinquencies (typically less than 1% or 2%) would not affect the payment of the securities.

Property owners (and their mortgage lenders) will not abandon their properties merely because of property tax increases. If property owners object to the taxes, they will sell their properties to new owners who will pay the taxes.

You may wish to gain assurance, however, from the review of available information in official statements and continuing disclosure documents that the community is diverse.

That is because certain smaller communities may be highly reliant upon one or two very large employers. Those employers would then pay a substantial proportion of the taxes, and in addition, would employ many community members who also pay taxes. If those employers were to fail or leave the community, then tax collections could become more difficult. That is not, however, the typical situation.

Official statements offering general obligation tax-secured municipal securities usually identify the top 10 or so real property taxpayers within the issuer's jurisdiction and those taxpayers' shares of the aggregate tax payments. Therefore, you should be able to determine easily whether a small number of taxpayers is liable for a disproportionate share.

In especially economically-damaged communities, there may be certain properties that have lost so much value to such an extreme degree that the properties are difficult to sell even in foreclosure merely for collection of delinquent taxes. This is a rare occurrence. Although this may be a reason for caution, even in such instances, it does not usually lead to payment difficulties for the general obligation securities, but rather in the case of unlimited tax securities, to local governments increasing ad valorem taxes on remaining properties.

What Are the Risks of Bankruptcy?

As noted earlier, precedent supports strong protection in bankruptcy for general obligation securities secured by obligated taxes supported by statutory liens. Those statutory liens should render the collection of taxes and payment of securities unaffected by a Chapter 9 bankruptcy filing.

Even when Chapter 9 proceedings involve local governments that do have outstanding general obligation securities (which is not the case in most proceedings), the proceedings generally have led historically to compromises between local governments and suppliers, employee unions, judgment creditors, and other creditors, but not to abrogation of general obligation securities benefiting from specifically-obligated tax sources of payment.

In the event that a statutory lien is not present, local governments often have voluntarily protected their general obligation investors in order to preserve their vital access to the market.

Is There Protection from Budgetary Problems?

Municipal general funds are the basic operational accounting entities through which local governments provide for their general governmental operations.

In contrast, certain governmental funds may relate, among other things, to specific enterprises (e.g., a water enterprise fund), to specific activities (e.g., a library fund), or to trust funds held by the governmental entity. Those other funds are segregated from the general fund.

Municipal securities that are payable from general funds (general fund securities) of general purpose local governments (such as cities and counties) are *not* general obligation bonds. Although sometimes certain parties may confuse the term *general obligation* so as to apply the term to municipal securities payable from local general funds, that usage is inaccurate. See Chapter 4, "General Fund and Other Municipal Securities."

In contrast to general obligation securities, general fund–supported municipal securities—leases, bonds or otherwise—are subject to greater risks associated with budgetary considerations. Even in this case, however, the historical record evidences very few defaults. Local governments in many states have a degree of flexibility to reduce spending and to raise taxes or fees within limits without voter approval.

Further, even for general fund securities, the necessity for local governments to have access to the municipal market in order to carry out their normal governmental functions on behalf of their citizens often strongly militates against default and bankruptcy risks.

Where Can I Find Tax Rate, Collection, and Delinquency Data?

In considering general obligation tax-supported municipal securities, you may wish to review, among other things, the issuer's historical property tax rates, collection and delinquency data, and property valuation trends in the community. Those data give you a picture of the issuer's success in collecting taxes and how the community is faring in terms of property values and trends.

Most issuers provide data reflecting their historical levels of taxes, collections, delinquencies, and property values.

The next pages contain hypothetical examples of historical property tax billing, collection, and delinquency information (Exhibit 3.1) and of historical property valuation data as the data might be presented in an official statement (Exhibit 3.2).

You may note that in the first table (Exhibit 3.1) the hypothetical total collections are shown in some years as exceeding 100 percent of the billings. This illustrates that delinquent taxes are collected following brief delays as foreclosures proceed. Thus, the sum of collections of delinquencies and collections of current taxes may exceed 100 percent of the currently-billed taxes.

Where Are Those Data Available?

At the time of a municipal securities offering, the tax rate, collection, delinquency, and property value data are contained typically in the official statement for the offering.

After offerings, the data often are available in continuing disclosure filings made by the issuers with the EMMA disclosure platform of the Municipal Securities Rulemaking Board (MSRB) at www.emma.msrb.org/.

What Are Double-Barreled Securities?

Sometimes, a municipal securities issuer will obligate more than one form of security for payment of a securities issue.

For example, for reasons of compliance with state laws or to obtain a better rating, a local government may secure an issue both with taxes and with enterprise revenues. In that case, you have the benefit of both forms of security. This book discusses security in the form of enterprise revenues under Chapter 5, "Revenue Securities."

Example of Real Property Tax Collection Data

Collection (Tax) Year	Current Taxes Billed	Current Taxes Collected	% Current Taxes Collected	Delinquent Taxes Collected	Total % Collected (Current & Delinquent)	Current Taxes	Accumulated (After Delinquent Tax Collections)
	Tax Billings & Collections					Delinquent	
2005–2006	$ 186,030,794	$ 184,347,441	99.10%	$ 1,250,233	99.77%	$ 1,683,353	$ 1,827,556
2006–2007	192,527,016	190,669,887	99.04	1,352,697	99.74	1,857,129	2,331,988
2007–2008	193,025,077	191,052,993	98.98	1,489,621	99.75	1,972,084	2,814,451
2008–2009	192,484,511	190,004,297	98.71	2,923,187	100.23	2,480,214	2,371,478
2009–2010	192,383,480	190,275,913	98.90	3,191,382	100.56	2,107,567	1,287,663

The 'Total Collected' in these years is more than 100% due to collection of delinquencies.

Exhibit 3.1

Example of Real Property Valuation Data

Collection (Tax) Year	Real Property	Personal Property	Public Utility	Total Assessed Valuation
2005–2006	$ 3,216,029,630	$ 825,904,701	$ 429,222,840	$ 4,471,157,171
2006–2007	3,259,967,850	865,315,906	431,259,654	4,556,543,410
2007–2008	3,266,973,550	871,441,801	433,661,588	4,572,076,939
2008–2009	3,262,983,870	872,692,157	436,128,977	4,571,805,004
2009–2010	3,259,626,330	873,534,596	437,258,963	4,570,419,889

Exhibit 3.2

For Additional Information

▪ As discussed under Chapter 4, "General Fund and Other Municipal Securities," the section entitled "What Are Special Tax and Assessment Securities?," tax-supported securities payable from taxes in undeveloped real estate developments present significantly different credit considerations from securities payable from taxes levied in established diverse communities.

▪ Standard and Poor's, "2007 Public Finance Criteria Book" at 60 (Standard & Poor's Financial Services LLP, Dec. 11, 2006).

CHAPTER 4

General Fund and Other Municipal Securities

Unlike general obligation securities, municipal general fund securities *are* payable from municipal general funds. Often, general fund securities take the form of lease obligations and certificates of participation (COPs) in the leases. Variations on these municipal securities may be called lease revenue bonds. These securities involve more risk than do general obligation securities, although again the historical record is strong. A key element to consider is the essential role of leased property, which in the municipal market is called essentiality. In addition, you should understand other forms of tax- and revenue-supported municipal securities and their sources of payment.

General fund municipal securities differ from other municipal securities in important respects. Once again, elements in your favor include the historical record of a very low level of defaults by governmental issuers issuing investment grade-rated securities for essential governmental purposes. They also include the necessity that governmental issuers have ready access to the market to serve their citizens.

What Are General Fund Securities?

General fund securities in the municipal market are different from general obligation securities. The similarity of the terms may have much to do with the confusion of the pundits and authors of some news reports.

As discussed above, municipal securities payable from local government general funds are *not* general obligation securities. (Securities payable from state general funds are, however, considered to be general obligations due to the variety of revenue sources available to states and the compelling necessity that states have access to the market continuously in order to function.)

Despite the absence of specific tax security such as exists in the local general obligation context, the mu-

DEFINITION:
Credit default swap

A credit default swap effectively insures against default by a borrower.

nicipal market considers state general fund obligations to be strong. This is indicated by the costs of credit default swap contracts (CDS) against default by the states. A credit default swap effectively insures against default by a borrower. The following tables (Exhibits 4.1 and 4.2) present Bloomberg data on August 4, 2011, regarding the prices of CDS for selected states and, in the second table, contrasts the price of a CDS on Illinois obligations versus the prices of CDS on obligations of selected European countries, notably Greece (*Note:* prices of CDS change throughout the trading day).

In brief, no U.S. state is another Greece! Or close to it. Not even in the ballpark. Or in the parking lot.

5-Yr Municipality CDS Contracts (as of 8/4/11)

Country/State	Price
State of Illinois	194,000
State of Nevada	143.57
State of California	141.35
State of Connecticut	130.25
State of New Jersey	127.11
City of New York NY	120.91
State of Michigan	117.90
Commonwealth of Massachusetts	108.59
State of Ohio	108.29
Commonwealth of Pennsylvania	107.72
State of New York	98.47
State of Wisconsin	93.20
State of Maryland	84.86
State of North Carolina	79.50
State of Minnesota	72.10
State of Texas	70.13

Prices provided by CMA (note: prices change constantly throughout the day).

Exhibit 4.1

Country/State	Price
Greece	1803.38
Ireland	862.81
Italy	395.00
State of Illinois	194.00

This puts Illinois in context with worldwide CDS. As Joe Mysak puts it, Illinois is not Greece. Nor Ireland.

Exhibit 4.2

Exhibit 4.3 presents Bloomberg data on August 5, 2011, regarding option-adjusted yields on various maturities of municipal securities of selected states. The yield differentials likely reflect credit considerations, as well as state income tax considerations and other factors. See Chapter 9, "Tax Exemption of Municipal Securities," in the section entitled "What Is the Role of State Income Tax Exemptions?"

Local government general fund securities are subject to budgetary risks, as they are paid from local governmental budgets, not from obligated taxes or dedicated revenues. Historically, however, local governments have

State Municipal Tax-Exempt G.O. Yields (on 8/5/11)

Comparison of Yields for Selected States (Aug. 5, 2011)							
Maturity	Virginia	New York	Texas	New Jersey	Florida	Wisconsin	California	Illinois
3M	0.11	0.24	0.17	0.35	0.21	0.38	0.30	0.72
6M	0.15	0.33	0.18	0.36	0.26	0.40	0.37	0.76
1Y	0.20	0.46	0.20	0.39	0.38	0.46	0.52	0.88
2Y	0.38	0.66	0.42	0.53	0.63	0.62	0.82	1.23
3Y	0.52	0.86	0.76	0.74	0.92	0.83	1.06	1.67
4Y	0.77	1.10	1.03	1.03	1.24	1.11	1.34	2.15
5Y	1.10	1.41	1.35	1.36	1.58	1.44	1.70	2.63
7Y	1.74	2.11	2.09	2.06	2.31	2.17	2.59	3.47
9Y	2.36	2.78	2.74	2.73	2.97	2.84	3.46	4.09
10Y	2.72	3.06	3.02	3.03	3.26	3.12	3.82	4.30
12Y	3.38	3.46	3.50	3.52	3.72	3.54	4.27	4.57
14Y	3.68	3.70	3.84	3.86	4.03	3.79	4.47	4.70
15Y	3.73	3.79	3.93	3.97	4.14	3.88	4.54	4.74
17Y	3.82	3.93	4.04	4.10	4.31	4.02	4.69	4.82
19Y	3.87	4.09	4.20	4.22	4.44	4.16	4.84	4.95
20Y	3.92	4.17	4.33	4.28	4.50	4.25	4.90	5.01
25Y	4.14	4.45	4.66	4.66	4.67	4.66	5.01	5.24
30Y	4.15	4.49	4.66	4.72	4.73	5.00	5.02	5.29

Note: Unlike the BVAL AAA Scale, these yields are *option-adjusted* for easy state-by-state comparison.

Exhibit 4.3

demonstrated that they will cut spending or raise revenues, rather than default on these securities. Defaults have occurred in only a few instances.

Exhibit 4.4 summarizes briefly certain contrasts between local government general obligation securities and local government general fund securities.

Local General Obligation Securities	Local General Fund Securities
Most commonly are bonds.	Usually are leases or participations in leases (called COPs) or lease revenue bonds.
Secured by pledged taxes, either unlimited tax or, in some states, limited tax.	No specific tax security; secured by issuer's general fund as another expenditure payable from the issuer's receipts allocable to the general fund.
Taxes or securities are often voter approved.	Voters rarely have a direct role in the issuance of general fund securities.
Future payment is protected by obligations to levy and collect taxes.	Annual appropriation usually is required in order to obligate monies for lease payments in each fiscal year (in California and Indiana, abatement leases may be used requiring lease payments if facilities are available for governmental use).

Local General Obligation Securities	Local General Fund Securities
Essentiality of financed governmental facilities is irrelevant due to obligation to levy and collect taxes to pay securities.	Essentiality of leased governmental facilities is a key credit consideration.
Tax levy enforceable under state law.	State law protection limited to agreement to pay from available and appropriated general fund monies.
Based upon precedent, should be protected in bankruptcy when state law provides a statutory lien.	No specially protected bankruptcy status.

Exhibit 4.4

Exhibit 4.5 presents Bloomberg data regarding the top 20 cities nationally by general fund receipts.. San Diego filed its annual information for 2010 shortly after the date of Bloomberg's screen. Seattle, WA, and Newark, NJ, have December 31 fiscal years and also filed their annual information.

The following two screens (Exhibits 4.6 and 4.7) from the Bloomberg Terminal show the balance sheet and general fund revenues and expenses of the City of New York for its fiscal years ended June 30, 2006 through 2010.

Top 20 Cities by Total General Fund Receipts   (8/1/11)

City	Latest Fiscal Year Published	Total General Fund Revenue (MM)
City of New York NY	2010	62,470.58
City of Los Angeles CA	2010	4,185.43
City of Philadelphia PA	2010	3,348.12
City & County of San Francisco CA	2010	2,798.65
City of Chicago IL	2010	2,610.85
City of Boston MA	2010	2,242.25
City of Houston TX	2010	1,786.43
City of Baltimore MD	2010	1,319.97
City of Detroit MI	2010	1,187.98
City & County of Honolulu HI	2010	1,185.79
City of Virginia Beach VA	2010	1,035.39
City of San Diego CA	2009	1,014.63
City of Jacksonville FL	2010	976.48
City of Dallas TX	2010	964.16
City of Seattle WA	2009	942.41
City of San Antonio TX	2010	857.49
City of Newark NJ	2009	856.13
City & County of Denver CO	2010	829.10
Metropolitan Government of Nashville & Davidson County TN	2010	751.52
City of Jersey City NJ	2010	700.52

Exhibit 4.5

<HELP> for explanation.   Equity**MIFA**
1<GO> to Show Charts, 2<GO> to Show Templates, Click numbers for transparency
5264Z US Equity   95) Defaults   96) Actions ▾   Financial Analysis
∿ Periods 20 Ann ▾   Filing MR ▾   Cur. USD ▾   Funds GEN ▾   City of New York NY
■ Estimates   ■ Current Values   Quick Field <Type a Field>   4) Fields

Balance Sheet	O:Jun 10 A	O:Jun 09 A	O:Jun 08 A	O:Jun 07 A	O:Jun 06 A
General Fund					
Period End Date	2010-06-30	2009-06-30	2008-06-30	2007-06-30	2006-06-30
Assets					
+ Cash & Near Cash	5,229.06	6,847.97	4,685.42	6,429.08	7,936.28
+ Marketable sec	349.23	712.11	2,150.18	136.73	258.40
+ Accounts & Notes Receivable	5,837.56	5,484.86	5,996.00	6,110.03	5,424.37
+ Other Receivables	8,100.20	6,068.88	5,158.89	4,211.52	4,211.30
+ Due from Other Funds	2,795.20	2,199.37	3,253.33	2,956.38	2,289.65
+ Other Assets	1,039.23	1,128.40	842.99	860.02	922.14
Total Assets	23,350.49	22,441.59	22,086.81	20,703.76	21,042.14
Liabilities					
+ Accounts Payable	9,792.49	10,220.56	10,251.22	9,196.93	9,517.81
+ Accrued Liabilities	353.27	323.31	394.83	375.29	394.24
+ Unearned Revenue	11,357.53	10,172.57	9,603.58	9,553.59	9,711.41
+ Due to Other Funds	n/a	n/a	n/a	n/a	n/a
+ Due to Other Component Units	88.24	13.33	22.93	15.72	8.51
+ Tax Overpayments	223.90	161.91	267.40	134.70	88.83
+ Other Liabilities	1,092.91	1,112.91	1,114.54	1,000.24	898.86
Total Liabilities	22,908.34	22,004.58	21,654.50	20,276.47	20,619.65
Fund Balances					

98) Units MLN ▾   Zoom 100% ▴▾

Australia 61 2 9777 8600 Brazil 5511 3048 4500 Europe 44 20 7330 7500 Germany 49 69 9204 1210 Hong Kong 852 2977 6000
Japan 81 3 3201 8900   Singapore 65 6212 1000   U.S. 1 212 318 2000   Copyright 2011 Bloomberg Finance L.P.
                                         SN 268301 CDT GMT-5:00 G515-401-2 10-Aug-2011 09:42:43

Exhibit 4.6

```
<HELP> for explanation.                                          EquityMIFA
1<GO> to Show Charts, 2<GO> to Show Templates, Click numbers for transparency
5264Z  US Equity        95) Defaults        96) Actions   ▾           Financial Analysis
 ⟊  Periods 20 Ann   ▾    Filing MR  ▾   Cur. USD  ▾   Funds GEN  ▾        City of New York NY
■Estimates     ■Current Values                          Quick Field ⟨Type a Field⟩    4) Fields
```

Income Statement	0:Jun 10 A	0:Jun 09 A	0:Jun 08 A	0:Jun 07 A	0:Jun 06 A
+ Other Tax Revenues	1,920.94	1,975.69	2,619.25	2,892.58	2,380.74
+ Charges for Services	2,538.98	2,244.92	2,125.87	1,920.75	1,836.96
+ Federal and Other Grants	20,700.80	19,495.41	18,330.13	16,625.63	15,930.75
+ Investment Earnings	22.16	123.90	376.80	473.06	362.20
+ Miscellaneous Revenues	2,007.67	2,112.28	1,990.18	1,849.50	1,559.69
Total Revenues	62,470.58	59,849.09	61,423.52	58,710.80	53,900.78
Expenses					
- General Government Expenses	2,038.52	1,917.78	1,827.65	1,619.92	1,530.07
- Health Expenses	1,661.16	1,843.33	1,587.84	2,272.48	2,757.80
- Education Expenses	19,130.00	18,432.73	17,475.85	16,325.22	15,344.62
- Human Resources Expenses	10,364.41	9,789.77	9,573.15	9,572.41	8,032.97
- Public Safety Expenses	8,000.45	7,683.11	7,258.57	6,841.91	6,693.91
- Public Service Expenses	210.54	366.31	266.40	330.06	261.14
- Social Services Expenses	12,370.11	12,151.26	12,511.34	11,078.05	10,147.67
- Transportation Expenses	1,223.87	1,269.99	1,187.10	1,020.89	954.15
- Judicial Expenses	568.25	623.19	625.39	564.04	516.80
- Recreation Expenses	434.35	445.19	450.15	410.67	376.81
- Community Development Expenses	813.88	796.80	679.58	641.22	721.48
- Environmental Expenses	2,667.04	2,199.57	2,082.73	1,943.30	1,836.40
- Other Program Expenses	-650.31	172.35	312.56	177.80	105.39
- Interest Debt Service	n/a	n/a	n/a	n/a	n/a

```
 98) Units  MLN  ▾                                                 Zoom  100%  ▴
```

Australia 61 2 9777 8600 Brazil 5511 3048 4500 Europe 44 20 7330 7500 Germany 49 69 9204 1210 Hong Kong 852 2977 6000
Japan 81 3 3201 8900   Singapore 65 6212 1000   U.S. 1 212 318 2000   Copyright 2011 Bloomberg Finance L.P.
                                          SN 268301 CDT GMT-5:00 G515-401-2 10-Aug-2011 09:45:28

Exhibit 4.7

What Are Leases, COPs, and Lease Revenue Securities?

Financing leases generally payable from municipal general funds often provide a means for municipal securities issuers to obtain funding for projects the issuers are constructing or purchasing. The credit structure of leases is different in key respects from that of other municipal securities.

Lease structures often are used in municipal finance to avoid state law restrictions on the creation of debt and requirements for voter approval.

To clarify in general terms, a financing lease serves as a vehicle for acquiring property, much as a loan. It provides security to the lender, in that the lender (lessor, which is you as an investor) generally holds title to the property until all payments have been made, at which time title passes to the borrower (lessee). In contrast, an example of a true lease is a lease of an apartment for a limited term, with the property owner continuing to own the property following termination of the lease.

Certificates of participation (COPs) and lease revenue bonds often provide mechanisms through which issuers subdivide leases into maturities and denominations for marketing to investors. (*Note:* In some states, another form of COPs may be used involving installment purchase agreements for revenue-producing governmental enterprises, but the revenue security generally is stronger and involves very different credit considerations from general fund leases.)

While most municipal securities may have taxes or dedicated revenues as long-term obligated (pledged) payment sources, in most states leases are used to avoid voter requirements and other limitations regarding taxes or debt. In many states, this occurs by the mechanism of the issuers' annual appropriation pledge of funds from a specific fund (usually the general fund) to pay the principal and interest (lease payments) to be paid in that fiscal year. In theory, if the issuer does not appropriate the funds in any year (a nonappropriation event), it is not required to make the payments in that year.

Municipal securities payable from obligated taxes (or dedicated revenues) bind future local government governing bodies (such as city councils, county commissions, and school boards). Appropriation leases do not.

Typically, the appropriation process involves initial budgeting steps by the executives or administrators of the issuers, followed by legislative approval of the budget by the issuer's governing body. Once a legislative appropriation occurs for a fiscal year, the issuer effectively has made provision for payment of amounts due under the lease for that year. That contrasts with security in the form of obligated taxes or dedicated revenues, which is binding upon the issuer under state law upon issuance of the securities. Sometimes, an issuer agrees to include lease payments in budgets submitted to the governing body for approval and to make its best efforts to appropriate monies for the lease payments.

A number of factors strongly discourage nonappropriation events in general fund lease transactions. First, if an issuer does not appropriate the funds to make lease payments in any year, it can lose the use of the leased property. For that reason, you may wish to satisfy yourself regarding the essentiality of the leased property to the issuer.

For example, a lease on a city hall is essential for the city's use. It would be almost unthinkable for a city to lose the use of its city hall. The same might be said for the use of key school facilities by a school district. There is the contrary, although unusual, risk that a court might decline, at least for a time, to deny an issuer the use of a key facility that is necessary for the public welfare.

A second factor strongly discouraging nonappropriation events is market pressures. When an issuer enters into a lease financing, the market's understanding is that the issuer does so with the good faith intention of appropriating funds for lease payments year after year until the lease is paid in full. An issuer that fails to appropriate would find that its access to the market in the future would be badly damaged. While nonappropriation is not the same as a default, in the view of investors and market participants, it is closely similar and would seriously harm the issuer's reputation for reliability. Nonappropriation would also impact the issuer's ability to function effectively and efficiently.

If an issuer were to make that choice, it may experience significant pressure from investors, rating agencies, any bond insurer, and state officials.

Nevertheless, having said that, an issuer is free to fail to appropriate funds if it so chooses. That necessitates a close review by you of the issuer's finances relating to the financial condition of the fund (usually the general fund) from which appropriations are expected to be made.

Financial trouble in a general fund (or other fund) serving as an expected source of appropriations for lease payments can lead to uncertain results in bankruptcy.

Note: There are a few states, such as California and Indiana, in which a different, more secure form of leasing is used. That is called an abatement lease. Abatement leases are viewed as stronger than appropriation leases because, in an abatement lease, the issuer is obligated under state law to make the lease payments so long as the leased facility is available for the issuer's use. Abatement lease structures generally incorporate casualty insurance and rental insurance to protect investors against the issuer's loss of use of the property due to fire, floods, and other disasters. They also may provide funds (called capitalized or borrowed interest) to pay interest on the lease during construction of leased property.

Nevertheless, you may wish to be careful to analyze the issuer's ability to pay amounts due from its general fund (or other designated fund). Lease securities, whether abatement or appropriation leases, are *not* secured by obligated taxes or dedicated revenues.

Why Are Essential Public Purposes Important?

Among the most critical aspects of evaluating a municipal securities issue is understanding the purpose for which it was issued and the security for payment of principal and interest.

budgeted and appropriated on an annual basis by the issuer's or obligor's governing body. The governing body is not legally obligated to make such appropriation in any year. An annual appropriation pledge typically is used only in connection with projects that are considered to be essential to the issuer's or obligor's operations and therefore the governing body is likely to appropriate the money needed to pay debt service on an on-going basis. This clause permits a borrowing entity to undertake a long-term certificate of participation or other lease revenue obligation financing without technically incurring debt. Such obligations are not considered debt in most states and therefore generally are not subject to debt limitations and referendum requirements because the lease payments are characterized as payments for use of the facilities rather than as payments on a promise to repay bonded debt.

Non-Appropriation Clause—A provision of a bond contract that allows the government to terminate a lease securing a long-term certificate of participation or other revenue obligation financing if its appropriating body does not appropriate funds for the lease payments. …

Municipal Securities Rulemaking Board (MSRB), *Glossary of Municipal Securities Terms* at www.msrb.org/msrb1/glossary/default.asp/.

This book points out the difference between municipal securities payable from obligated taxes or dedicated revenues, on the one hand, and from issuers' appropriations of general (or other) funds, on the other. The essentiality of projects becomes especially important in the latter case.

When municipal issuers can be denied ready utilization of essential facilities, there is additional assurance that payments will be forthcoming.

Essentiality of projects and programs or services, therefore, is one important tool upon which professional municipal securities analysts focus. A city hall, key school facilities, a key bridge, and facilities for water and wastewater services are all examples of projects that have a high degree of essentiality to local issuers. As a general rule, issuers cannot afford to go without those types of facilities. In contrast, a park, a softball field or a skating rink may not be as essential.

You may wish to evaluate the essentiality to issuers of financed projects, especially in the cases of leases and other obligations payable from local general fund annual appropriations.

As I have mentioned, there are many types of municipal securities and many purposes for which municipal securities may be issued. The screens in Exhibits 4.8 and 4.9 from the Bloomberg Terminal illustrate partially some of the broad variety of municipal securities and purposes for which the securities may be issued.

What Are Securities Payable from Specific Taxes?

Municipal securities may be payable from obligated taxes that are not ad valorem taxes. For example, municipal securities may be payable from sales taxes or excise taxes.

When considering these structures, you may wish to identify factors that affect the specific taxes. For example, sales taxes are considered to be volatile and dependent upon economic conditions affecting sales. Current relatively high levels of sales taxes might be affected adversely in the event of another recession.

What Are Tax Increment Securities?

Tax increment or tax allocation municipal securities are payable from real property taxes collected above a prior base level following the construction of improvements. In general, the base level of taxes is the taxes that were collected prior to the construction of the improvements. The theory is that the improvements will increase the value of the property subject to taxation, and that it is appropriate for those increased taxes to be used to pay for those improvements.

To the extent that the property subject to taxation is already developed, you would wish to consider the potential for taxes to be collected at a higher level following the construction. Among other things, you may wish

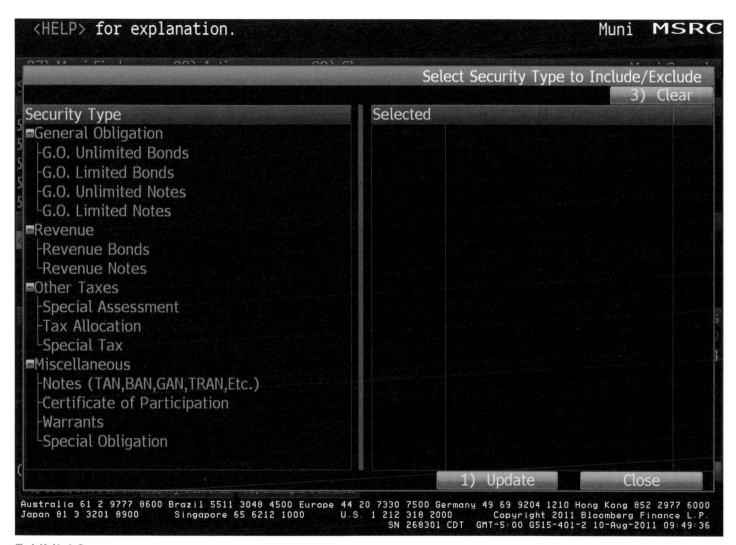

<HELP> for explanation.

Muni **MSRC**

Select Security Type to Include/Exclude

3) Clear

Security Type

- ▣General Obligation
  - G.O. Unlimited Bonds
  - G.O. Limited Bonds
  - G.O. Unlimited Notes
  - G.O. Limited Notes
- ▣Revenue
  - Revenue Bonds
  - Revenue Notes
- ▣Other Taxes
  - Special Assessment
  - Tax Allocation
  - Special Tax
- ▣Miscellaneous
  - Notes (TAN,BAN,GAN,TRAN,Etc.)
  - Certificate of Participation
  - Warrants
  - Special Obligation

Selected

1) Update   Close

Australia 61 2 9777 8600 Brazil 5511 3048 4500 Europe 44 20 7330 7500 Germany 49 69 9204 1210 Hong Kong 852 2977 6000
Japan 81 3 3201 8900   Singapore 65 6212 1000   U.S. 1 212 318 2000   Copyright 2011 Bloomberg Finance L.P.
SN 268301 CDT GMT-5:00 G515-401-2 10-Aug-2011 09:49:36

Exhibit 4.8

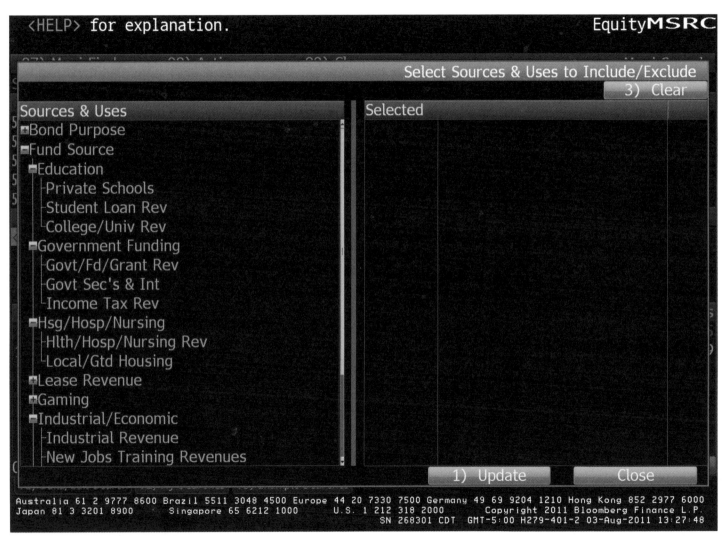

to review historical tax rates, collections, delinquencies, and values in the developed area.

To the extent that the property is not developed, you may wish to identify and also consider the property's potential for further development as a result of the improvements, so that the increased taxes will eventuate and be collected. In doing so, you may wish to consider also the potential for fluctuations in real property values and the capabilities and willingness of developers to develop the property and to pay the taxes. Bankruptcy of a developer or an especially significant taxpayer in a district with concentrated real property ownership could affect tax payments.

Tax increment securities for real estate developments also are discussed under Chapter 6, "Greater Rewards and Greater Risks."

What Are TRANs, BANs, VRDNs, VRDOs, and Other Municipal Notes?

Several types of notes are issued by state and local governments. The notes are expected to be paid from varying sources that you may wish to understand when you purchase the notes. The following is a brief outline of the notes and their common sources of payment.

Some of these forms of notes often are not considered to be debt under state law for purposes of state law restrictions on obligation issuance subject to voter approval. Nevertheless, you should receive in official statements bond counsel opinions that the notes are payable and enforceable according to their terms. When making an investment in notes, you may wish to understand the notes' terms and, as noted, the specific source of repayment.

TRANs. "TRANs" is an acronym for tax and revenue anticipation notes. TRANs commonly are issued to assist governments coping with fluctuating seasonal receipts, while the governments must pay expenses on a continuing basis.

In order to have adequate funding to cover expenditures during low revenue seasons early in fiscal years, governments commonly borrow by issuing short-term notes (TRANs) that are payable from taxes and revenues received at other times later in the fiscal years.

For example, a city with a June 30 fiscal year may receive property tax payments semiannually in December and April, but still must pay expenses from July through November. Various revenue sources may also be seasonal. A resort community may receive greater revenues during a tourist season. The community, however, must pay employees and other expenses of operation throughout the year.

The governments' contractual agreements and their historic patterns of tax and revenue receipts are your assurance of repayment, so you may wish to review those historic patterns as presented in the official statement.

RANs. Like TRANs, RANs are a form of short-term notes issued in anticipation of revenue receipts.

TANs. Like TRANs, TANs are a form of short-term notes issued in anticipation of tax receipts.

BANs. BANs (bond anticipation notes) also are short-term notes, but their maturity may extend beyond the current fiscal year. BANs are anticipation notes payable from the proceeds of future long-term securities issues. BANs are often issued to allow a governmental issuer to proceed with a project during its early planning and construction phases.

For example, BANs may be issued to cover project planning, design, and similar costs. BANs also may be issued to cover initial stages of construction. BANs may be issued so the issuer can avoid borrowing the full amount of a project's cost before the entire funding amount is needed. In addition, BANs may be issued before all costs are fully quantified. In that event, the longer-term securities may be issued once the project has progressed far enough to enable the issuer to define project costs more precisely. At that time, the issuer will repay the BANs, as well as provide for remaining anticipated project costs, from the proceeds of sale of the long-term bonds.

When you purchase BANs, you may wish to evaluate the issuer's ability to issue the longer-term obligations. That may bring into play a number of variables, such as the issuer's credit, its capabilities and performance record, potential increases in interest rates, other market costs that may have the potential to impede the later long-term bond issuance, and unforeseen project cost increases that may interfere with the later issuance.

GANs. GANs are grant anticipation notes. GANs are less common than other forms of governmental note issuance.

Sometimes, governmental issuers receive a grant award, but may not receive the grant funding until a later date or until certain conditions are satisfied. Grant conditions may require that the issuer proceed with project or program implementation to predefined stages prior to release of grant funding. Grants may also require that the issuer contribute certain of its own funds toward the project or program. To satisfy such conditions, and to advance funds to be repaid from the grant, the issuer may borrow funds through the issuance of the GANs.

You may wish to understand the grant and conditions imposed upon the issuer, and whether the grant funds are sufficiently obligated to provide for repayment of the GANs.

Rollover Notes. Rollover notes in the municipal market are an equivalent of commercial paper in the corporate securities market. Some governmental issuers use these notes to implement short-term borrowing as a portion of their debt profile. That enables them to take advantage of short-term interest rates, which (barring unusual circumstances) are lower than long-term rates. The issuers are accepting the risks of future rising interest rates, and if necessary, the issuers' ability to pay off the notes from internal funds or long-term borrowing.

The issuers of these notes roll them over periodically, such as every 6, 9, or even 12 months, often paying down some principal with each rollover, as well as the remaining balance of the outstanding notes.

VRDNs and VRDOs. VRDNs (variable-rate demand notes) and VRDOs (variable-rate demand obligations) are a form of longer-term borrowings that pay investors short-term interest rates.

The securities generally have highly-rated credit quality, at times provided by bond insurers. VRDNs and VRDOs also may provide third-party liquidity support. VRDNs and VRDOs are subject to interest rate resets by a remarketing agent periodically, such as daily, weekly, or monthly. In a remarketing structure, VRDNs and VRDOs offer investors the ability to tender the securities to the remarketing agents.

Some varieties of variable-rate securities are not subject to remarketing structures. In such cases, the securities may pay short-term interest rates based upon formulae tied to indices that are intended to approximate short-term market interest rate conditions. You should be aware that, as occurred during the financial crisis, interest rate indices may behave in unexpected patterns under certain market conditions, especially under conditions of economic stress.

VRDNs and VRDOs are likely to be sold institutionally, being designed especially for money market funds. Retail investors are not likely to have significant direct contact with them.

Issuers and borrowers in variable-rate structures commonly, but not always, enter into derivatives known as interest rate swaps in order to hedge their variable interest rate risks. These are discussed later.

Auction-Rate Securities. Auction-rate securities were another form of long-term borrowing in a structure intended to take advantage of short-term interest rates. Instead of relying upon remarketings when investors wished to sell their securities, dealers were to re-offer the securities through an auction process. A number of dealers provided a degree of support to the auctions by buying the auction-rate securities themselves if investor demand lagged. When, however, the bond insurers began to experience rating downgrades, investors avoided the auction-rate securities, and auctions failed. Dealers were unwilling to purchase the increasing quantities of the securities that investors would not purchase.

You are unlikely ever to encounter auction-rate securities in the future. If, however, you do, you may wish to be especially careful in considering the risks of low liquidity and often unfavorably low interest rates. See Chapter 6, "Greater Rewards and Greater Risks," in the section entitled "What Are Auction-Rate Securities?"

What Are Roles and Risks of Derivatives?

Although this book is not about derivatives, I note that, as discussed earlier, some issuers and borrowers utilize short-term municipal securities structures to achieve long-term financing goals. As a part of their financing structures, those issuers and borrowers may seek to hedge their risks of interest rate fluctuations by entering into derivatives in the form of interest rate swaps.

Essentially, in those swaps, the issuers and borrowers generally make fixed payments to swap counterparties and receive variable payments based upon short-term interest rate indices. The issuers and borrowers intend usually to use the variable payments to pay variable interest on their short-term securities.

Those issuers and borrowers are engaging in complex financial activities that introduce substantial risks. For example, there may be a mismatch between the interest rates payable on the issuers' or borrower's obligations, on one hand, and the payments the issuers or borrowers receive pursuant to the interest rate swaps, on the other. As some issuers and borrowers have learned to their dismay, unexpected events may cause what is usually a minor mismatch to become significant. In addition, some issuers and borrowers found during the financial crisis that, due to rating downgrades on either side of the swaps (including on the issuers' and borrower's side, downgrades of bond insurers or other credit enhancers), the issuers and borrowers were subject to substantial unanticipated liabilities associated with unscheduled termination of interest rate swaps. Those liabilities proved to be burdensome and, in a few cases, led to significant unfavorable financial consequences for the issuers and borrowers.

There are other risks associated with interest rate swaps that are beyond the scope of this book. You should be aware, however, that interest rate swaps introduce more than plain vanilla credit risks into municipal securities structures.

Sophisticated issuers and borrowers are likely to be able to understand and manage more intelligently those risks and their potential financial consequences as part of the issuers' and borrowers' overall financial programs.

That generally is not true for less sophisticated governmental issuers (which includes the vast majority of governmental issuers in the market). For those issuers, you may wish to exercise caution when you see that they are engaging in significant levels of interest rate swap activity. That caution certainly relates to the tens of thousands of smaller, less frequent governmental issuers, but also extends to many larger issuers, as well.

What Are Special Tax and Assessment Securities?

Special tax and special assessment securities are payable from taxes or special assessments levied only on properties within specially delineated districts to pay for improvements for the districts. In general, special assessments are levied according to the benefits provided by the improvements to the respective properties within a district. Special taxes usually are not constrained by reference to benefits to properties, although generally a reasonableness standard may apply.

Depending upon state law, the permitted infrastructure may be streets, curbs and gutters, sidewalks, sewers, water lines, lighting, parks, schools, and other facilities of a public character.

These municipal securities commonly are described as land-secured or land-based, which refers to the ability of issuers to foreclose in order to collect delinquent taxes or assessments. There is no mortgage collateral backing the securities.

A key factor to consider is whether the properties upon which taxes or assessments are levied are or are not developed. If a district encompasses a substantially developed community, and if the aggregate property on which taxes or assessments are levied has a reasonable size and diversity, the securities may be analogous to a general obligation security, and the risk of nonpayment may be relatively small.

Prior development is not, however, the most common set of facts for these types of municipal securities. In an undeveloped district, you may wish to take into account the potential for future fluctuations in real estate values and developer behavior in response.

Municipal securities are permitted by the federal income tax laws and many state laws to be issued to pay for various types of infrastructure intended also to serve future residents and possibly businesses in the new real estate subdivisions under development or planned to be developed. If the property is not yet developed, in order for the plan of finance to work effectively over the long term, the development must be successful. That means ideally that the developed properties will be sold to the ultimate users.

Until parcels are sold to the ultimate future residents and business owners, the current owners of the land (often, but not always the developers) must pay the taxes or assessments to avoid foreclosure. Intervening recessions in the housing market may inhibit development at the anticipated pace, or at all.

If the real estate loses substantial value, developers may decide not to proceed with development and the developers (or other property owners) may decline to pay the taxes or assessments. They also may not be able to obtain additional needed bank financing. If that occurs, much will depend upon the issuer's ability to sell the undeveloped (or not-fully-developed) real estate at a sufficient price in a foreclosure proceeding to pay the delinquencies, penalties, and costs of the sale.

If real estate values plummet sufficiently, developers or other property owners may choose to abandon the properties, and, in more serious cases, the issuers of the securities may be unable to sell delinquent properties to collect taxes (plus costs, penalties, and interest) at foreclosure sales.

While delinquent real estate often can be foreclosed in order to collect delinquent taxes or assessments, the process can be delayed and complex. If developers or property owners enter into bankruptcy, the process may be delayed further.

Therefore, you may wish to determine the capabilities and willingness of the developers or property owners to complete the developments and sell the developed real estate to new owners who will pay. This works best for developers with strong development records, reputations, and financial strengths. Developers that have significant equity investments in development projects have a direct financial interest in the success of the projects that may prove helpful.

These real estate development securities are discussed under Chapter 6, "Greater Rewards and Greater Risks."

What Are Moral Obligation Securities?

Moral obligation securities involve an indication that, or perhaps a set of circumstances, but not an enforceable obligation, in which, one governmental entity would pay obligations of another governmental entity if the second governmental entity were to fail to do so. The reason for use of a moral obligation often is to avoid state law restrictions on explicit debt creation.

In considering moral obligations as another level of credit support for municipal securities, you may wish to identify why the morally-obligated governmental entity would pay the other governmental entity's obligations, as well as its ability to do so. Relevant factors may include the relationship between the two (e.g., a state for its local government) or the essentiality of the project to the morally-obligated governmental entity.

What Are Revenue Securities?

Municipal securities payable from enterprise or project revenues are discussed in Chapter 5, "Revenue Securities."

Private Involvement

Private parties, both profit-making and nonprofit, are permitted by federal tax law and state law to borrow through municipal securities in certain circumstances. In addition, the success of governmental or mixed public-private projects may be dependent upon the performance of private parties in other ways, such as pursuant to management contracts, arrangements for the development of real property, or the success of private projects generating users for public projects (e.g., shopping malls served by public parking facilities). The involvement of private parties may introduce risks that are much more significant than are the governmental risks highlighted in prior chapters.

How Do Public Credits Contrast with Private Credits?

Not all municipal securities are issued for purely governmental purposes or are payable solely from obligated taxes or dedicated revenues from the performance of essential governmental services.

A common element of some categories of municipal revenue securities is involvement of private parties, including as borrowers, developers of projects benefiting from funded infrastructure, and management companies.

For example, special tax, special assessment, tax increment, or tax allocation securities may be issued to provide funding for infrastructure that will serve or otherwise benefit real estate projects of private developers. Industrial development bonds are issued to provide loans to private companies. Many hospitals, nursing homes, and assisted living facilities are owned by nonprofit companies, but are funded through municipal securities issues. Sports teams use stadiums and arenas.

Why Can Private Borrowers Benefit from Tax-Exempt Securities?

The federal tax laws and state laws permit limited private participation in projects funded from proceeds of sale of municipal securities.

The applicable federal tax laws, in particular, are quite strict and complex regarding private use. The presence of bond counsel, who provides an opinion that is contained typically in official statements, is your assurance that the securities offering complies with federal and state legal requirements.

What Are the Risk Implications of Private Borrowers?

As is reflected in Chapter 1, "Introduction," the significant participation of private parties with financial interests in a project often (but not always) presents the potential for somewhat greater risks, as well as potentially greater rewards, than municipal securities issued purely for essential public purposes. See also Chapter 6, "Greater Rewards and Greater Risks." Private parties are not eligible for bankruptcy under Chapter 9, but rather generally file under Chapters 7 or 11.

The risks presented by private parties involved in municipal securities issues are comparable to the risks of private parties in the corporate securities market.

It is relevant to point out that, ironically, the pundits and many media stories are not making predictions regarding municipal securities involving significant private participation, which as discussed in Chapter 1, "Introduction," may increase risks considerably in some cases. Rather the pundits are focused upon the public purpose securities that have been exceedingly sound and strong historically.

Revenue Securities

Chapter 5 is divided into two parts. The first part discusses traditional municipal utility revenue securities, which generally are extremely safe. The second part identifies other types of municipal revenue securities that bring into play a wide variety of additional and often unique considerations.

Traditional Revenue Securities

Traditional municipal revenue securities, like general obligation securities, are extremely strong. The securities are payable from revenues based upon user fees, such as water and wastewater rates. Municipalities are required to collect the user fees. That obligation generally is enforceable under state law and protected in bankruptcy. Additional protections include rate covenants requiring that rates be collected at specific levels affording investors coverage after issuer payments for operation and maintenance of the utilities. Limitations on the issuance of additional obligations payable from the same revenues provide more protection.

Municipal securities payable from traditional essential enterprise revenue sources are quite sound. They are even stronger when the enterprises are monopolies and the securities are rated at investment-grade levels.

The sale of these traditional revenue securities provides funding for facilities for critical municipal enterprises, such as governmentally-owned water and wastewater systems. Governmentally-owned retail gas and electric utilities may be viewed as similar.

Why Are Traditional Revenue Securities Extremely Safe?

The first part of Chapter 5 discusses traditional municipal revenue securities, which generally are extremely safe.

What Are Dedicated Revenues?

Municipal revenue securities are payable from dedicated revenue sources. Those are user fees collected for the provision of services by municipal enterprises. This is a highly reliable securities structure that, in the case of traditional municipal securities, virtually never experiences default in typical circumstances, generally because virtually all users pay their utility bills and do so on time. Those circumstances involve established monopolistic enterprises in developed diverse communities.

You may gain confidence from strong securities structures, discussed later, in conjunction with state law enforceability and bondholder protections in Chapter 9 bankruptcies.

Neither general fund pension obligations nor general fund budgetary issues should prevent the payment of these traditional municipal revenue securities.

This is one of the key reasons that various pundits and certain media have failed to present an accurate portrayal of municipal securities.

You should recognize, however, that as occurred in the case of the Jefferson County, Alabama, sewer system, environmental requirements can become extremely burdensome, requiring costly and expansive additions and modifications to water and wastewater systems. In such cases, you may wish to review financial feasibility studies. See Chapter 10, "Understanding Expert Work Products." Those considerations are not among those that the pundits or media have asserted, so again, they missed important information and subtleties of the municipal market.

Jefferson County's financial problems were magnified by official corruption and the County's extensive use of interest rate swaps that, among other things, introduced significant, unanticipated County liabilities upon termination of the swaps when bond insurers encountered financial difficulties and rating downgrades. See Chapter

4, "General Fund and Other Municipal Securities," in the section entitled "What Are Roles and Risks of Derivatives?"

How Are Enterprise Revenue Securities Protected in Bankruptcy?

Enterprise revenues dedicated to payment of municipal securities are treated as "special revenues" in Chapter 9 bankruptcy. As a result, the payment of the securities should not be impacted by a Chapter 9 filing.

What Are Rate Coverage Requirements?

Another of the key reasons that various pundits and the media have failed to present an accurate portrayal of municipal securities is their disregard of revenue coverage requirements.

Local governments can be compelled pursuant to their contractual agreements protecting revenue securities to increase their user fees, if necessary, both to pay system expenses and to pay the securities.

Coverage requirements necessitate user fee increases as needed not only to pay principal of and interest on the municipal securities (and any other securities on a parity with the municipal securities), but also to provide an additional level of protection. For example, a coverage requirement for a water system financing might require that the system's "net" revenues (after payment of operational expenses, including maintenance) be collected at least at, or if necessary increased to, 115% or 125% of the system's total debt service on all of its outstanding parity securities (including the specific securities issue). The term *parity* refers to equality in priority of payment from the source of payment of the municipal securities.

These coverage requirements are used widely in municipal securities issues payable from user fees. With coverage requirements, especially in the case of enterprises providing essential services in diverse communities as established monopolies, such as water and wastewater utility systems, the chances of default are virtually nil. You may wish to review the official statement for securities you are considering to determine that a coverage requirement is present (which will generally be the case) and how strong it is.

What Restrictions Are Placed on Additional Securities?

As another protection, municipal revenue securities financings commonly contain restrictions on the issuance of additional securities payable from the same revenues unless historical or projected coverage tests can be satisfied.

In order to protect against dilution of the coverage of debt service by available revenues, the coverage requirements generally are supplemented by these restrictions on an issuer's ability to issue additional obligations payable from the same revenue sources. If additional debt can be issued without your consent, your credit protection can

be eroded seriously as additional claims emerge to be asserted against the same revenues upon which you depend.

For example, as pointed out by Tim Schaefer of Magis Advisors, if an issuer has annual revenues of $200,000 after paying operation and maintenance costs, and the issuer owes you $100,000 in debt service, you have "two times" (2.0×) coverage ($200,000 to pay $100,000). If the issuer is permitted to issue (without your approval) additional debt with annual debt service of another $100,000, then your "coverage" would fall to only "one times" (1.0×) coverage ($200,000 to pay $200,000). That level of coverage would leave no room for error by the issuer in managing its enterprise.

This is a good reason to examine the additional debt restrictions in securities you are considering, as well as to review the issuer's capital plan for future improvements and issuance of additional debt.

Are Revenue Securities Protected from Budgetary Problems?

Municipal enterprises, being separate funds, are not included in local government general fund budgets. Consequently, general fund difficulties due to pension liabilities or other budgetary problems will not affect the collection of user fees to pay the securities. This is another municipal market subtlety that has been missed by pundits and some media.

Budgetary issues within the enterprise funds are, however, relevant.

(continued)

STEP-BY-STEP

As another protection, municipal revenue securities financings commonly contain restrictions on the issuance of additional securities payable from the same revenues.

You may wish to look for the additional debt restrictions as outlined in the official statement.

The following is a simplified hypothetical example of protective additional debt provisions in traditional municipal revenue securities issues—

The Enterprise may issue Additional Bonds on a parity with the Bonds, provided:

(1) The Enterprise is in compliance with all terms of the Bonds and all other Bonds on a parity with the Bonds; and

(2) The Enterprise Revenues net of Operation and Maintenance Costs (Enterprise Net Revenues) for the last completed Fiscal Year equal at least 120% of the Maximum Annual Debt Service of the Bonds, and all other Bonds on a parity with the Bonds, and the Additional Bonds.

The Enterprise may adjust the foregoing Enterprise Net Revenues to reflect:

(a) an allowance for increased or decreased Enterprise Net Revenues arising from any increase or decrease in the rates, fees and charges of the Enterprise

What Is the Strength of Credit Diversity in Communities?

As with general obligation securities, traditional revenue securities for essential purposes are especially strong in diverse communities with large numbers of rate paying residences, commercial businesses, and industries.

Users of essential municipal services will not abandon their homes or communities merely because they find charges for the services to be expensive and distasteful. The user charges are likely only minor components of rate payers' budgets.

What Are Enforcement Mechanisms for Revenue Securities?

In general, local governments have access to various enforcement mechanisms to facilitate collection of the user fees. Depending upon state law, these may include denial of service or imposition of property liens. User fees may be supplemented for certain disadvantaged rate payers.

What User Fee Collection and Delinquency Data Is Available?

As with historical data for general obligation securities relating to tax rates, collections and delinquencies, local governments prepare similar historical data regarding user fee levels, collections and delinquencies.

Exhibit 5.1 is an example of a presentation of those data.

Example of Billing and Collection Data

Fiscal Year Ended June 30,	Bi-Monthly Revenues Billed	Bi-Monthly Revenues Collected	Percentage of Bi-Monthly Billings Collected
2006	$ 1,918,735	$ 1,914,302	99.77%
2007	1,923,175	1,943,132	*101.04*
2008	1,919,218	1,945,229	*101.36*
2009	1,970,672	1,960,962	99.51
2010	1,950,647	1,983,946	*101.71*

Exhibit 5.1

As shown, in some years, collections may exceed billings as delinquent payments are received.

Where Are Those Data Available?

Again, as with tax data relating to general obligation securities, historical user fee data are available typically in official statements for securities offerings and, after offerings, in many local government continuing disclosure filings.

Why Are Essential Services Important?

Municipal revenue securities generally are strongest when they provide funding for projects facilitating the provision of essential services under monopoly conditions.

When services may not be essential or when monopoly conditions are not present, you may wish to consider the possibility of user options to avoid paying the fees. For example, in the case of toll roads or bridges, there may be alternative highways or bridges, even if less convenient. Airlines and passengers may avoid airports if fees are excessive. Health consumers may have choices of hospitals or nursing homes. These are discussed later under "Other Revenue Securities."

In the case of certain projects owned or operated by private parties, coverage requirements may be present, but less effective in practice. This may be illustrated by hospitals, nursing homes and assisted living communities for which user fee increases may be limited by law (e.g., federal Medicare law for health care providers), or may be limited by competition, affordability or other factors (e.g., in the case of private borrowers in industrial development bonds). These private undertakings are not the types of projects, however, that have given rise to adverse comments by pundits or certain media about municipal securities.

What Is the Risk of Start-Up Projects?

The principal exceptions to the strength of traditional municipal revenue securities for essential projects include: (1) a very small number of issues for start-up or rapidly-expanding projects (e.g., Jefferson County and the Washington Public Power Supply System) for which user bases, and the capacity of users to pay new or substantially increased user charges, are less certain or for which project costs may exceed projections; (2) a few small communities with little diversity; (3) communities that are dependent upon a small number of employers; and (4) issuers utilizing exotic instruments.

The exception for start-up projects is perhaps more apparent when projects are entirely new in small communities, as in the case of a start-up wastewater project in a small rural area previously served totally by septic systems. Other less traditional, less essential examples, with a lower degree of revenue flexibility, may be a new monorail transportation system and toll roads in geographical regions unaccustomed to toll roads, especially when the toll roads run parallel to existing freeways.

Securities for start-up projects, or for projects in tiny communities, generally are not rated at investment grade levels or at all.

The provision of funding for rapidly-expanding projects, even with some history of operations, sometimes is only a few steps removed.

When these types of projects are funded, expert work products, such as feasibility studies, financial projections, and appraisals, discussed later under Chapter 10, "Understanding Expert Work Products," may assume an important role. You may wish to review those studies closely.

Other Revenue Securities

This second part of Chapter 5 identifies other types of municipal revenue securities that bring into play a wide variety of additional and often unique considerations.

that was duly adopted prior to the date of issuance of the Bonds but which, during all or any part of the last completed Fiscal Year, was not in effect, in an amount equal to the amount by which the Enterprise Net Revenues would have been increased or decreased if such increase or decrease in rates, fees and charges had been in effect during the whole of that Fiscal Year; and

(b) an allowance for Enterprise Net Revenues that, according to a study of [a qualified professional], would have been derived from each new use or user of the Enterprise that during any part of that Fiscal Year, was not in existence, in an amount equal to the estimated additional Enterprise Net Revenues that would have been derived from each such new use or user if it had been in existence for the entire Fiscal Year.

Nothing contained in this Section shall limit the issuance or incurrence of any Subordinate Bonds.

There is a considerable diversity of municipal revenue securities beyond the traditional revenue securities discussed in the first part of this Chapter 5. Investors may wish to consider a number of variables, including the essentiality of projects, the roles, if any, of private parties and the importance of private involvement, rate coverage requirements and additional obligation restrictions, competition, factors that may lead to revenue declines, and the like.

Rate coverage requirements function more effectively in traditional municipal revenue securities issues than in other types of revenue issues. When rate covenants and coverage requirements are likely to be less effective, the issuers or borrowers may be required to employ management consultants in the event of financial or operational difficulties.

What Is the Diversity of Revenue Securities?

There are many varieties of municipal revenue securities beyond those for traditional utility enterprises providing essential services.

These are not, however, the types of municipal securities upon which pundits and certain news media are focusing.

The following is a listing of some of the variations in purposes for which municipal revenue securities may be issued, each of which presents its own unique credit considerations:

- Industrial development bonds
- Economic development securities, such as for designated economic development zones, or infrastructure to benefit private facilities and dependent upon the success of the private facilities (*e.g.*, parking garages for shopping malls, convention centers in conjunction with hotels)
- Education, including among others, public and private colleges, universities, and dormitory authorities
- Student loans
- Airports
- Ports
- Transit agencies
- Toll roads and bridges
- Solid waste systems
- Hospitals
- Nursing homes and assisted living communities
- Housing, both single-family and multi-family
- Power generation and distribution
- Stadiums and arenas
- Various forms of PPP (public-private partnership) projects

See the Appendix, which discusses resources that may assist you in considering the unique features and risks of the diverse types of municipal revenue securities.

Why Is It Important to Understand Revenue Credits?

The listing given previously of diverse categories of municipal revenue securities identifies many types of securities with substantially different structures, risks and credit criteria.

It is important for you to understand the specific revenue securities you are considering buying, selling or continuing to hold in your investment portfolio and relevant factors and risks relating to those securities.

For example, although various revenue securities listed above may incorporate coverage requirements in their structures, the practicality for some of the requirements in terms of ease of raising user fees may differ significantly from the relative ease of raising user fees by traditional water and wastewater utility enterprises. Others may be more flexible. Securities, known as "dou-

bled-barreled securities," for certain of the projects may be secured also by taxes. These are discussed in Chapter 3, "General Obligation Securities," in the section "What Are Doubled-Barreled Securities?"

The Appendix to this book provides you with resources that you may wish to use—and that I recommend that you research—if you wish to gain a better understanding of specific municipal securities credits and relevant investment considerations for each.

In that connection, published rating agency criteria by market sector and Best Practices in Disclosure published by the National Federation of Municipal Analysts (NFMA) at www.nfma.org can guide you with respect to key factors that professional municipal securities analysts consider important relating to various municipal market sectors. The Appendix provides information as to how you are able to access these resources.

Greater Rewards and Greater Risks

A number of categories of municipal securities often involve greater risks than do traditional municipal securities. Some of those categories are identified in this chapter. When considering securities in those categories, you may wish to consider also whether greater rewards are in order.

As advised by Tim Schaefer of Magis Advisors, "If the yield seems too good to be true, then you are dealing with greater risk!"

On the other hand, *risk* is not inherently something to be avoided. Indeed, no matter what decisions you make, you cannot avoid risk. Like life, all investments involve risks and trade-offs for low or high returns. A key goal is to understand the risks you are taking and to assume them in an informed, reasonable manner.

Are Riskier Municipal Securities Readily Identifiable?

Certain municipal securities have greater risks and usually, as compensation, offer greater rewards. Through careful investing, those investors who are less risk-averse than others, may reduce, although not eliminate, the risks. Some considerations are discussed in this section.

I am not advocating that you not invest in any of the municipal securities discussed in this chapter. Rather, I am suggesting that, if and when you do so, you make your decisions understanding the risks of those securities, credit, and other considerations relevant to those specific securities, and the diversity of credits in the municipal securities market.

Most (although, of course, not all) of the riskier municipal securities have certain readily-identifiable characteristics. I discuss in this chapter some of the factors for which you might remain alert.

What Are High Yield Securities?

You may wish to consider municipal securities offering higher returns than more traditional municipal securities. These are known in the market as high yield securities.

That is a valid choice, so long as you make it understanding that higher yields suggest that the market views the securities as incorporating greater risks. It bears re-emphasis that, ironically, these are not the types of municipal securities upon which pundits and media are focusing.

If interest rates on municipal securities you are considering seem to be very attractive, look closely to determine whether the yields are reflective of the risks you are willing to accept.

If you choose intelligently and with awareness of the risks, your portfolio, and you, may benefit from the higher yields. You may be able to identify securities that are poorly structured and ill-conceived.

If you are a conservative investor, you may wish to avoid these securities.

When you make a choice to accept the risks, you may do so on a better-informed basis by understanding the differences among municipal securities and by engaging in your own research and analysis. The Appendix to this book is intended to assist you in doing so by directing you to a wealth of important resources available in the market.

What Municipal Securities Deserve Closer Review?

Throughout this book, I have attempted to direct your attention to municipal securities that deserve a closer look. Those include, but are not limited to, municipal securities that are from categories with the highest rates of default. Some of those also are discussed in Chapter 1, "Introduction." Other securities may pose risks of poor liquidity or otherwise less favorable treatment in terms of market pricing.

The most apparent of the readily-identifiable municipal securities that pose default risks warranting special care are:

- Securities involving significant private participation
- Securities to fund infrastructure for real estate developments
- Securities payable from revenues of start-up or rapidly-expanding projects

In addition, you may wish to look carefully at securities in the following categories:

- Securities for which issuers or borrowers have not filed required continuing-disclosure reports or have a record of repeated failures to file in a timely manner
- Securities for which the latest audited financial statements are stale

- Securities issued for other than essential governmental purposes
- Securities with surety bond reserve funds
- Unrated securities and securities rated below investment grade
- Securities issued to pay judgments
- Securities issued to pay pension or other post-employment obligations
- Tobacco settlement bonds
- Securities with credit enhancement, but no underlying rating
- Securities for which the financial statements are not audited at all
- Securities for which auditors or other experts are not identified as experts or for which auditors or experts have not consented to the use of their work
- Auction-rate securities
- Securities of issuers investing in exotic instruments (see Chapter 4)

What about Private Participation?

As discussed previously under Chapter 1, "Introduction," and Chapter 4, "General Fund and Other Municipal Securities," in the section entitled "Private Involvement," when private performance is important directly or indirectly to municipal securities structures, you may wish to identify and understand the nature, extent, and credit implications of private party involvement.

The securities may be payable solely from revenues to be paid by private parties, the projects may be managed by private parties, or the securities may fund projects that depend upon the success of private facilities.

What about Real Estate Developments?

Municipal securities issued for real estate developments may be secured by special taxes, special assessments, or incremental taxes. Those securities are discussed further under Chapter 4, "General Fund and Other Municipal Securities," in the sections entitled "What Are Special Tax and Assessment Securities?" and "What Are Tax Increment Securities?," and under Chapter 10, "Understanding Expert Work Products."

Historically, in the municipal securities market, real estate development projects have proved more difficult for investors. The history extends back more than 150 years through successive real estate booms and busts and even to the construction of the railroads and canals. This is a classic high yield type of security.

In the case of municipal securities payable from taxes or assessments in real estate developments, you may wish to understand the strengths, weaknesses and intentions of the developers, as well as their financial and development plans.

Until the property is subdivided or developed further, and sold to other land owners, such as numerous home owners or commercial property owners, the land-based securities will be payable from special assessments or special taxes levied upon the property of that small number of owners and developers. You will be dependent upon them for payment. Further, they generally are not obligated to pay the assessments or taxes.

Of course, the property can be sold by the issuer at tax foreclosure sales, but those may require significant time during which you may not be paid, especially if debt service reserve funds are depleted. Further, a downturn in the real estate market may result in difficulties for sale at a foreclosure sale for all amounts owing with respect to the property.

Among other things, you may wish to consider the developers' reputations and experience, financial capabilities, and level of commitment to the projects. The financial capabilities include not only the developers' internal financial strengths, but also the level of equity the developers have invested in the projects and commitments they have received for bank and other loans or lines of credit for the development. While the municipal securities provide funding for certain infrastructure of a public character, the developers must still obtain funding in order to develop their projects.

A caution: The presence of a well-known, recognized developer without a good business plan and invested equity and access to other funding does not necessarily suggest good credit, just higher quality of management. You may wish to focus your investigation on the developer's business plan—development and marketing—as well as on financial capabilities and developer experience.

You may also want to know about the status of permits and other governmental approvals for the projects, what environmental and market studies the developers have received, and the appraised values of the properties as anticipated to be improved with proceeds of sale of the securities, as well as much more information.

A good source of suggested information you may wish to know may be found in "Recommended Best Practices for Disclosure for Land Secured Debt Transactions" published in 2000 by the National Federation of Municipal Analysts. You can find the document online at www.nfma.org under "Publications—Disclosure Guidelines" along with many other such documents published by NFMA that will assist you in reviewing municipal securities.

What about New or Significantly Expanding Projects?

Likewise, you may wish to look closely at municipal securities funding start-up or rapidly expanding projects. Those are discussed in Chapter 5, "Revenue Securities."

New or rapidly-expanding revenue projects, even those of a governmental character, have been associated with defaulted municipal securities in many securities issues, for example, for power and wastewater utilities, a steam utility, a telecom system, toll roads, arenas, charter schools, a monorail system, and the like.

Depending upon the type of financing, you may wish to review closely financial feasibility studies and projections and appraisals. Those are discussed further in Chapter 10, "Understanding Expert Work Products."

What about Reserve Funds Backed by Insurer Surety Bonds?

Except for general obligation securities, the structures of most long-term municipal securities include reserve funds. Reserve funds exist to protect investors by affording issuers or borrowers time to work through financial difficulties. In the worst cases, most reserve funds provide approximately one year's debt service. The issuers or borrowers usually are required to use future revenues to replenish draws on the reserves.

Sometimes, rather than borrowing to fund reserve funds with invested cash, issuers or borrowers will purchase a surety bond from a bond insurer. Those reserve funds consist solely of the surety bonds. That is a reason to be cautious. Among other things, bond insurers are private companies.

One consequence of the financial crisis is that all seven, formerly triple-A rated, bond insurers have been downgraded. In a few cases, bond insurers have experienced severe financial difficulties or even bankruptcy.

When considering municipal securities, you may wish to investigate whether the reserve funds consist solely of bond insurer surety bonds. If so, you may wish to investigate further the status of the insurers.

When debt service reserve funds consist of insurers' surety bonds, adverse consequences of financial difficulties of insurers may be magnified, if any such difficulties occur. Not only will the credit-enhanced ratings of the municipal securities suffer if insurers' credit ratings are downgraded, but the financial integrity of the municipal securities underlying the insurance may be damaged if reserve funds become less credit-worthy. If the underlying municipal securities are rated, those ratings also may be downgraded if the reserve funds become less secure.

In new issues, you should be aware of this issue in the event the surety bond reserve fund structure is used.

See Chapter 7, "Considerations When Buying," in the section entitled "What Is the Significance to Me of the Bond Insurance Industry's Decline?" See also Chapter 12, "Investor Questions and Answers (Q&As)," in the section entitled "What Are Debt Service Reserve Funds?"

What Are Securities for Nonessential Purposes?

As discussed previously under Chapter 4, "General Fund and Other Municipal Securities," and Chapter 5, "Revenue Securities," you may wish to look carefully at general fund municipal securities and revenue securities issued for other than essential governmental purposes. This is especially applicable in, but not limited to, the case of leases, lease certificates of participation (COPs) and lease revenue bonds payable from issuer general funds and in the case of nontraditional revenue securities.

What about Nonrated and Lower-Rated Securities?

Securities warranting closer examination include nonrated securities, and securities rated below investment grade. These municipal securities are sold most often, but not exclusively, to institutional or professional investors who are best equipped to evaluate the risks disclosed to them. If securities with higher yields in relation to prevailing market conditions are being offered to you as a retail investor, you may wish to look closely at the securities.

Although one sometimes hears that municipal securities are not rated due to the cost, that is a rare occurrence. The rating agencies accommodate small municipal securities issues, and there are cost savings for issuers and borrowers in terms of interest rates when municipal securities are rated. Even issues in the neighborhood of $5 million or less may be rated if they are credit-worthy.

Accordingly, I recommend that you exercise caution to be informed when you are offered nonrated municipal securities. That is true even, or perhaps especially, when the interest rates appear to be very good.

What about Judgment Bonds, Pension Bonds, and Tobacco Bonds?

Communities with legal difficulties may borrow to fund judgments against them. On rare occasions, communities may be subject to sizeable judgment awards that cannot be paid from current budgets. The communities then may borrow, in effect to pay for the judgments over time. Since the judgment bonds require payments from taxes and other sources that otherwise would be used for the benefit of the citizens, this means that the citizens may be receiving a lower level of services. Taxes or revenues may be increased, and budgets may be under stress.

Pension bonds, and their close cousins, bonds issued to pay for other post-employment benefits (OPEBs), such as retiree health care, suggest that the issuers have not been providing adequately for the payment of their actuarially-determined pension, health care, and other obligations for retirees. Again, communities may be borrowing to pay in the future for current liabilities. Such practices spread current costs to future budgets and can place strains on those future budgets.

Tobacco settlement bonds are a different and special case. The securities are payable from proceeds expected to be received over time from tobacco companies as due under a prior settlement with various states. Some states distribute tobacco settlement proceeds to local governments. The tobacco companies' liabilities to make payments are framed with reference to their revenues from sales of tobacco products. As, and to the degree, tobacco usage decreases (a decrease in usage that states receiving tobacco companies' payments publicly encourage), the payments also would decrease. In turn, that would reduce available revenues from the tobacco settlement for use in payment of the securities, an important investment risk. These securities have complex financial structures, and are not for the faint-hearted.

What about Securities with Credit Enhancement, but No Underlying Rating?

Securities backed by bond insurance, letters of credit, or other credit enhancement, but having no underlying rating, are at risk of illiquidity in the event of a rating downgrade of the credit enhancers.

Experience in the municipal securities market shows that credit enhancement alone, which is provided by corporate obligors, may be at greater risk of significant fiscal stress than are investment-grade-rated securities of many governmental issuers.

Why Do Audited Financial Statements Matter?

Virtually all municipal securities issuers and most private borrowers are audited annually. (Audits, relatively current information, and subsequent events reviews are routine

in registered corporate securities offerings.) (See "For Additional Information" at the end of the chapter.)

In those cases in which financial statements have not been audited, you should be aware that there has not been an expert third-party review of whether the financial statements are prepared in accordance with applicable generally accepted accounting principles. It can be a sign that either the issuer or borrower does not wish to, or cannot afford to, spend the money necessary to pay auditors or that the issuer's or borrower's financial records are not in a condition to be audited.

In those circumstances, you may wish to be cautious. If you decide to accept risks associated with unaudited financial statements, you may wish to expect greater rewards for the greater risks.

When Is Financial Information Stale?

Similarly, you may wish to be cautious when issuer or borrower financial statements are stale.

When financial statements are stale, you should be aware of the risk that there may be changes in the financial results or condition of the issuer or borrower since the date of the financial statements. The longer the period since the date of the financial statements, the greater the risk of significant issuer or borrower financial changes.

If you decide to accept risks associated with stale financial statements, you may wish to expect greater rewards for the greater risks. At least when considering general obligation securities supported by statutory liens and traditional revenue securities, it remains, however, largely a matter of rewards. Although current information is always desirable in order to minimize your default risks, you at least have the security protections discussed throughout this book relating to those traditional municipal securities.

In those cases, the greater risks are less likely to be default risks, and are more likely to be associated with liquidity and market pricing. Still, if an issuer of even traditional municipal securities publishes only stale financial information, you may wonder with justification whether that issuer may lie within the universe of those issuers more likely to follow less effective financial management practices, and therefore, more prone to financial difficulties and potentially default, as well.

How can you know the risks of that issuer without current information? The problem is that stale information denies you access to that issuer's most recent financial results.

For other municipal securities, given developments associated with the aftermath of the financial crisis, even though widespread defaults are unlikely among investment-grade-rated municipal securities issued for essential purposes, you may wish to weed out from your consideration, or to seek additional yield from, the less credit-worthy issuers and borrowers, and to do that, you may need current financial information.

When it comes to deciding to seek greater rewards in return for exposure to greater risks, it is worth noting that a number of SEC enforcement actions in the municipal securities market are associated with stale financial information. Before a disclosure document was released

by the issuer or borrower, significant undisclosed financial changes may have occurred relating to the issuer or borrower subsequent to the end of its most recent audited fiscal year for which financial statements were included in the disclosure document.

Many municipal issuers and borrowers complete and publish their audits within six months after the ends of their fiscal years, although financial transactions (including your trade) may occur somewhat later.

Richard Ciccarone of Merritt Research Services found in a survey of more than 6,500 audits for 16 municipal market sectors that the average time it took for audit reports to be completed was a little under five months (141.3 days). Publication of the audited financial statements required slightly more time. (See "For Additional Information" at the end of the chapter.)

These timing issues may arise in at least two contexts—in initial offerings of securities and in secondary market transactions.

In initial offerings, audited financial statements sometimes may be 9 months old, 12 months old, or even older. (See "For Additional Information" at the end of the chapter.) To some degree, that staleness may be ameliorated somewhat with respect to governmental issuers because financial information in the state and local governmental sector often does not change rapidly. Yet, it is not always the case. That became apparent following the beginning of the financial crisis in which real estate values fell quickly; property, sales and income tax collections fell, as did the valuations of employee pension portfolios; and some state and local governments experienced sudden financial stress. Changes may (or may not) be publicized on issuer websites or in local press reports. Risks of rapid changes for private borrowers often are even greater, and may not be publicized at all.

In the case of both governmental and private borrowers, it is possible that the only financial information that is available is annual financial information filed with the Electronic Municipal Market Access (EMMA) platform maintained by the Municipal Securities Rulemaking Board (MSRB). That is especially true for many smaller issuers or borrowers.

In connection with secondary market trades, the time frame within which an issuer or borrower agrees to file annual financial information with the MSRB's EMMA assumes importance. Although many issuers file their annual information within six months, it is not uncommon for filings to be made nine months or longer following fiscal year ends.

See Chapter 2, "Basic Information Resources," in the subsections entitled "What Continuing Disclosure Is Available?, What Have Issuers or Borrowers Promised To Disclose and When?," and "How Can I Find Identities of Cooperative Issuers/Borrowers?"

As discussed, other potential information sources include issuer or borrower websites and local press information, if any. Each of those might be identified through internet resources. See Chapter 2, "Basic Information Resources," in the sections entitled "What Information Is Available on Issuer Websites?" and "What Information Is Available through Local Press Reports?"

What about Securities for Which Issuers/Borrowers Have Not Honored Continuing Disclosure Agreements?

Securities for which issuers or borrowers have not filed required continuing disclosure reports, or have a record of repeated failures to file in a timely manner, are at risk of illiquidity.

Securities for which required continuing disclosure filings have not been made are increasingly difficult to trade.

Those securities for which the issuers or obligors are late repeatedly in making filings are avoided by some investors. Given the laws of supply and demand, that impacts the liquidity and market prices of those securities.

As stated by the Financial Industry Regulatory Authority (FINRA), "Investors should treat missing or past-due financial information from a bond issuer as a potential red flag."

What Are Auction-Rate Securities?

Auction-rate securities are no longer issued, but some remain outstanding. These securities involve substantial risks. In general, auction-rate securities involved long-term securities bearing short-term interest rates. The securities could be re-offered periodically though an auction process. That process broke down, among other things, in conjunction with rating downgrades of bond insurers and cessation of dealer support for the auctions. Most auction-rate securities are illiquid, and some bear low interest rates. See Chapter 4, "General Fund and Other Municipal Securities," in the section entitled "What Are TRANs, BANs, VRDNs, VRDOs, and Other Municipal Notes?"

You are unlikely ever to encounter auction-rate securities in the future. If, however, you do, you may wish to be especially careful in considering the risks of low liquidity and often unfavorably low interest rates.

For Additional Information

▪ Corporate securities issuers active in the corporate securities market routinely complete their audits within 90 days following their fiscal years, provide quarterly unaudited financial statements more rapidly following ends of fiscal quarters, and even provide information on an interim basis. One explanation given by municipal issuers for their longer delays in completing audits is that state law requirements relating to the audits sometimes may cause some delay.

Privately-owned private borrowers in the municipal market, on the other hand, sometimes may not release financial information at all, unless required to file that information with the MSRB's EMMA.

▪ Richard Ciccarone," Timing of Municipal Bond Financial Audits Leaves Room for Improvement" (Oct. 2011 Merritt Research Services LLC). Mr. Ciccarone

also found that individual issuers were able to complete their audits within much shorter periods, stating:

Many smaller entities were among the fastest to have their audits completed, while others were among the slowest. The four fastest audit times in 2010 were all linked to relatively small entities. Pulaski Electric Division, Tennessee, for example, was able to complete its audit within only 16 days of the close of its fiscal year. Titus County Fresh Water Supply District #1 in Mount Pleasant, Texas had its audit signed in 22 days, while two school districts, Newaygo Public Schools, Michigan and Maple Shade School District, New Jersey, both completed their audits in 23 days.

Many large municipal bond issuers also were able to have their audits signed within the 60-day window required by the Securities & Exchange Commission (SEC) for large, public corporate borrowers. A sample of those entities included Sacramento Power Authority (49 days), Indiana Municipal Power Agency (56 days), Port Authority of New York & New Jersey (56 days), Syracuse University (29 days), Mayo Clinic (48 days) and Santa Barbara County, California (55 days).

… [T]he State of New York and New York City, two obvious complex credits, were able to make the 120-day audit time guideline [set by the Municipal Securities Rulemaking Board for special recognition on EMMA] for the past two years (the State of New York for the last four years, and New York City in three of the last four years).

One way in which issuers or borrowers may provide a degree of assurance against financial changes after fiscal year ends is through a procedure known as a subsequent events review by the auditors. The review occurs most commonly (but not always) in a context in which disclosure documents state that auditors have consented to the use of their audit reports or refer to the auditors as experts. A subsequent events review process is not as thorough as an audit. It does involve, however, certain question-asking and investigation by the auditors regarding potential significant changes.

If an auditor has not consented to designation as an expert, or if an issuer or borrower has not asked for that consent, that information should, but may not, be disclosed. If you do not see an identification of the auditor as having given its consent to the use of its audit report or designating the auditor as an expert, then it is highly likely either that the issuer or borrower has not asked for that consent or that the auditor has refused to give it. In that event, it also is highly likely that no subsequent events review has been conducted. The issuer or borrower also should, but may not, make disclosure if no subsequent events review has been conducted.

In those circumstances, you may wish to be cautious. The longer the period since the end of the audited fiscal year, the greater the risks of significant changes. If you decide to accept risks associated with the absence of a subsequent events review (or the absence of an expert's consent to being identified as an

expert), you may wish to expect greater rewards for the greater risks of undetected financial changes.

For other potential information sources that may post-date the audit, see Chapter 2, "Basic Information Resources," in the sections entitled "What Continuing Disclosure Information Is Available?"; "What Information Is Available on Issuer Websites?"; and "What Information Is Available through Local Press Reports?"

Addendum to Chapter 6— Certain 2011 Bankruptcy and Financial Developments

Several noteworthy bankruptcy and financial developments occurred in 2011 affecting municipal securities. Taken as a whole, the developments support the analysis of this book that the greatest threats to municipal securities investors are in securities issues with one or more of the following characteristics: significant private party involvement; start-up or rapidly expanding revenue-producing projects; real estate development projects; and significant issuer involvement with interest rate swaps or other exotic financial products.

In terms of private sector-supported municipal debt, American Airlines filed a Chapter 11 proceeding affecting certain airport bonds supported by leases and other obligations of the Airline and its parent.

In Florida, the Court in Chapter 11 bankruptcy proceedings brought by a private real estate developer did not consider municipal investors to be creditors of the private developer. A community development district had provided funding for infrastructure benefiting the developer's start-up real estate development project. The Court considered the district to be the private developer's creditor. The developer paid assessments levied by the district on the developer's land.

Certain state tobacco bond issues, reportedly including California and Ohio, experienced draws on debt service reserve funds as tobacco usage decreased more than anticipated. That, in turn, affected the revenues of private tobacco companies making tobacco litigation settlement payments that the States pledged to the payment of the bonds.

In the governmental sector, the Harrisburg (PA) Chapter 9 bankruptcy petition brought by the City Council (and opposed by the Mayor and the Commonwealth) was dismissed. The Commonwealth had appointed a receiver for the City, and Commonwealth law withheld permission for the filing. Harrisburg has outstanding general obligation securities (also backed in part by a County obligation and bond insurance) that the City had expected to pay from revenues of a start-up waste incinerator project.

In Rhode Island, the City of Central Falls filed a Chapter 9 petition intended primarily to manage substantial pension liabilities. City employees and unions oppose adjustments to retiree benefits, and are challenging Rhode Island's enactment of statutory protection for taxes pledged to the payment of general obligation securities. Rhode Island appointed a receiver for the City. The State also is seeking to reduce its own pension liabilities.

The Jefferson County (AL) Chapter 9 bankruptcy filing remains contested as of this writing. Creditors are asserting that the State of Alabama has not granted permission for issuers of "warrants," as opposed to voter-approved "bonds," to make Chapter 9 filings. Jefferson County issued "warrants" without voter approval in the form of both general obligation and sewer revenue securities. Jefferson County's sewer system project was rapidly expanding with substantial improvements in order to satisfy outstanding environmental mandates. In addition, Jefferson County had participated in substantial interest rate swap transactions relating to the sewer warrants. An Alabama State Court appointed a receiver for the County's sewer system. The County is challenging that appointment and is arguing against the "special revenue" protected status of the sewer revenue securities.

The City of Detroit is experiencing significant financial challenges under scrutiny by the State of Michigan. The State has taken actions that potentially could lead to appointment of an emergency manager of the City over the City's objections. Detroit also participated in substantial interest rate swap transactions.

In an obscure Chapter 9 bankruptcy for a small special health care district, Sierra King, the Court protected general obligation bonds secured by pledged taxes backed by a statutory lien.

In Washington, the Greater Wenatchee Regional Events Center Public Facilities District defaulted on bond anticipation notes (BANs) issued to provide funding for a start-up arena project.

CHAPTER 7

Considerations When Buying

Y ou may have questions about selected technical topics when you make municipal securities investments. There are a number of important considerations beyond simply credit risks. Those include, for example, risks that the value of the securities may change due to market movements in prevailing interest rates, risks associated with optional redemptions (especially when investors pay a premium for the securities), and risks of illiquidity in a market that may be traded thinly.

This chapter is intended to highlight certain matters that you may wish to consider when buying municipal securities

Where Should I Begin?

When you are considering buying municipal securities, the place to begin is to obtain and review available information. Based upon that information, you may wish to consider carefully whether the securities belong in your portfolio at all in light of their yields, your tax position,

your investment horizon, and risks of the securities, including among them, risks identified below.

As discussed in Chapter 2, "Basic Information Resources," you should read the official statement for the offering and continuing disclosure documents filed by the issuer or borrower.

You can obtain the official statement from the broker or dealer who sold you the securities, as well as later from the Electronic Municipal Market Access (EMMA) platform maintained by the Municipal Securities Rulemaking Board (MSRB) at www.emma.msrb.org. If there is a preliminary official statement, as is usually the case, you should request it from the broker or dealer offering the securities to you. The broker or dealer then is obligated to provide it to you. The preliminary official statement will precede the official statement, which is the final version of the document containing pricing information for the offering. The continuing disclosure documents are available at EMMA. EMMA also can give you access to information as to how the issuer's or borrower's outstanding securities (if any) are trading, which will give you an insight into liquidity of those securities.

You also may wish to search on the Internet for the issuer's or borrower's website so that you can review other, perhaps more current, information regarding the issuer or borrower.

What Are Some of the Factors I Should Consider?

When you purchase municipal securities, as a guide to appropriate investment you may wish to consider several risks associated with the securities. Those risks include, among others, issuer or borrower credit risks, default risks, credit enhancer and liquidity provider credit risks, pricing and yield risks, duration risks, liquidity risks, redemption (prepayment or call) risks, and tax risks.

The information available to you should be adequate for you to evaluate the securities intelligently. If adequate information is not available, then you may wish to consider other municipal securities.

When you buy municipal securities, you may wish to follow the practices of professional analysts and look closely at the credit-worthiness of the issuers and borrowers, even when the securities are insured, as well as at the terms of the securities.

By way of example, as discussed throughout this book, especially given the wide credit diversity within the municipal securities market, you should pay close attention to the source of payment and security for the municipal securities you are considering.

Therefore, among other things, you may wish to consider whether the municipal securities are secured by obligated taxes supported by a statutory lien or by dedicated revenues. In the cases of general fund securities or securities payable from an enterprise fund, you may wish to consider the financial condition of the fund and its results for the past several years.

You may wish to examine the essentiality of the project for the issuer and, in the case of revenue securities offerings, of the services that will generate revenues to pay you. You may wish to consider whether the community is diverse.

In addition, you may wish to consider whether factors such as are described in Chapter 6, "Greater Rewards and Greater Risks," may be present. If so, you may wish to consider what the implications of those factors may be in terms of rewards and risks for you.

Among other factors, there are securities terms that you may wish to consider. An example is the optional redemption feature of many municipal securities pursuant to which issuers or borrowers may redeem (prepay) the securities at the sole option of the issuers or borrowers. If the securities can be redeemed after a period of years, as is generally the case for long-term municipal securities, then you should be aware that any premium you pay for the securities could result in a loss if the redemption price is lower than the price you pay.

A similar outcome may occur when the securities are subject to mandatory redemption at their outstanding par (principal) amounts. See the section following entitled "What Are Municipal Securities Premiums and Discounts?"

For example, if you pay 105% for a municipal security, you are paying 5% more than the principal amount of the security. If the security is subject to redemption (also called *prepayment* or *call*) at the option of the issuer at 101% of the principal amount of the security, you may lose up to 4% of the principal amount. (Technically, if the municipal securities are *priced correctly* (sometimes a significant assumption) to the lower of the yield to the applicable call date or to maturity, then you are compensated by the greater current yield, and during the period between your purchase and the redemption, there may be an *amortization* of all or a portion of the premium you paid when you purchased the securities. For purposes of simplicity, however, I am ignoring that, but the caution still applies.)

You should also be aware of where your securities fall on the yield curve, which is discussed later. You may wish to gain an understanding of where on the yield curve the remaining life of the securities falls and how that may affect the pricing and yield of the securities and their duration. Duration is a measure of their price responsiveness to changes in market conditions, as discussed in Chapter 12, "Investor Questions and Answers (Q&As)," in the section entitled "What Is 'Duration'?"

The Municipal Securities Rulemaking Board (MSRB) has published a fact sheet entitled "Seven Questions to Ask When Investing in Municipal Bonds."

The seven questions identified by the MSRB for municipal securities investors are:

1. What information is available about a municipal bond?
2. What should I know about credit quality?
3. What should I know about yield?
4. Is the price I am being offered fair?
5. How is my financial professional compensated?
6. Is the investment appropriate for my tax status?
7. Is the bond callable?

From the MSRB, "Seven Questions to Ask When Investing in Municipal Bonds" (2011). The complete document is contained on the MSRB's website through a link at a page with more extensive information for investors. The page is entitled "Preparing to Invest in Municipal Securities" at www.msrb.org/Municipal-Bond-Market/Investor-Resources/Preparing-to-Invest.aspx/.

There are, of course, many other factors that you may wish to consider. The Appendix directs you to resources to assist you in identifying them.

What Is the Appropriate Role of Ratings?

When municipal securities are rated, as is usually the case, the ratings are one tool, but only one, to assist you. Long-term securities ratings of municipal securities that are regarded as safest are triple-A and double-A. Municipal securities that are A-rated, or BBB or Baa-rated also are considered to be investment grade. Long-term municipal securities at lower ratings, such as BB or Ba, are not considered to be investment grade.

Rating agencies stress that their ratings are *not* recommendations that you buy, sell, or hold any security. Ratings agencies do not engage in substantial active due diligence. Instead, they rely largely upon information provided to the agencies by securities issuers or borrowers or by underwriters.

I recommend that you not regard ratings as a substitute for gaining your own understanding of the securities.

What Are Rating Categories?

Rating categories are used by the rating agencies as a short-hand mechanism to express credit opinions regarding securities issues. The rating agencies often publish detailed analyses explaining their rationales for the ratings.

The major rating agencies are Standard and Poor's (S&P), Moody's Investors Service (Moody's), and Fitch Ratings (Fitch). The major rating agencies generally are paid by the issuers or borrowers. Other, less-well-known rating agencies also publish ratings. Some of them are paid differently, such as by investors. You may wish also to investigate those other rating agencies, their rating practices and records, and their rating scales.

The long-term rating categories of the major rating agencies include the following table.

Certain Rating Categories

AAA/Aaa	
AA/Aa	
A/A	Investment Grade
BBB/Baa	
BB/Ba	
B/B	Below Investment Grade

The ratings below those levels (such as C and D) indicate even more substantial risks of default and actual default status.

Each rating category contains other scaled indicators, such as + and –, or 1, 2, or 3 designations, such as A+ and A– or A1 and A3.

As one progresses down the rating scales, experience of the rating agencies demonstrates increasingly greater risks of default or late payment.

There also are short-term ratings for municipal securities. Standard and Poor's uses short-term ratings of A, B, C, and D, with 1, 2, and 3 designations within those categories. For notes, S&P uses SP-1, SP-2, and SP-3. Moody's Investors Service uses short-term ratings of MIG 1, MIG 2, and MIG 3, and for municipal securities with variable interest rates, VMIG-1, VMIG-2, and VMIG-3. Fitch Ratings uses F1, F2, and F3, with lower ratings for securities having, in Fitch's view, greater credit risks.

Municipal securities with credit enhancement—bond insurance, bank letters of credit, or occasionally, other forms of enhancement (such as guarantees)—are rated generally with the ratings of the credit enhancers, unless that is lower than the rating, if any, of underlying securities. As discussed below, you also may wish to consider the credit and underlying ratings of the issuers or borrowers. If underlying ratings are not present, you may experience illiquidity in the event credit enhancers are downgraded.

As discussed in the Appendix, you are able to obtain the ratings for the securities from rating agencies (as well as EMMA and, upon initial issuance, official statements) and to review the rating criteria of various rating agencies for municipal market sectors.

What Are Investment-Grade Ratings?

Investment grade ratings are ratings that span the credit quality ranges considered credit-worthy by various mutual funds, casualty insurance companies, banks, and other institutional investors, as well as by many retail investors.

As indicated in the table earlier, the long-term ratings of the major rating agencies that qualify generally as investment grade vary from AAA/Aaa at the highest rating level to BBB-/Baa3 at the lowest.

To What Degree Are Investment Grade Ratings a Useful Guide?

Some investors will limit their investments only to the highest levels, such as triple-A, double-A, and perhaps single-A.

Ratings below BBB–/Baa3 are considered to be below investment grade and subject to risks that many inves-

tors (but not all) avoid. Securities at those levels deserve especially careful examination and higher yields.

As stated by Fitch Ratings, municipal securities that are not rated at investment-grade levels "are approximately 10 times more likely to default" than are investment grade municipal securities. (See "For Additional Information" at the end of the chapter.)

Having noted that investment grade ratings are a helpful factor for cautious investors, however, it bears restating that you should make your own review and analysis of the municipal securities you consider. There are numerous factors in addition to credit quality that you may wish to consider, some of which are discussed in this Chapter.

How Do I Know When Ratings of My Securities Change?

You are able to monitor your securities for rating changes on the MSRB's EMMA at www.emma.msrb.org. That is one of the categories of event notices that issuers and borrowers are required to file on EMMA. S&P and Fitch also provide information to EMMA.

What Are Underlying Ratings, and Why Do They Matter?

Municipal securities with credit enhancement—bond insurance, bank letters of credit, or occasionally, other forms of enhancement (such as guarantees)—are rated generally with the rating of the credit enhancers. In the past, that meant that insured municipal securities usually were rated

at triple-A levels (a few bond insurers, and other credit enhancers, had lower ratings such as double-A or single-A).

The issuers or borrowers in those securities transactions commonly were able to obtain ratings for their
own securities, although they did not always do so.
When those ratings were assigned to the securities, they
were known as underlying ratings. The underlying ratings should be disclosed in official statements.

Many professional municipal securities analysts did
not review the bond insurers' or other credit enhancers'
ratings alone. Instead, the analysts also paid attention
to the underlying ratings resulting from the issuers' or
borrowers' participations in the transactions.

Further, many analysts rarely relied solely upon the
credit enhancers' and underlying ratings. They also conducted their own internal review of information con-
cerning both the credit enhancers and the underlying
issuers or borrowers.

Those practices were due to a number of considerations. First, the credit enhancers were private corporations, and at the time, ironically given contrasting
historical default experience, rating agencies rated
corporate obligors more favorably overall than municipal obligors. That has changed somewhat, although not
entirely.

In addition, professional analysts discounted the insured ratings and believed the credit-worthiness of the
underlying issuers and borrowers mattered. This proved
to be the case when all of the bond insurers' ratings were
downgraded.

When you buy credit-enhanced municipal securities,
you may wish to follow the practices of professional analysts and also look at the underlying credit-worthiness
of the issuers and borrowers, including but not limited
to, their underlying ratings.

In the long run, the underlying credit-worthiness of
the issuer or borrower is your primary source of security,
with the bond insurer or other credit enhancer stand-
ing in the background. If and when the credit enhancer's
rating declines significantly, you may find that, like a
broad universe of other municipal investors, the credit-
worthiness of your investment will depend more upon
the issuer and borrower than the insurer.

Another reason that underlying ratings matter is
that the liquidity of the municipal securities may be
affected without the underlying ratings, especially if
the bond insurers or other credit enhancers are downgraded at some point. That illiquidity will affect adversely the price you can receive if you decide to sell
the securities.

What Is the Relevance of the Spread between Bid and Asked Prices?

A *bid price* is the price that a potential investor offers for
a security. The *asked price* is the price for which a potential seller proposes to sell the security. In this context,
the difference between the bid price and the asked price
is the *spread* between them.

You may wish to consider the size of the spread between bid and asked prices for municipal securities.

A wider spread is viewed by some traders as indicating reduced liquidity for a municipal security. See the sections entitled "Why Does Liquidity Matter?"; "What Enhances Liquidity?"; and "How Does the Size of My Purchase Affect the Price?"

What Is the Relationship between Interest Rates (Coupons) and Yields?

The stated interest rate or coupon of your municipal securities is an annual percentage applied to the principal amount of the securities. See Chapter 12, "Investor Questions and Answers (Q&As)," in the section entitled "What Is the Coupon of My Securities?"

When you buy municipal securities, whether in initial offerings or in trading transactions, you may pay a price that is different from the principal amount (par) of the securities. Similarly, when you sell municipal securities, the price you receive may be different from the principal amount.

When the price you pay or receive on municipal securities is different from the principal amount, the yields of the securities will be different from the interest rate (coupon) borne by the securities.

Pursuant to Municipal Securities Rulemaking Board (MSRB) rules, the yields are calculated to the lower of the yields to maturity of the securities or the yields to the first redemption date.

Exhibit 7.1 illustrates municipal yields as published in Bloomberg Brief: Municipal Market on July 20, 2011. The index is Bloomberg Valuation AAA Benchmark Municipal Yields (BVAL).

What Is the Relationship between Yields and Prices?

Yields on and prices of municipal securities move in opposite (inverse) directions.

For fixed rate securities, as the price of a municipal security falls, the yield rises, and conversely, when the price rises, the yield falls.

What Is a Basis Point?

Municipal securities interest rates and yields are expressed in basis points. A basis point is $1/_{100th}$ of a percentage point, or .01%.

What Are Total Return and Buy-and-Hold Strategies?

Purchasers of individual municipal securities, especially individual (retail) investors, commonly have a *buy-and-hold* approach to investing. Their ownerships, and their risks, may be concentrated in fewer securities issues than may be the case when investing in mutual funds. They may make their own investment choices or may invest upon advice of a broker-dealer or financial advisor.

Bloomberg Valuation AAA Benchmark Yields

Description	Current	Current Date	Previous	Previous Date	Net Change
BVAL 1Y	0.19	07/19	0.18	07/18	+0.01
BVAL 2Y	0.39	07/19	0.37	07/18	+0.01
BVAL 3Y	0.67	07/19	0.64	07/18	+0.02
BVAL 4Y	0.90	07/19	0.93	07/18	−0.02
BVAL 5Y	1.22	07/19	1.21	07/18	+0.01
BVAL 6Y	1.54	07/19	1.53	07/18	0
BVAL 7Y	1.94	07/19	1.97	07/18	+0.03
BVAL 8Y	2.24	07/19	2.25	07/18	−0.01
BVAL 9Y	2.50	07/19	2.49	07/18	0
BVAL 10Y	2.65	07/19	2.63	07/18	+0.02
BVAL 20Y	3.82	07/19	3.82	07/18	0
BVAL 30Y	4.35	07/19	4.31	07/18	+0.05

Exhibit 7.1
Source: "Bloomberg Brief: Municipal Market" (July 20, 2011). Chart reprinted with permission. Copyright 2011 Bloomberg L.P. All rights reserved.

For these investors, *total return* considerations associated with price volatility in the market may be viewed as largely irrelevant, as they do not intend to sell. As a result, they are less sensitive to liquidity and to changes in market values over time. They intend to look only to receipt of the interest they sought upon their original purchases.

Investors in mutual funds, on the other hand, may be concerned with total return considerations, meaning that they look not only to interest earnings, but also take into account changes in the value of securities in fund portfolios and the prices at which the funds can sell portfolio investments.

What Are Municipal Securities Premiums and Discounts?

When municipal securities are sold or purchased at prices that are higher than the principal amount (par) of the securities, the price includes a premium that is represented by the difference between the principal amount and the higher price.

Because prices and yields move in opposite (inverse) directions, the premium has the effect of reducing the yield on fixed-rate securities below their stated interest rates. The greater the premium, the lower the yield.

Similarly, when the securities are sold at a price that is lower than the principal amount, the difference is a discount. The discount has the effect of raising the yield above the stated interest rates. The greater the discount, the higher the yield.

What Is the Impact of Redemptions?

Redemption provisions are very important to municipal securities investors. A redemption means that you no longer will own the securities and that you may not be able to re-invest the funds at the same yield.

Most municipal securities are subject to redemption (also described as *prepayment* or *call*). The redemption price may be the principal amount of the securities or may include a small redemption premium.

Optional redemption occurs at the sole option of the issuer or borrower. You have no say in the matter. In general, you will receive your principal (plus any prescribed redemption premium, but no more), plus interest accrued to the redemption date.

Mandatory redemptions are a frequent facet of long-term municipal securities structures. For example, a term security maturing in 2030 may be subject to mandatory redemption in 2026, 2027, 2028, and 2029 in predetermined and fully-disclosed principal amounts. Most commonly, mandatory redemptions occur at the principal amount redeemed, plus interest accrued to the redemption date. Regarding *term securities*, see the descriptions above and in Chapter 12, "Investor Ques-

tions and Answers (Q&As)," in the section and subsection entitled "What Are Basic Provisions in Securities Structures?, What Are Term Securities?"

Depending upon the price you paid for the municipal securities, you may incur a capital gain or loss upon redemption. If you paid a premium for the securities, you may lose money upon a redemption at a lower redemption price. See the earlier discussion of "premiums" and the related example in the section entitled "What Are Some of the Factors I Should Consider?"

The trustee or paying agent for the securities generally is required to give prior notice of a redemption for a period, such as 30 days, which will give you an opportunity to plan for reinvesting the redemption payment.

Why Does Liquidity Matter?

Many municipal securities are illiquid. Especially securities of smaller and less well-known issuers or borrowers may not have a ready market when and if you wish to resell them. Ernesto A. Lanza, deputy executive director and chief legal officer to the Municipal Securities Rulemaking Board (MSRB), testified that "On a typical trading day, there are about 40,000 trades in 14,000 different [municipal] securities. This means that over 99 percent of municipal securities do not trade on a given day. In fact, over 90 percent typically do not trade in a given month. The individual municipal securities that are traded each day change as new issues come to market, are traded, and eventually are purchased by investors that hold them as long-term investments, in many cases with the intention of retaining until maturity."

In turn, that illiquidity can affect the price you may receive on resale of the securities.

In other words, there is a higher price for liquid securities, in part due to the greater demand for the securities and in part because parties buying them have a higher level of confidence that they will be able themselves to resell the securities more readily and at a more favorable price.

As noted, many retail investors are buy-and-hold investors who purchase municipal securities and hold them to maturity. Those investors generally are not highly concerned with liquidity issues most of the time. If, however, the investors find it necessary or desirable to sell their securities unexpectedly, liquidity can become a very serious pricing and sales issue for them.

To illustrate contrasting liquidity in the secondary market, the next three pages contain screens (Exhibits 7.2, 7.3, and 7.4) from the Bloomberg Terminal showing (1) an example of a relatively high level of liquidity for a bond of a state issuer (California), reflecting numerous trades in larger blocks in the brief period from July 1, 2011, through July 20, 2011; (2) an example of a lower level of liquidity resulting from fewer trades for a security in smaller blocks in the longer period from February 20, 2011, through August 10, 2011; and (3) a security without any trades in the period from January 30, 2011 through July 20, 2011.

What Enhances Liquidity?

If you are concerned about liquidity, you may wish to consider municipal securities of larger, more frequent issuers, such as states, state agencies, and larger cities, counties, school districts, airports and the like. The same is true of larger, better-known private borrowers. Those are likely to have more active trading patterns and tend to be more liquid than securities of smaller, less frequent issuers. Other factors that may affect liquidity of your securities include the size of blocks you trade and the maturity of the securities. You may find that larger blocks (e.g., $100,000, $250,000 or more) and shorter maturities (e.g., 10 to 12 years or less) have more appeal (greater liquidity) in the market. (See "For Additional Information" at the end of the chapter.)

If you are not a buy-and-hold municipal securities investor, or if you must sell your securities unexpectedly and suddenly, such considerations may impact you upon resale of your securities.

The MSRB's EMMA facility at www.emma.msrb.org is a recent enhancement in the market that is intended in part to improve liquidity by providing real-time trading and pricing data on municipal securities.

In addition, underwriters of securities upon initial issuance generally remain interested in those securities in the secondary market and may assist with trading, although they do not guarantee liquidity.

```
<HELP> for explanation.                              Muni   TDHM
<MENU> to Return
   1) Export                      Trade Disclosure History (As Reported by MSRB)
Issuer    CALIFORNIA ST                              Cusip   13063A4Y7
Issue     VAR PURP
Coupon    6.00000    Maturity  04/01/38    Issued  04/01/09    State  CA
```

Range 07/01/11 – 07/20/11			View Price	Trade Size All Sizes	
Agg. Volume (M)	Agg. Trades	Trade Days	High		Low
2,625	44	8	110.784		105.210

Date	Volume (M)	Trades #	High	Low	Average
3) 07/18/11	400	5	109.510	106.330	107.649
4) 07/14/11	145	2	109.322	109.322	109.322
5) 07/12/11	620	8	110.784	107.123	109.339
6) 07/11/11	240	12	109.037	105.878	107.446
7) 07/08/11	450	8	107.546	105.210	106.696
8) 07/07/11	280	1	106.396	106.396	106.396
9) 07/06/11	265	4	106.875	106.470	106.571
10) 07/05/11	225	4	109.011	106.971	107.494

```
     Average Price calculated by Bloomberg. Volume may not include trades over 1 million
Australia 61 2 9777 8600 Brazil 5511 3048 4500 Europe 44 20 7330 7500 Germany 49 69 9204 1210 Hong Kong 852 2977 6000
Japan 81 3 3201 8900      Singapore 65 6212 1000      U.S. 1 212 318 2000      Copyright 2011 Bloomberg Finance L.P.
                                              SN 268301 CDT   GMT-5:00 G515-401-2 10-Aug-2011 10:30:10
```

Exhibit 7.2

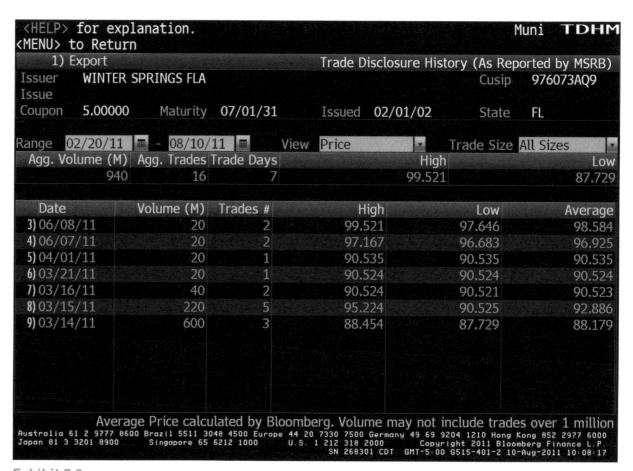

<HELP> for explanation.   Muni **TDHM**
<MENU> to Return

| 1) Export | Trade Disclosure History (As Reported by MSRB) |

Issuer   WINTER SPRINGS FLA   Cusip   976073AQ9
Issue
Coupon   5.00000   Maturity   07/01/31   Issued   02/01/02   State   FL

Range   02/20/11   ▦ - 08/10/11   ▦   View Price   ▾   Trade Size All Sizes   ▾

Agg. Volume (M)	Agg. Trades	Trade Days	High	Low
940	16	7	99.521	87.729

	Date	Volume (M)	Trades #	High	Low	Average
3)	06/08/11	20	2	99.521	97.646	98.584
4)	06/07/11	20	2	97.167	96.683	96.925
5)	04/01/11	20	1	90.535	90.535	90.535
6)	03/21/11	20	1	90.524	90.524	90.524
7)	03/16/11	40	2	90.524	90.521	90.523
8)	03/15/11	220	5	95.224	90.525	92.886
9)	03/14/11	600	3	88.454	87.729	88.179

Average Price calculated by Bloomberg. Volume may not include trades over 1 million
Australia 61 2 9777 8600 Brazil 5511 3048 4500 Europe 44 20 7330 7500 Germany 49 69 9204 1210 Hong Kong 852 2977 6000
Japan 81 3 3201 8900   Singapore 65 6212 1000   U.S. 1 212 318 2000   Copyright 2011 Bloomberg Finance L.P.
                          SN 268301 CDT   GMT-5:00 G515-401-2 10-Aug-2011 10:08:17

Exhibit 7.3
Reprinted with permission from Bloomberg. Copyright 2011 Bloomberg L.P. All rights reserved.

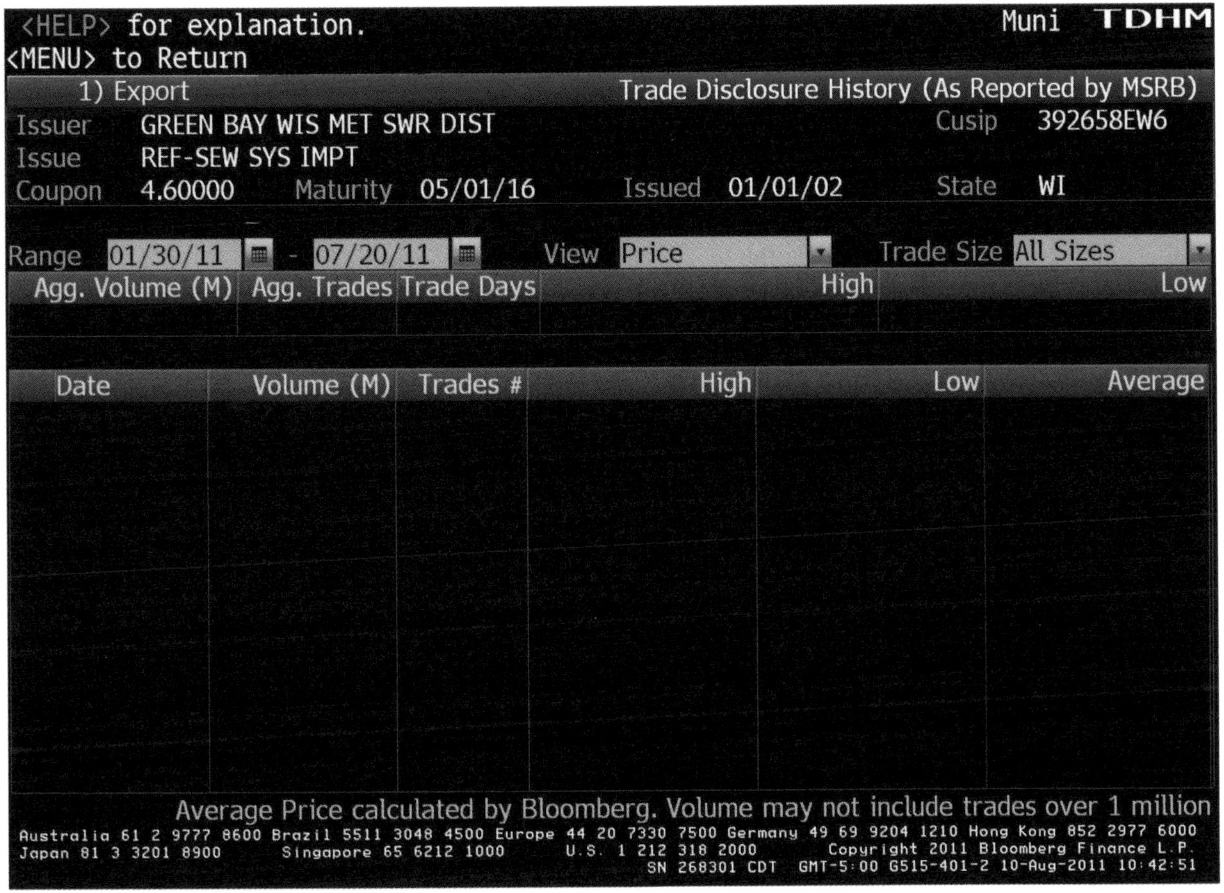

```
<HELP> for explanation.                                          Muni  TDHM
<MENU> to Return
   1) Export                          Trade Disclosure History (As Reported by MSRB)
Issuer    GREEN BAY WIS MET SWR DIST                   Cusip    392658EW6
Issue     REF-SEW SYS IMPT
Coupon    4.60000      Maturity  05/01/16    Issued  01/01/02    State   WI

Range  01/30/11  ▦ - 07/20/11  ▦    View  Price      ▾   Trade Size  All Sizes    ▾
  Agg. Volume (M)  Agg. Trades Trade Days              High                     Low


   Date         Volume (M)  Trades #         High            Low         Average
```

Average Price calculated by Bloomberg. Volume may not include trades over 1 million

Australia 61 2 9777 8600 Brazil 5511 3048 4500 Europe 44 20 7330 7500 Germany 49 69 9204 1210 Hong Kong 852 2977 6000
Japan 81 3 3201 8900   Singapore 65 6212 1000   U.S. 1 212 318 2000   Copyright 2011 Bloomberg Finance L.P.
                                       SN 268301 CDT GMT-5:00 G515-401-2 10-Aug-2011 10:42:51

Exhibit 7.4
Reprinted with permission from Bloomberg. Copyright 2011 Bloomberg L.P. All rights reserved.

How Does the Size of My Purchase Affect the Price?

In general, a broker or dealer must work disproportion-
ately to sell $5,000 of securities, as opposed to selling
$1 million or $10 million of securities. Thus, smaller purchases have higher execution costs per $1,000 of prin-
cipal amount. In order to make a profit, the broker or
dealer is likely to provide a less favorable price for the
smaller sale, within regulatory limits.

In general, smaller principal amounts of securities
(blocks) are less liquid than are larger blocks You may
find that blocks of $100,000 or more are more liquid than
are municipal securities in smaller blocks.

When Should I Consider Mutual Funds and ETFs?

Due to the execution costs of smaller municipal securities sales, if you are interested in investing smaller
amounts in municipal securities, you may wish to consider the alternative of investing in municipal bond
funds or exchange-traded funds.

Those funds are discussed in Chapter 12, "Investor
Questions and Answers (Q&As). What Is a Yield Curve?
When considering specific municipal issues, the yield
curve—a graphic depiction of yields expressed across
periods—reflects relationships among different maturities of debt securities and interest rates. Under normal
economic conditions, shorter-term debt securities gen-

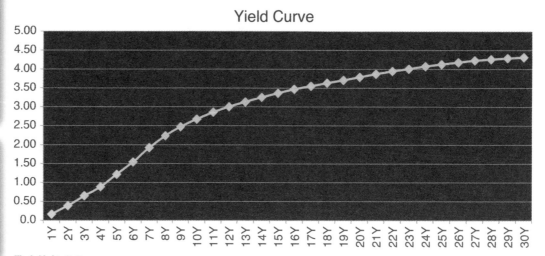

Exhibit 7.5

Reprinted with permission from Bloomberg L.P. Copyright 2011 Bloomberg L.P. All rights reserved.

erally have lower yields than do longer-term securities for which there are greater inflation and other risks. The generally greater appeal and liquidity of securities with shorter maturities is reflected in the yield curve.

The upward slope of the normal yield curve, can be affected, however, by general investor (market) expectations for inflation or by general economic and political developments. In unusual conditions, the slope can become inverted, signaling possible future economic difficulties. The slope of the yield curve can tell you what the market expects yields may be in the future. You may wish to research yield curves and the significance of a variety of yield curve slopes in terms of how market professionals view them.

To illustrate, Exhibit 7.5 shows a yield curve based upon BVAL (the "Bloomberg Valuation AAA Benchmark Municipal Yields") on August 1, 2011.

What Is the Significance to Me of the Bond Insurance Industry's Decline?

Bond insurers are private companies. You may wish to evaluate the presence of bond insurance in a municipal securities structure just as you would evaluate the presence of any other private credit.

Bond insurance has proved to be one of the greatest disappointments in the history of the municipal securities market. After participating in the municipal market significantly for decades, the bond insurance industry experienced significant decline. That impacted directly and adversely large numbers of municipal securities investors.

This is, of course, quite different from the assertions by certain pundits and media sources regarding municipal securities. Bond insurance companies are not government entities.

Before the financial crisis, many investors relied upon bond insurance as an all-purpose homogeneous substitute for active review of their investments. Among other things, bond insurance homogenized municipal securities at triple-A levels. Many investors made the serious mistake of looking no further than an insurance company's triple-A rating.

Bond insurer practices and financial conditions led to rating downgrades of all of the formerly triple-A rated insurers, most of them substantially and even, in a few cases, to the point of insolvency and bankruptcy or close to it. Those occurrences impacted municipal securities prices, and led to large investor losses in terms of market prices. With only one exception, all the monoline insurers, have ceased active insurance underwriting, although some would like to re-enter the market.

For many years, half or more of municipal securities issues were insured as they were offered to the market. Today, the percentage is very low, even in single-digit percentages.

Exhibit 7.6 and Exhibit 7.7 present, based upon Bloomberg data, the volumes of insured long-term, fixed-rate municipal securities issued annually from 2003 through 2010.

Year	Annual Bond Ins. %
2003	55
2004	56
2005	62
2006	52
2007	47
2008	21
2009	9
2010	6

Exhibit 7.6
Reprinted with permission from Bloomberg L.P. Copyright 2011
Bloomberg L.P. All rights reserved.

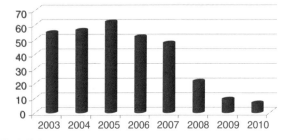

Annual Bond Insurance Percent

Exhibit 7.7
Reprinted with permission from Bloomberg L.P. Copyright 2011
Bloomberg L.P. All rights reserved.

To the extent that some investors relied solely upon the bond insurers and rating agencies to perform the investors' due diligence for them, it has been a bitter lesson. Although to date, most bond insurance companies have continued to pay claims, investors paid a significant price in terms of market valuations of their securities, sometimes leading to quite substantial losses.

With the emergence of bond insurer credit difficulties, the perception of homogeneity of municipal securities has disappeared. In today's market, it is even more important that you read and understand the information that is provided to you in official statements and issuer and borrower continuing disclosure documents. That will help you distinguish among issuers and borrowers.

The relevance to you of bond insurance in a municipal securities structure can be magnified even more when the issuer's debt service reserve fund consists solely of a surety bond issued by a bond insurer. Regarding the practice of some issuers or borrowers in structuring reserve funds consisting solely of bond insurer surety bonds, see also Chapter 6, "Greater Rewards and Greater Risks," in the section entitled "What About Reserve Funds Backed by Insurer Surety Bonds?" See also Chapter 12, "Investor Questions and Answers (Q&As)," in the section entitled "What Are Debt Service Reserve Funds?"

As discussed earlier, it is also important for you to pay attention to the credits and ratings of municipal securities underlying bond insurance and other forms of credit enhancement.

How Can I Use CUSIP Numbers?

In researching information regarding municipal securities, issuer and borrower disclosure filings, pricing and trading data and other information, you are likely to find CUSIP numbers to be very useful.

What Are CUSIP Numbers?

CUSIP numbers are important to securities investing. They are a widely-used means of identifying securities according to specific traits, such as differing maturities, and of gaining ready access to substantial information for specific securities issues. The Municipal Securities Rulemaking Board (MSRB) estimates that there are over 1.3 million CUSIP numbers.

As described by the SEC, "The CUSIP system—owned by the American Bankers Association (ABA) and operated by Standard and Poor's—facilitates the clearing and settlement process of securities." The term *CUSIP* refers to the ABA's Committee on Uniform Securities Identification Procedures.

CUSIP numbers are electronic identifiers for every municipal security (and virtually all other securities, including not only corporate debt obligations, but also stocks and debt securities of national governments). A separate CUSIP number is issued for each maturity in a municipal securities issue. If municipal securities have been refunded (refinanced), or if changes have been made to the credit (such as certain securities of an issue being insured, while others are not), the affected securities may be assigned distinct CUSIP numbers.

How Can CUSIP Numbers Be Used?

CUSIP numbers make it possible to buy, sell, trade, and track every municipal security.

When you wish to identify municipal securities in specific terms, CUSIP numbers make that specific identification possible.

For example, the use of CUSIP numbers facilitates searches for data and documents on municipal securities on the MSRB's EMMA website.

The numbers also make it possible for investors and brokers or dealers to communicate the specific identities of securities.

Where Can I Locate CUSIP Numbers?

You can locate CUSIP numbers on purchase and sale confirmations. In addition, most issuers or borrowers provide CUSIP numbers on the covers of official statements in tables showing the securities maturities offered, together with the interest rates and prices or yields.

On the EMMA website maintained by the Municipal Securities Rulemaking Board, you can search for information using issuer names. If you know the name of your securities, as well as the maturity, you can locate the CUSIP number.

Six-digit CUSIP numbers are associated with the issuers or borrowers. Three additional characters are attached for specific securities. For example, the format of a six-digit CUSIP number for a specific issuer or borrower is 000000. With the addition, the entire nine-digit CUSIP number may have a format of 000000 XX0.

For Additional Information

▪ Fitch Ratings, "Default Risk and Recovery Rates on U.S. Municipal Bonds" at 2 (January 9, 2007).

▪ Ernesto A. Lanza, deputy executive director and general counsel to the Municipal Securities Rulemaking Board (MSRB), written testimony at the Securities and Exchange Commission's Field Hearing in Jefferson County, Alabama, on the State of the Municipal Securities Market, at 6 (July 29, 2011).

▪ Ernesto A. Lanza, deputy executive director and chief legal officer to the Municipal Securities Rulemaking Board (MSRB), in written testimony at the Securities and Exchange Commission's Field Hearing in Jefferson County, Alabama, on the State of the Municipal Securities Market, at 7 (July 29, 2011), testified: "In terms of trading, the small par value transaction—$100,000 or less—accounts for about 8.4 million or 81 percent of the transactions that occur each day. However, ... 78 percent of the par value traded each day is in transactions of $1 million or greater."

▪ The yield curve is also a general tool used in the market reflecting, as market barometers, yields for 10-year U.S. Treasury securities or other benchmark securities. See Chapter 8, "Municipal Securities and Trading," in the section entitled "What Is the Yield Spread?"

Municipal Securities Pricing and Trading

Many investors wish to have greater transparency in the pricing and trading of municipal securities. The Municipal Securities Rulemaking Board's EMMA website is a tool that now gives you access to virtually real time trading data.

This chapter is intended to describe certain municipal securities market pricing and trading practices and to answer certain investor questions regarding those practices.

Where Can I Find Trading and Pricing Information?

The Municipal Securities Rulemaking Board (MSRB) has created and maintains real-time municipal securities trading and pricing information at the MSRB's EMMA platform at www.emma.msrb.org/.

This excellent facility is discussed also in Chapter 2, "Basic Information Resources" and in the Appendix.

The MSRB's facility has encouraged the development of useful market products using information from EMMA.

To illustrate, Exhibit 8.1 from the Bloomberg Terminal provides information regarding trades of certain securities issued by the Alaska International Airport Authority, with information regarding dates, numbers and volumes of trades, and trading price data.

Exhibit 8.2 provides another type of trading information. This table from "Bloomberg Brief: Municipal Market" identifies the "Most Active Bonds" traded as of July 20, 2011.

What Pricing Information on EMMA Should I Consider?

As discussed in Chapter 7, "Considerations When Buying," in the section entitled "Why Does Liquidity Matter?" many municipal securities issues are illiquid. That may

<HELP> for explanation.   Muni TDHM
<MENU> to Return
     1) Export   Trade Disclosure History (As Reported by MSRB)
Issuer   ALASKA ST INTERNATIONAL ARPTS   Cusip   011842QF1
Issue   REF-SER D
Coupon   4.75000   Maturity 10/01/16   Issued 03/14/06   State   AK

Range 02/20/11 ▦ - 08/10/11 ▦   View Price ▾   Trade Size All Sizes ▾
     Agg. Volume (M) Agg. Trades Trade Days   High   Low
            8,630   50   22   114.252   104.799

Date	Volume (M)	Trades #	High	Low	Average
3) 07/29/11	140	2	114.252	112.895	113.574
4) 07/21/11	525	3	113.045	112.783	112.923
5) 07/01/11	1,500	2	112.180	112.120	112.150
6) 06/28/11	750	2	112.310	112.310	112.310
7) 06/23/11	3,000	2	111.855	111.802	111.829
8) 06/14/11	15	1	111.603	111.603	111.603
9) 06/09/11	35	2	111.885	110.794	111.340
10) 06/06/11	25	1	110.447	110.447	110.447
11) 05/25/11	25	1	112.067	112.067	112.067
12) 05/24/11	50	1	112.520	112.520	112.520
13) 05/17/11	50	1	110.728	110.728	110.728
14) 05/16/11	20	2	112.537	112.437	112.487

Average Price calculated by Bloomberg. Volume may not include trades over 1 million
Australia 61 2 9777 8600 Brazil 5511 3048 4500 Europe 44 20 7330 7500 Germany 49 69 9204 1210 Hong Kong 852 2977 6000
Japan 81 3 3201 8900   Singapore 65 6212 1000   U.S. 1 212 318 2000   Copyright 2011 Bloomberg Finance L.P.
                                      SN 268301 CDT GMT-5:00 G515-401-2 10-Aug-2011 10:17:32

The circled transactions are small, relatively isolated secondary market trades.

Exhibit 8.1

Trading

Most Active Bonds

Description	Selling Date	State	Dated	Coupon	Maturity	Volume	Price Average	Yield Average	Number of Trades
Metro Trans Auth-A		NY	07/20/11	5.000	11/15/37	8,670,000	100.347	4.955	112
Met Trans Auth		NY	10/15/09	5.871	11/15/39	7,315,000	104.624	5.545	87
Nj Trn Sys Ser A-Amba		NJ	09/27/07	5.000	12/15/32	7,215,000	102.582	4.530	83
Nyc Mun Wtr Ser B		NY	12/08/04	5.000	06/15/36	6,955,000	103.226	3.974	40
Liberty Dev Goldman		NY	10/12/05	5.250	10/01/35	6,400,000	101.400	5.148	45
Hudson Yards-A-Agm-Cr		NY	12/21/06	5.000	02/15/47	6,395,000	99.173	5.050	64
Metro Trans Auth-A		NY	07/20/11	5.000	11/15/46	6,265,000	99.340	5.040	72
Ny Dorm Auth-A		NY	06/09/11	4.250	03/15/32	6,060,000	98.138	4.388	53
Palmdale Cops-Pk Impt		CA	12/10/02	5.000	09/01/32	5,870,000	93.062	5.562	18
Pr Infra-Ser B		PR	09/28/06	5.000	07/01/37	5,624,000	93.168	5.497	66
Tavares-A-Osprey Ldge		FL	07/21/11	9.000	07/01/46	5,145,000	97.340	9.000	112
Phila Hosp & Hgr-A		PA	08/17/07	5.500	07/01/30	5,090,000	91.794	6.244	39
Il St Txb-Pension		IL	06/12/03	4.350	06/01/18	4,675,000	99.705	4.399	36
Golden Tob Sr-A-1		CA	03/14/07	5.750	06/01/47	4,575,000	73.380	8.019	19
Nj Tpk Auth-Ser A		NJ	07/09/03	4.750	01/01/25	4,350,000	102.331	3.497	75

Volume numbers do not include trades > $1mm due to MSRB reporting restrictions.

Exhibit 8.2

Source: "Bloomberg Brief: Municipal Market" (July 20, 2011). Chart reprinted with permission. Copyright 2011 Bloomberg L.P. All rights reserved.

be especially so for smaller issuers and issues. Further, smaller trades and isolated transactions reported on EMMA are not necessarily reflective of optimal market pricing conditions. See also Chapter 7, "Considerations When Buying," in the sections entitled "What Enhances Liquidity?" and "How Does the Size of My Purchase Affect the Price?"

For those reasons, among others, not all trading prices reported on EMMA are necessarily good guides to accurate pricing for particular municipal securities.

Pricing can become a complex subject. It is an art, and not a science. I do not intend to discuss all relevant pricing ramifications.

Nevertheless, key dynamics include emphasizing trades between dealers (known as *inter-dealer trades*) and larger trades (say, $100,000, $250,000, or more). Small customer trades may be with individuals who are less sophisticated about market conditions and who are not sensitive to market subtleties, so prices in those trades may not provide optimal pricing guidance. The dealer trades reflect dealer sophistication, and the larger trades are likely with more sophisticated individuals or with institutions.

Within those parameters, the more recent trades are likely to be more indicative of current pricing. How recent a trade may be is not dependent solely upon the time that has passed since the trade in relation to your trade, but also upon whether market conditions have changed since the trade and whether there are intervening reported informational changes relating to the issuer or borrower.

> **KEY POINT:**
>
> Pricing can become a complex subject. It is an art, and not a science.

If the municipal securities you are considering are not associated with significant recent trading or pricing information, you may wish to consider information relating to similar securities. Such a step requires the exercise of care in terms of a variety of factors such as, among other things, similarity of credit quality, nature of security, maturity, duration, redemption (prepayment) provisions, size of the issue, federal and state tax treatment, and yield spread in relation to U.S. Treasury securities. Regarding the yield spread in relation to U.S. Treasuries, see "What Is the Yield Spread?"

If you wish to investigate further the subject of municipal securities pricing, you may wish to review information associated with the MSRB's Rule G-30. The Rule governs dealer responsibilities regarding municipal securities pricing. The MSRB publishes interpretations of the Rule that may be useful to you in discussing pricing considerations. You can review those interpretations at http://msrb.org/Rules-and-Interpretations/MSRB-Rules/General/Rule-G-30.aspx/.

How Is Interest Calculated on Municipal Securities?

Interest on municipal securities generally is calculated assuming a 360-day year composed of twelve 30-day months. For certain short-term securities, such as variable-rate securities and notes, interest may be calculated based upon actual days, that is 365- or 366-day years and actual days within months.

What Is Accrued Interest, and Why Must I Pay It?

Accrued interest is unpaid interest on a municipal security from the last date, if any, on which interest was paid in full to the settlement date of your trade. As the buyer, you are entitled to interest income from that date forward. The buyer must pay the accrued interest because the seller of the security is entitled to it for the period the seller owned the municipal security.

Interest accrues on new issues of municipal securities from the date of the securities, sometimes the first day of a month. The dates of issuance generally are provided on the covers of official statements. A date of issuance may predate the trade for the convenience of the parties participating in the offering (for example, to compensate for the possibility of changing transactional closing dates). In effect, you pay the accrued interest from that date of the securities to your settlement date, and then receive it back (without interest) when the issuer makes the first interest payment.

In the secondary market, as noted, the seller is entitled to the interest for the period the seller owns the security. The buyer pays the accrued interest because the buyer will receive it from the issuer or borrower on the next interest payment date and is not entitled to the portion of the interest for the period of the seller's ownership.

What Is the Yield Spread?

When yield curves for different securities types are compared, the difference between the curves at a particular point (e.g., the 10-year maturity) is called a *spread*. Municipal market professionals often measure the yields on municipal securities in relation to the yields on U.S. Treasury securities with the same maturities. The spread in that case is the difference, expressed in basis points, between the yield on the Treasury securities and the yield on the municipal securities of the same maturity

Exhibit 8.3 presents Bloomberg data regarding yield relationships in August of selected years between triple-A–rated municipal securities of the indicated maturities and U.S. Treasury securities of the same maturities. Among other things, the contrasts between the yield relationships in 2001 and 2002, which predated the financial crisis, versus 2009, 2010, and 2011, which postdated the crisis, demonstrate that, following the financial crisis, the yield relationships have not returned to previously traditional relationships.

The screen in Exhibit 8.4 from the Bloomberg Terminal compares two yield curves as of July 20, 2011. The yellow curve is for the Bloomberg Valuation AAA Benchmark Municipal Yields (BVAL). The orange curve is for yields of U.S. Treasury securities.

To illustrate graphically, the screen in Exhibit 8.5 from the Bloomberg Terminal illustrates the spreads expressed in basis points as of July 20, 2011, between (1) the Bloomberg Valuation AAA Benchmark Municipal Yields (BVAL); and (2) U.S. Treasuries. In addition to a

Muni AAA Yields as % of Treasury Yields

Maturity	% 8/1/01	% 8/1/2002	% 8/1/09	% 8/1/10	% 8/1/11
1Y	76.9	66.8	169.8	127.6	83.7
2Y	79.0	81.3	94.0	106.5	104.1
3Y	80.1	82.3	81.1	100.1	118.8
5Y	79.8	84.4	74.9	91.4	91.8
10Y	84.1	86.5	88.1	95.9	97.5
30Y	92.0	95.1	110.6	107.9	105.7

This chart shows how the traditional relationship between munis and Treasuries has changed (and not yet settled down) since 2007/2008 meltdown.

Exhibit 8.3

Reprinted with permission from Bloomberg. Copyright 2011 Bloomberg L.P. All rights reserved.

yield curve depiction, the graphic adds a bar graph representation of the relationships between the two curves at different maturities. The reason for the gap in the bar graph is due to the absence of intervening Treasury yields. Regarding basis points, see Chapter 7, "Considerations When Buying," in the section entitled "What Is a Basis Point?"

The next two following screens (Exhibits 8.6 and 8.7) from the Bloomberg Terminal illustrate the spreads in basis points as of July 19, 2011, between (1) triple-A rated municipal general obligation securities and U.S. Treasury securities; and (2) A-rated municipal general obligation securities and U.S. Treasuries.

Sometimes, spreads are discussed in terms of yield relationships among municipal securities of differing rating levels, such as a spread in basis points between the yields on particular municipal securities and the yields of triple-A municipal securities of the same maturity.

Why Do Values of Municipal Securities Change in My Portfolio?

When you receive reports on your portfolio from your broker or dealer, you will see that the reflected values change for the municipal securities you hold in your portfolio. Sometimes, there are substantial changes from period to period.

It is important for you to realize that municipal securities prices change. This occurs as interest rates and yields available in the market for similar maturities and rating categories of municipal securities change in response to economic and political developments and the effects of those developments upon securities supply and demand in the market.

For example, Federal Reserve policies affect municipal securities prices. Economic conditions affect prices.

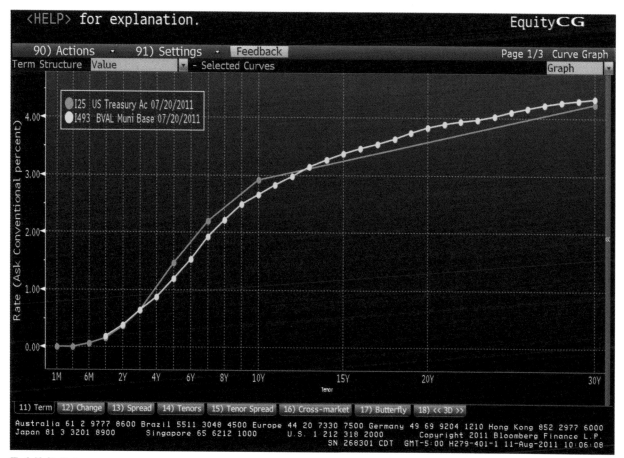

<HELP> for explanation.   Equity**CG**

90) Actions   ▾   91) Settings   ▾   Feedback   Page 1/3   Curve Graph
Term Structure Value   ▾ - Selected Curves   Graph   ▾

● I25 US Treasury Ac 07/20/2011
● I493 BVAL Muni Base 07/20/2011

Rate (Ask Conventional percent)

4.00

3.00

2.00

1.00

0.00

1M   6M   2Y   4Y   6Y   8Y   10Y   15Y   20Y   30Y

Tenor

11) Term   12) Change   13) Spread   14) Tenors   15) Tenor Spread   16) Cross-market   17) Butterfly   18) << 3D >>

Australia 61 2 9777 8600 Brazil 5511 3048 4500 Europe 44 20 7330 7500 Germany 49 69 9204 1210 Hong Kong 852 2977 6000
Japan 81 3 3201 8900   Singapore 65 6212 1000   U.S. 1 212 318 2000   Copyright 2011 Bloomberg Finance L.P.
                                            SN 268301 CDT GMT-5:00 H279-401-1 11-Aug-2011 10:06:08

Exhibit 8.4
Reprinted with permission from Bloomberg. Copyright 2011 Bloomberg L.P. All rights reserved.

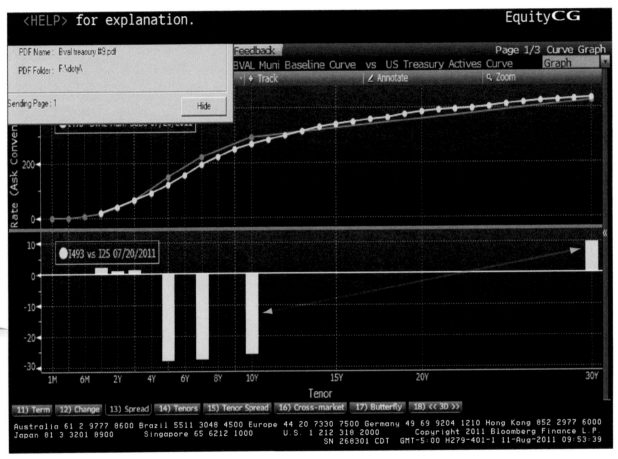

The arrows point to bar graph illustrations of yield spreads in basis points at specific points on the yield curve.

Exhibit 8.5

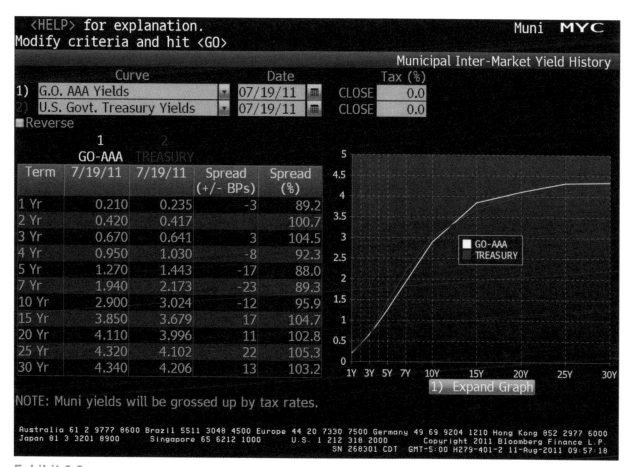

<HELP> for explanation.
Modify criteria and hit <GO>

Muni MYC

Municipal Inter-Market Yield History

Curve	Date	Tax (%)
1) G.O. AAA Yields ▼	07/19/11	CLOSE 0.0
2) U.S. Govt. Treasury Yields ▼	07/19/11	CLOSE 0.0

■Reverse

	1 GO-AAA	2 TREASURY		
Term	7/19/11	7/19/11	Spread (+/- BPs)	Spread (%)
1 Yr	0.210	0.235	-3	89.2
2 Yr	0.420	0.417		100.7
3 Yr	0.670	0.641	3	104.5
4 Yr	0.950	1.030	-8	92.3
5 Yr	1.270	1.443	-17	88.0
7 Yr	1.940	2.173	-23	89.3
10 Yr	2.900	3.024	-12	95.9
15 Yr	3.850	3.679	17	104.7
20 Yr	4.110	3.996	11	102.8
25 Yr	4.320	4.102	22	105.3
30 Yr	4.340	4.206	13	103.2

■ GO-AAA
TREASURY

1) Expand Graph

NOTE: Muni yields will be grossed up by tax rates.

Australia 61 2 9777 8600 Brazil 5511 3048 4500 Europe 44 20 7330 7500 Germany 49 69 9204 1210 Hong Kong 852 2977 6000
Japan 81 3 3201 8900   Singapore 65 6212 1000   U.S. 1 212 318 2000   Copyright 2011 Bloomberg Finance L.P.
SN 268301 CDT GMT-5:00 H279-401-2 11-Aug-2011 09:57:18

Exhibit 8.6
Reprinted with permission from Bloomberg. Copyright 2011 Bloomberg L.P. All rights reserved.

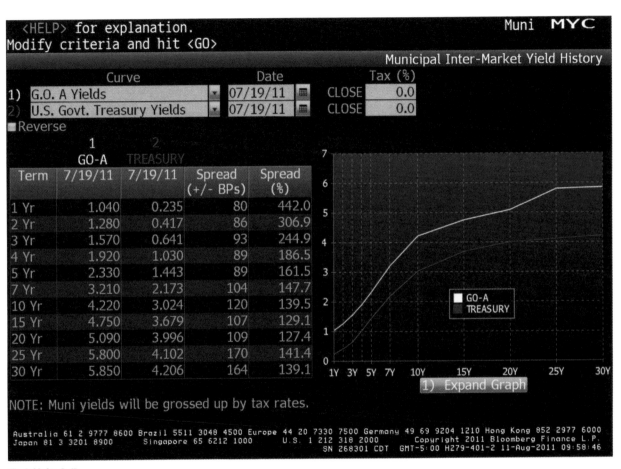

<HELP> for explanation.   Muni **MYC**
Modify criteria and hit <GO>

Municipal Inter-Market Yield History

	Curve		Date		Tax (%)
1)	G.O. A Yields	▼	07/19/11 ▦	CLOSE	0.0
2)	U.S. Govt. Treasury Yields	▼	07/19/11 ▦	CLOSE	0.0

■ Reverse

| | 1 | 2 | | |
| | GO-A | TREASURY | | |
Term	7/19/11	7/19/11	Spread (+/- BPs)	Spread (%)
1 Yr	1.040	0.235	80	442.0
2 Yr	1.280	0.417	86	306.9
3 Yr	1.570	0.641	93	244.9
4 Yr	1.920	1.030	89	186.5
5 Yr	2.330	1.443	89	161.5
7 Yr	3.210	2.173	104	147.7
10 Yr	4.220	3.024	120	139.5
15 Yr	4.750	3.679	107	129.1
20 Yr	5.090	3.996	109	127.4
25 Yr	5.800	4.102	170	141.4
30 Yr	5.850	4.206	164	139.1

1) Expand Graph

NOTE: Muni yields will be grossed up by tax rates.

Australia 61 2 9777 8600 Brazil 5511 3048 4500 Europe 44 20 7330 7500 Germany 49 69 9204 1210 Hong Kong 852 2977 6000
Japan 81 3 3201 8900   Singapore 65 6212 1000   U.S. 1 212 318 2000   Copyright 2011 Bloomberg Finance L.P.
SN 268301 CDT   GMT-5:00 H279-401-2 11-Aug-2011 09:58:46

Exhibit 8.7
Reprinted with permission from Bloomberg. Copyright 2011 Bloomberg L.P. All rights reserved.

Inflation affects prices. Rating changes affect prices. Information released by issuers and borrowers affects prices.

New information may have been released by the issuer or borrower in press releases, on the issuer's or borrower's website, or in continuing disclosure annual or event reports filed with the MSRB's EMMA disclosure platform. Significant information may become public through news reports. Due to the changes in information that will affect your securities, you may wish to monitor information regarding your securities on EMMA and on issuer or borrower websites.

As with equity securities and U.S. Treasuries, the prices of municipal securities change continuously, not only on a daily basis, but within trading days. Often, the changes are relatively small. On other occasions, there can be rapid changes in prices and, consequently, market values of outstanding municipal securities.

The screen in Exhibit 8.8 from the Bloomberg Terminal illustrates general changes over the 1-year period from July 21, 2010, to July 20, 2011, in prices bid for 10-year maturities of triple-A municipal securities.

What Are Tax Consequences of Trading?

Trading may lead to tax consequences. The tax exemption of the interest on municipal securities does not protect you from capital gains or losses for income tax purposes.

In general, when you sell municipal securities at a different price from the price at which you purchased the securities, you may incur capital gains or losses, with corresponding tax implications.

You may wish to consult with your tax advisor regarding these tax impacts.

The arrow identifies the highest BVAL 10-year yield during the 12-month period

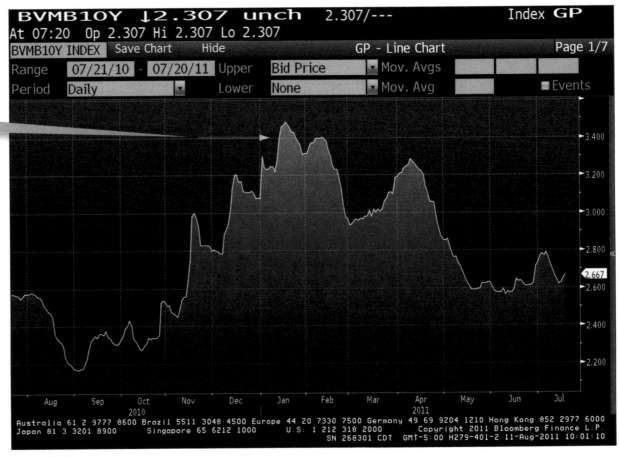

Exhibit 8.8

Reprinted with permission from Bloomberg. Copyright 2011 Bloomberg L.P. All rights reserved.

CHAPTER 9

Tax Exemption of Municipal Securities

Most municipal securities bear interest that is exempt from federal and state income taxation. That is a valuable feature of those municipal securities. Some municipal securities are subject to the alternative minimum tax. Social security (and railroad retirement) recipients may wish to consult tax advisors about tax treatment of interest they receive on municipal securities. Some taxable municipal securities are issued. The incidence of taxable municipal securities increased during the financial crisis with the availability of certain federal subsidy programs (now expired).

What Is the Importance of the Federal Income Tax Exemption?

With the exception of a minority of municipal securities issued in taxable form, an outstanding feature of most municipal securities is the exemption of the interest from federal income taxation. Literally, the tax exemption is an exclusion from gross income for federal income tax purposes. (See the "Additional Information" section at the end of the chapter.)

Additionally, the income tax laws of most states also exempt interest on securities of issuers within those respective states (but generally not of issuers in other states).

The federal income tax exemption (with corresponding state income tax exemptions) is a key reason to purchase tax-exempt municipal securities, particularly for higher-income taxpayers.

In order to qualify for the exemption, municipal issuers and private borrowers are required to satisfy exceptionally complex tax regulations. Bond counsel may assist issuers and borrowers with respect to compliance with those requirements at least at the time of issuance (but may not be employed with respect to continuing compliance). Bond counsel provide opinions to investors regarding the tax exemption. The bond counsel opinions are included in official statements.

A few categories of municipal securities are subject to the alternative minimum tax. When that is the case, it should be disclosed clearly in official statements and in bond counsel opinions contained in the official statements.

Do All Municipal Securities Bear Tax-Exempt Interest?

No. There are several special categories of municipal securities that bear taxable interest.

The categories of taxable municipal securities include certain municipal securities issued in 2009 and 2010 that are subsidized pursuant to the American Recovery and Reinvestment Act of 2009 (ARRA). For example, taxable securities include Build America Bonds (BABs), Qualified School Construction Bonds, Qualified Zone Academy Bonds, and Recovery Zone Economic Development Bonds, as well as a few other types of municipal securities. Official statements should indicate when municipal securities are taxable. (See the "Additional Information" section at the end of the chapter.)

The following table (Exhibit 9.1) and graphs (Exhibits 9.2 and 9.3), based upon Bloomberg data, present the annual volumes (in billions of dollars) of taxable municipal securities issued from 2003 to 2010 in relation to the total volumes of long-term, fixed-rate municipal securities issued. The increased volumes in 2009 and 2010 reflect the issuance of federally-subsidized taxable Build America Bonds pursuant to ARRA.

Year	Annual LT Fixed-Rate Issuance	Annual Taxable Bond Issuance
2003	293	9
2004	267	4
2005	312	4
2006	296	4
2007	338	4
2008	281	5
2009	379	21
2010	408	37

Exhibit 9.1

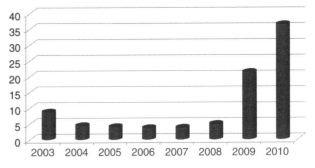

Annual Taxable Bond Issuance

Exhibit 9.2

The second graph illustrates the issuance of taxable bonds (in red) in relation to the total volume of long-term, fixed-rate municipal securities issued.

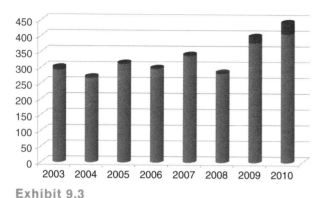

Exhibit 9.3
Reprinted with permission from Bloomberg L.P. Copyright 2011 Bloomberg L.P. All rights reserved.

The following table (Exhibit 9.4) presents Bloomberg data regarding the issuance, by state, of federally-subsidized Build America Bonds during 2009 and 2010. The data show that the five most active states in the issuance of BABs were responsible for more than 50% of the issuance.

There also are unusual municipal securities that are intended to bear tax-exempt interest, but that violate prohibitions against arbitrage practices, private use, or other proscriptions. Those very unusual violations may arise either at the time of issuance of the municipal securities or later. Bond counsel opinions provide protections against violations at the time of issuance. Bond counsel generally structure municipal securities, and obtain representations and agreements by issuers or borrowers, against later practices that may lead to unintended results. Issuers or borrowers may not, however, employ bond counsel to assist them on a continuing basis. In practice, difficulties regarding the tax-exemption of interest on municipal securities have proved to be rare. When those difficulties occur, responsible parties almost always enter into agreements with the Internal Revenue Service to remedy the problem, so as to protect investors.

Build America Bond Program (2009–2010)

Statewide BAB Issuance	Total Issuance ($Millions)	% of Total	
California	39,034	20.80%	
New York	20,757	11.06%	
Texas	16,6780	8.89%	
Illinois	11,770	6.27%	
Ohio	8,962	4.78%	51.80%

The boxed states accounted for a majority of the federally subsidized BABs issuance.

(continued)

New Jersey	16,680	8.89%	
Washington	6,213	3.31%	
Florida	5,778	3.08%	
Pennsylvania	5,054	2.69%	
Massachusetts	4,852	2.59%	
Colorado	4,140	2.21%	
Georgia	3,950	2.11%	
Virginia	3,881	2.07%	
Maryland	3,494	1.86%	
Missouri	3,184	1.70%	
Kentucky	3,052	1.63%	
Michigan	3,039	1.62%	
Utah	2,947	1.57%	
Nevada	2,626	1.40%	
Wisconsin	2,227	1.19%	
Indiana	2,143	1.14%	
District of Columbia	2,040	1.09%	
Tennessee	2,020	1.08%	
Connecticut	2,002	1.07%	
Arizona	1,999	1.07%	
North Carolina	1,896	1.01%	
Kansas	1,679	0.89%	
Minnesota	1,581	0.84%	
Hawaii	1,333	0.71%	
South Carolina	1,268	0.68%	

Puerto Rico	1,106	0.59%	
Nebraska	1,085	0.58%	
Oregon	1,026	0.55%	
Louisiana	953	0.51%	
Alabama	839	0.45%	
Mississippi	833	0.44%	
Oklahoma	816	0.43%	
Iowa	795	0.42%	
Delaware	519	0.28%	
New Hampshire	449	0.24%	
South Dakota	419	0.22%	
Alaska	370	0.20%	
New Mexico	286	0.15%	
Wyoming	193	0.10%	
Vermont	161	0.09%	
Idaho	143	0.08%	
North Dakota	121	0.06%	
West Virginia	108	0.06%	
Maine	104	0.06%	
Rhode Island	80	0.04%	
Montana	63	0.03%	
Arkansas	40	0.02%	
United States	187,660	100.00%	

Exhibit 9.4

Reprinted with permission from Bloomberg L.P. Copyright 2011 Bloomberg L.P. All rights reserved.
This exhibit includes direct-issuer subsidy-build America bonds issued in the first round of the American Recovery and Reinvestment Act.

What Is the Role of State Income Tax Exemptions?

Municipal securities issued by issuers within states having income taxation generally (but not always) bear interest that is exempt from those states' income taxation. Bond counsel tax opinions usually speak to this exemption, as well as to the federal exemption. State exemptions carry more benefit for investors in states with higher state income tax rates.

Normally, investors in one state are unable to take advantage of a state tax exemption for municipal securities issued in another state.

Interest on obligations of federal jurisdictions, such as Puerto Rico, may be exempt from state income taxation. When you are considering those securities, you may wish to consult your tax advisor as to their state tax treatment.

The following table (Exhibit 9.5) presents Bloomberg data showing effective high state income tax rates for individuals and corporations as of August 2011. The Bloomberg data adjust the state rates to present net rates after taking into account the federal income tax deduction. Bloomberg adds that the boxed states issue state taxable municipal bonds for both individuals and corporations.

State/Region Income Tax Rates (August 2011)

State/Territory	Individual Rate (net of 35% Federal Income Tax)	Corporate Rate
Alabama	3.25	6.50
Alaska	none	9.40
Arizona	2.95	6.97
Arkansas	4.55	6.50
California	6.70	8.84
Colorado	3.01	4.63
Connecticut	4.23	7.50
District of Columbia	5.53	9.98
Delaware	4.52	8.70
Florida	none	5.50
Georgia	3.90	6.00
Guam	none	none

Hawaii	7.15	6.40
Idaho	5.07	7.60
Illinois	3.25	7.30
Indiana	2.21	8.50
Iowa	5.84	12.00
Kansas	4.19	7.05
Kentucky	3.90	6.00
Louisiana	3.90	8.00
Maine	5.53	8.93
Maryland	3.58	8.25
Massachusetts	3.45	9.50
Michigan	2.83	4.95
Minnesota	5.10	9.80
Mississippi	3.25	5.00
Missouri	3.90	6.25
Montana	4.49	6.75
Nebraska	4.45	7.81
Nevada	none	none
New Hampshire	3.25	8.50
New Jersey	5.83	9.00
New Mexico	3.19	7.60
New York	5.83	7.10
North Carolina	5.04	6.90
North Dakota	3.16	6.50
Ohio	3.85	8.50
Oklahoma	3.58	6.00

According to Bloomberg, the boxed states do not exempt from income taxation interest on municipal securities issued within those states.

(continued)

Oregon	7.15	6.60
Pennsylvania	2.00	9.99
Puerto Rico	none	none
Rhode Island	3.89	9.00
South Carolina	4.55	5.00
South Dakota	none	none
Tennessee	3.90	6.50
Texas	none	none
Utah	3.25	5.00
Vermont	5.82	8.50
Virgin Islands	none	none
Virginia	3.74	6.00
Washington	none	none
West Virginia	4.23	8.50
Wisconsin	5.04	7.90
Wyoming	none	none

Exhibit 9.5

Reprinted with permission from Bloomberg. Copyright 2011 Bloomberg L.P. All rights reserved.

For additional information regarding state taxation, see the website of the Federation of Tax Administrators at www.taxadmin.org/.

How Can the Alternative Minimum Tax Affect Me?

The majority of municipal securities are not subject to the alternative minimum tax.

The federal alternative minimum tax applies, however, to interest on municipal securities that are issued for certain private benefits. If you are subject to the alternative minimum tax, you may be required to include the interest on those municipal securities for purposes of calculating the alternative minimum tax. You may wish to consult your tax advisor regarding the alternative minimum tax.

If the alternative minimum tax applies to municipal securities, the bond counsel opinion contained in the official statement should so state. Again, you can obtain the preliminary official statement and official statement from your broker or dealer in connection with the initial offering of the securities, and for trading transactions, you can obtain the official statement from the Municipal Securities Rulemaking Board's (MSRB) EMMA website at www.emma.msrb.org/.

Particularly if private parties are involved with the municipal securities, you may wish to check whether the alternative minimum tax may apply to municipal securities you are considering.

In addition, if you invest in municipal bond funds, you may wish to check their policies and portfolios regarding potential alternative minimum tax exposure.

How Does Tax-Exempt Interest Compare to Taxable Interest?

While interest rates on municipal securities are often lower than interest rates on securities bearing taxable interest, the after-tax equivalency benefits of the tax exemption can be significant.

Exhibit 9.6 illustrates generally the federal equivalency yields on tax-exempt municipal securities bearing the designated interest rates, without taking into account state income tax rates or the impacts of the federal deduction for state income taxes or the reverse at the state level.

Federal Marginal Income Tax Rates

Interest Rate	25%	28%	33%	35%
3%	4.00%	4.17%	4.48%	4.62%
4%	5.33%	5.56%	5.97%	6.15%
5%	6.67%	6.94%	7.46%	7.69%

Exhibit 9.6

Does My Receipt of Social Security Affect Tax-Exemption of My Municipal Securities?

It can. This is of greatest interest to retirees and to individuals planning for retirement.

You may wish to consult with your tax advisor regarding whether your receipt of social security (or railroad retirement) payments affects the tax-exemption of interest you receive on municipal securities. There are also a few other circumstances that may have a similar impact.

For Additional Information

■ Recently, certain proposals have been made to eliminate or weaken the tax exemption for interest paid on municipal securities. Those proposals have not advanced far as of this writing.

■ The ARRA authorizations of federal subsidies for additional issuances of taxable municipal securities have expired (although outstanding issues continue to be subsidized). Legislative proposals, if enacted, would reauthorize various forms of taxable municipal securities at lower subsidy levels. Certain taxable municipal securities continue to be authorized apart from the ARRA.

10

Understanding Expert Work Products

Expert work products—for example, feasibility studies and real estate appraisals—offer expert validation regarding the future performance of municipal securities and projects. When conducted appropriately, expert work products can be valuable tools, although they should not be used without consideration of other important information. Expert work products cannot predict the future with certainty. Further, there are a number of key factors to which you may wish to pay careful attention in relying upon the work products.

Expert work products presented in official statements have the appearance of highly authoritative expert analyses regarding the security for a municipal securities issue. Especially in riskier municipal securities offerings, which often involve expert work products, you may wish to exercise care in reviewing and relying upon expert work products.

When prepared appropriately, as occurs most of the time, expert work products can be useful in evaluating municipal securities, but only in conjunction with other information.

As with ratings, it is advantageous not to place undue emphasis upon the conclusions in expert work products. Some parties tend to look only at the bottom line conclusions in expert work products, rather than examining the work products as a whole. Among other things, many expert work products, such as financial feasibility studies or projections, are forward looking. That is, they are forecasts or projections into the future and are based upon certain present assumptions that may not be supported by actual future experience. The future outcomes may vary, sometimes significantly, from the forecasts or projections.

This chapter is intended to suggest factors that you may wish to identify and consider when deciding whether to place reliance upon an expert work product and, if so, how much to rely upon it.

What Are Expert Work Products?

Expert work products used in marketing municipal securities are presented in official statements as authoritative reports or analyses, such as feasibility studies and forecasts, financial projections, and real estate or other asset appraisals.

Another type of expert work product that is presented in a majority of municipal securities offerings is an audit report on issuers' or borrowers' financial statements. Some, but not all, of the considerations that follow apply to the work of auditors.

What Is the Role of Feasibility Studies and Financial Projections?

Feasibility studies and financial projections are presented in offerings for revenue producing projects with several quite different characteristics

Start-up projects. For example, a wastewater treatment system in a rural community that previously relied on septic systems or a new sports arena in a city that has not previously had a professional sports team.

Rapidly expanding projects. For example, a substantial expansion of an existing city-owned wastewater system to sizable new subdivisions planned for development or a substantial reconstruction of the system in response to environmental concerns.

Other project expansions on less substantial scales. For example, incremental upgrades to an existing water sys-

tem with an established user base or additions of gates to an airport that has operated for decades.

These varying circumstances present differing histories and levels and characteristics of risks. The histories may or may not facilitate feasibility studies that are able to make projections or forecasts reasonably taking into account, at least in part, prior experience.

What Is the Role of Appraisals?

Appraisals are used most often in financings for real estate developments.

The appraisals generally value both the current value of the real estate and the expected value once the infrastructure to be funded has been completed. More precisely, the appraisals are opinions regarding the current value of real estate based upon the assumption that the infrastructure financed with proceeds of the securities issue is completed (a hypothetical condition that should be noted as such in the appraisals).

Since real estate markets are sometimes susceptible to rapid change, the appraisals generally are expected to demonstrate that the property, after completion of the proposed infrastructure, is expected to have a value that exceeds, by a substantial margin, amounts owing on the securities. This often is called the *value-to-lien ratio*. A common ratio used as a minimum rule of thumb is at least three- or four-to-one.

The valuation is intended to provide a cushion for real estate market volatility and for the uncertainty inherent in an appraisal of hypothetical values.

What Is the Role of Audit Reports?

Audit reports are used in a significant majority of municipal securities offerings and annual continuing disclosure documents.

The reports provide opinions by private certified public accountants (CPAs), or sometimes state officials, on the financial statements of issuers or borrowers. The reports almost always recite that the auditors have audited the financial statements in accordance with generally accepted auditing standards (GAAS).

In addition, the audit reports also almost always recite that an issuer's or borrower's financial statements have been prepared in accordance with generally accepted accounting principles (GAAP). Those standards differ for governments, which primarily follow standards of the Governmental Accounting Standards Board (GASB), and private parties, which should follow standards prepared under the auspices of the Financial Accounting Standards Board (FASB). Sometimes, governmental entities in certain states follow standards prescribed under state authority, which may differ from GAAP for governments. The differences, and their impacts on the financial statements, may or may not be disclosed to you.

If you see a qualification in an audit report regarding an issuer's or borrower's compliance with GAAP, it indicates that you should be careful in reviewing the financial statements and in evaluating the municipal securities.

A caution: a compilation is not an audit report, but merely a presentation of the issuer's or borrower's unaudited financial statements or projections without an audit report.

When Are Expert Work Products Important?

Expert work products are especially important in the case of funding for start-up or rapidly-expanding projects and real estate developments. Those projects may present greater risks that are not present in the case of long-established undertakings with successful historical records and pre-existing customers.

Audit reports are important in providing auditors' opinions regarding an issuer's or borrower's financial statements.

What Should I Consider in Expert Work Products?

You may wish to consider several factors that are important with reference to expert work products. The following discussion is intended to highlight some of them briefly. Some of the considerations do not apply to audit reports, such as consideration of assumptions.

You may wish also to review factors discussed in the White Paper on Expert Work Products published in 2011 by the National Federation of Municipal Analysts (NFMA) at www.nfma.org under "Publications-Disclosure Guidelines."

The following is a checklist of factors that you may wish to consider in reviewing and relying upon expert work products:

✔ Expert's experience with subject matter
✔ Expert's licenses, qualifications
✔ Identity of professional standards, if any, applied by experts
✔ Statement that experts have complied with those standards
✔ Description of expert's methodologies
✔ Identity of assumptions used by experts
✔ Identification of expert's sources of assumptions
✔ Statement that experts believe assumptions to be reasonable or, if not, why not
✔ Expert's consents
✔ Expert's potential conflicts of interest, including relationships with parties and professionals involved in project or offering and contingent or unpaid compensation
✔ Statement of issuer or borrower, underwriter, and financial advisor review of expert work product

What Are Experts' Qualifications and Experience?

The first factor to consider is the identity and qualifications of the experts. You will want to rely upon qualified experts who have successful experience in preparing expert work products of the nature of the work products you are reviewing and in the same fields (e.g., airports, stadiums, arenas, convention centers, transportation systems, toll roads, relevant utilities [water, wastewater, gas, electric], hospitals, or nursing homes).

It is reasonable for you to expect experts to identify projects on which they have worked. With that information, you can investigate how those projects have fared. With the identification of the earlier projects, you may be able to search for information regarding the earlier projects on the Internet or to find continuing disclosures at the EMMA website maintained by the Municipal Securities Rulemaking Board regarding the municipal securities offerings for those projects. If so, you may be able to learn whether investors continue to be paid in those securities offerings.

Expert work products should also present the experts' qualifications, including their training, professional licenses, education, and experience with similar work products.

Auditors should be qualified as certified public accountants (CPAs).

What Professional Standards Are Applied?

Expert work products should identify the professional standards, if any, applied by the experts.

A number of organizations publish professional standards for the preparation of expert work products. These include the Appraisal Institute with respect to appraisals, and the American Institute of Certified Public Accountants with respect to audits and studies prepared by accounting firms.

In other cases, there may not be applicable professional standards published by national professional organizations. Some experts may simply apply standards that they have developed internally. When that is the case, in the absence of your ability to determine whether an expert work product was prepared appropriately, there is a correspondingly greater emphasis that you may wish to place upon the qualifications and experience of the experts.

In some cases, there may be the appearance of professional standards, but the standards may not apply specifically to the type of study an expert prepares. For example, a feasibility study for a parking garage to serve a shopping mall or commercial area may apply standards designed to facilitate multiple uses of the property.

The expert may be able to conclude that there are enough parking spaces to accommodate shopping in the daytime and restaurants and movie theaters at night. The standards may say nothing, however, about whether there are too many spaces.

The standards also may not provide guidance for financial feasibility analyses of parking garages. That is, the standards may not discuss how to determine appropriately whether the revenues from the garage will be able to pay both operation and maintenance costs, on the one hand, and debt service on the securities, on the other. Further, such a financial feasibility determination for a parking garage may require that the feasibility of a related shopping mall also be studied because the primary source of parkers may be the expected customers of the mall. A mere assumption that the mall will be successful may represent an enormous leap of faith.

What Are Experts' Methodologies?

Professional standards and experts' methodologies are not the same thing. Methodologies are the specific steps that the experts undertake in conducting their research, developing their assumptions, and forecasting or projecting revenues and expenses for the project, or reaching other conclusions, based upon those assumptions.

The experts should be able to articulate how they conducted their analyses and reached their conclusions. Expert work products should describe the experts' methodologies.

What Assumptions Are Used?

Financial forecasts and projections, and appraisal conclusions of value, are only as good as the assumptions upon which the forecasts, projections, and appraisals are based. Assumptions are critical foundations for the validity of expert work products and the opinions experts express.

You may wish to identify all of the assumptions used by experts in connection with their work products. Experts should provide clear statements identifying for you, preferably in a single section of their work products, all of the assumptions upon which the conclusions in their work products are based.

What Are Sources of Assumptions?

You may wish to identify the sources of experts' assumptions. Those sources may include professional sources, the results of experts' research, and information in identified documents (such as contractual terms).

In addition, assumptions may be provided by issuers, borrowers, property owners, developers, underwriters, financial advisors, or others interested financially or otherwise in the success of the project or completion of the municipal securities offering. When assumptions are provided by parties interested in the success of the project or the securities offering, a potential conflict is apparent.

It is possible that an expert may have been provided certain assumptions about which the expert is not knowledgeable. For example, the expert may have been informed by the issuer of the start date for construction of a project and the expected date for completion. Those dates may matter because the completion date is important information regarding when the issuer will begin receiving revenues to pay the securities. If revenues begin too late, the issuer might not be able to make even the first payment. The expert may or may not have checked the assumptions against available information, such as construction contracts. If not, the expert should say so.

Are Assumptions Reasonable?

You may wish to identify a clear statement that the experts consider to be reasonable the assumptions from which conclusions are drawn. The experts may rely upon others, or upon documents like construction contracts, with respect to certain assumptions, such as the anticipated dates of beginning and completion of construction or anticipated costs of a project. Nevertheless, the experts should be able to express professional judgments as to reasonableness of the assumptions or, if not, should be able to explain why not.

If the experts do not do so, then you may wish to be cautious in relying upon the conclusions in the expert work products unless you have your own firm basis for concluding from your own knowledge that the assumptions are reasonable. That may be an impossible task.

This is a definite case in which an analysis can be tainted by inappropriate information and methodology. The assumptions are the foundation of the analysis and conclusions. If the assumptions are not reasonable, then there is little basis for reliance upon the conclusions. As the saying goes, garbage in, garbage out.

Have Experts Given Their Consents?

Another factor is whether the experts are described in official statements as "experts" and whether their work products are presented in official statements with their consents.

This applies to auditors, as well as other types of experts.

Look for affirmative statements in official statements that the experts have given these consents.

An absence of those consents may present issues in some states regarding your ability to rely upon the expert work products and upon their analyses and conclusions.

If purported "experts" are not presented to you as experts, then a relevant question is why you, the party investing your funds in the project, should rely upon them as such.

There are plenty of experts who are willing to accept full responsibility for their status as experts. Therefore, you may wish to look for municipal securities offerings involving those less reticent experts or, alternatively, may wish to expect to receive additional yield in return for assuming a greater risk.

Do Experts Have Potential Conflicts of Interest?

In addition to conflicts that may arise when interested parties provide assumptions to experts, there are a variety of other conflicts that you may wish to identify and consider.

What Are Relationship Conflicts?

Experts may have a variety of conflicts of interest. These may relate to past, present, or anticipated relationships with parties interested in the success of the project or the municipal securities offering. These should be identified in the expert work products, if there are any.

For example, engineers preparing feasibility studies may also have performed engineering services for an interested party. An appraiser may have prepared appraisals in multiple prior engagements for a developer or a party related to a developer, or may have been engaged repeatedly in other securities offerings through efforts of an underwriter or financial advisor.

How May Conflicts Relate to Experts' Compensation?

You may wish to identify the parties who employed and who are paying the experts, and how the experts are paid, including the timing and amounts of payments. If significant payments have not yet been made, or if compensation is contingent, you may wish to take that into account.

Why Are Issuers', Financial Advisors', and Underwriters' Reviews Important?

You may wish to avoid securities when issuers or borrowers, financial advisors, and underwriters in municipal securities offerings say they have not reviewed the expert work products.

It is important to note at this point that the financial advisors I am describing are *not* stock brokers or other advisors who advise you. These financial advisors advise issuers or borrowers, and are registered as "municipal advisors" under requirements of the Dodd-Frank Act with the Securities and Exchange Commission and the Municipal Securities Rulemaking Board. See Chapter 11, "Municipal Securities Regulation," in the section entitled "What Changes Were Made by the Dodd-Frank Act?"

The parties who are bringing the securities to market have the best opportunities, in addition to the experts themselves, to review and evaluate the expert work products, to ask questions, and if advisable, to request that experts clarify certain matters and conduct additional work.

If a statement is made that issuers or borrowers and underwriters have not reviewed the expert work products or have not made a determination regarding reasonableness of the experts' assumptions, you may have to determine on your own, based upon information available to you, whether the experts' assumptions are reasonable and whether the expert work products are appropriate for your investment.

Since you have no contact with the experts and are not involved in putting the securities offering together, that is not something you are likely to be able to do.

CHAPTER 11

Municipal Securities Regulation

Municipal securities are not subject to the regulatory pattern applicable to corporate securities. The Securities and Exchange Commission (SEC) does not have the same regulatory authority over either municipal securities offerings or continuing disclosure by municipal issuers or borrowers. In addition, the SEC, and to a more significant degree, the Municipal Securities Rulemaking Board (MSRB) are subject to certain explicit restrictions against devising regulations for municipal securities issuers. Nevertheless, there are legal and market requirements of accuracy and completeness in disclosure of important information in disclosure documents ("official statements") used in municipal securities offerings. There also is regulation to the effect that, with respect to most issues, issuers and borrowers make certain continuing disclosure. A growing body of resources are used in a voluntary disclosure system for the market.

This chapter discusses, in broad outlines, regulation of the municipal securities market. It also mentions a number of resources available to assist you. The Appendices present information on how to gain access to those resources.

In general, as noted, the municipal securities market is not subject to the same level of regulation as are other securities markets. Even private borrowers in municipal securities transactions are subject to the lower level of regulation.

What Is the Role of the Securities and Exchange Commission?

Municipal securities are not subject to the statutory and regulatory requirements of the Securities Act of 1933 that securities offerings be registered with the Securities and Exchange Commission (SEC).

Further, municipal securities are not subject to statutory and regulatory requirements of the Securities Exchange Act of 1934 applicable to corporate issuers regarding filing of periodic and other reports with the SEC following offerings.

Federal and state laws require municipal securities issuers and private borrowers to make accurate and complete disclosure of important information to investors in offerings of municipal securities and in other communications to investors. Those requirements are contained in laws and regulations prohibiting fraud in general terms (and, in some cases, negligence) in disclosing important information.

Under a provision of the 1934 Act known as the Tower Amendment, the SEC is prohibited from requiring issuers to file official statements or other information or documents with it prior to offerings.

The more significant restriction with respect to the SEC's authority to regulate municipal securities issuers and private borrowers is a lack of affirmative regulatory authority.

The SEC has been able to achieve indirect regulation over issuers and private borrowers in its Rule 15c2-12 by prohibiting dealers from underwriting most municipal securities offerings unless the issuers or borrowers take certain steps in terms of preparing official statements. The issuers and borrowers also must agree to prepare and file with the Municipal Securities Rulemaking Board (MSRB) certain continuing disclosure documents. The ability to enforce those agreements, however, is weak.

The continuing disclosures are annual financial and operational information and notices of the occurrence of certain events. The required event disclosures are identified in Chapter 2, "Basic Information Resources," in the section entitled "What Continuing Disclosure Is Available?"

Rule 15c2-12 was amended most recently, effective December 1, 2010, to tighten to 10 days the time frames for filing continuing disclosures giving notice of the occurrence of events and to add additional events of which issuers or borrowers must agree to give notice. Agreements effective prior to December 1, 2010, are not required to contain those additional protections.

While the SEC's direct regulatory authority over issuers and private borrowers in the municipal market is weaker than the SEC's powers over issuers in the corporate securities market, the SEC does have direct authority over municipal dealers and a newly-regulated group of "municipal advisors," who advise issuers and borrowers. Additionally, a key securities law provision prohibiting fraud, SEC Rule 10b-5, applies in transactions involving municipal securities. Almost all state securities laws contain similar antifraud provisions.

The SEC is able to undertake enforcement actions against issuers and private borrowers, their officials, dealers, municipal advisors, and others involved in municipal transactions, and has done so with increasing aggressiveness over the years. The SEC has also increased its regulatory and enforcement staffing and funding, and created a special enforcement unit devoted to municipal securities. Having said that, it must still be recognized that the SEC is limited both in terms of staff and funding.

What Is the Role of the Municipal Securities Rulemaking Board?

The Municipal Securities Rulemaking Board (MSRB) was formed in the mid-1970s at the time of the New York City financial crisis. At that time, the MSRB was created by Congress as a self-regulatory body for municipal securities dealers and dealer banks. The Tower Amendment restricts the MSRB from imposing disclosure requirements upon municipal securities issuers.

Until enactment of the Dodd-Frank Act, the MSRB's membership consisted of 10 representatives of dealers and banks and 5 public members. After Dodd-Frank's enactment, the MSRB consists of 21 members, with a majority of public members, including at least one investor representative and one issuer representative, and in addition to regulated dealers and banks, includes representatives of the newly-regulated "municipal advisors."

Over the years, the MSRB has adopted a number of rules favorable to investors, including among others, rules governing professional qualifications, requirements for delivery of official statements (Rule G-32), fair dealing (Rule G-17), securities pricing (Rule G-30), executions of transactions with customers (Rule G-18), and suitability (Rule G-19). Rules governing municipal advisors are likely to add to the protections. You can find the MSRB's rules and interpretations of the rules at http://msrb.org/Rules-and-Interpretations/MSRB-Rules.aspx.

The MSRB does not enforce its rules. The SEC (www.sec.gov) and FINRA (www.finra.org) enforce the MSRB's rules.

The MSRB has taken a number of other actions to assist and protect investors. Those actions include the provision on the MSRB's website of information for investors, and notably, the creation of the MSRB's Electronic Municipal Market Access website (EMMA) at www.emma.msrb.org. In addition to other enhancements, as discussed in the Appendix, EMMA provides access to issuer and borrower official statements and continuing disclosure documents and to real-time pricing and trading data on municipal securities.

The screen in Exhibit 11.1 from the Bloomberg Terminal illustrates MSRB transaction reports relating to securities of certain Massachusetts issuers.

What Is the Role of FINRA?

The Financial Industry Regulatory Authority (FINRA) was formed from the National Association of Securities Dealers (NASD) and the New York Stock Exchange (NYSE). FINRA regulates securities dealers, enforces its own rules, and together with the SEC, enforces the MSRB's rules.

Like the MSRB, FINRA's governing body has a majority of public members.

FINRA provides a BrokerCheck service (www.finra.org/Investors/ToolsCalculators/BrokerCheck/) through which you are able to check on the regulatory records,

KEY POINT:

In most offerings, issuers and borrowers must agree to prepare and file with the MSRB annual financial and operational information and notices of the occurrence of certain events. The ability to enforce those agreements, however, is weak.

KEY POINT:

The MSRB has adopted a number of rules protective of municipal securities investors.

SMART INVESTOR TIP

The MSRB's website contains information to assist investors and notably EMMA, which provides access to municipal securities official statements and continuing disclosure documents and to real time pricing and trading data on municipal securities. The website is located at www.emma.msrb.org/.

KEY POINT:

The MSRB does not enforce its rules. The SEC (www.sec.gov) and FINRA (www.finra.org) enforce the MSRB's rules.

<HELP> for explanation.   dgp Muni **MSRB**

MSRB TRANSACTION REPORTS   Page   4/   62

MA   LISTINGS

1) 121835YA4 BURLINGTON MASS MUN PURP LN   7/19/11 MA
   N.A.   DTD: 7/26/2011 Cpn: 4.125% Mat: 7/15/2031 Vol: 115,000 (3x)
   Price/Yield Hi:100.375/ 4.078 Lo:100.375/ 4.078 Avg:100.375/ 4.078 (3x)
2) 121835YF3 BURLINGTON MASS MUN PURP LN   7/19/11 MA
   N.A.   DTD: 7/26/2011 Cpn: 4.500 Mat: 7/15/2036 Vol: 215,000 (4x)
   Price/Yield Hi:100.000/ 4.500 Lo:100.000/ 4.500 Avg:100.000/ 4.500 (4x)
3) 132285YF8 CAMBRIDGE MASS MUN PURP LN   7/19/11 MA
   AAA   DTD: 2/ 1/2005 Cpn: 4.000 Mat: 1/ 1/2015 Vol: 40,000 (4x)
   Price/Yield Hi:110.450/ 0.902 Lo:110.085/ 1.004 Avg:110.258/ 0.955 (4x)
4) 192450VA9 COHASSET MASS MUN PURP LN   7/19/11 MA
   N.A.   DTD: 8/ 1/2009 Cpn: 4.000 Mat:11/15/2016 Vol: 100,000 (1x)
   Price/Yield Hi:112.721/ 1.497 Lo:112.721/ 1.497 Avg:112.721/ 1.497 (1x)
5) 236469P22 DANVERS MASS MUN PURP LN   7/19/11 MA
   AA+   DTD: 7/ 7/2011 Cpn: 4.000 Mat: 7/ 1/2026 Vol: 200,000 (3x)
   Price/Yield Hi:102.726/ 3.670 Lo:101.726/ 3.790 Avg:102.309/ 3.719 (3x)
6) 236469P97 DANVERS MASS MUN PURP LN   7/19/11 MA
   AA+   DTD: 7/ 7/2011 Cpn: 4.375 Mat: 7/ 1/2033 Vol: 30,000 (3x)
   Price/Yield Hi:100.375/ 4.328 Lo: 97.750/ 4.538 Avg: 98.708/ 4.468 (3x)

Yields & Average Trade Price calculated by Bloomberg   * Floater
Volume may not include trades over 1 million   Rating is Bloomberg Composite

Australia 61 2 9777 8600 Brazil 5511 3048 4500 Europe 44 20 7330 7500 Germany 49 69 9204 1210 Hong Kong 852 2977 6000
Japan 81 3 3201 8900   Singapore 65 6212 1000   U.S. 1 212 318 2000   Copyright 2011 Bloomberg Finance L.P.
SN 268301 CDT GMT-5:00 G515-401-2 10-Aug-2011 10:05:41

Exhibit 11.1

and certain other information regarding, individual and firm brokers and dealers.

FINRA also has become increasingly active in protecting investors with respect to enforcement of municipal securities rules and disclosure requirements. It is an unusual month in which FINRA does not take action against one or more dealers for violation of rules of the MSRB or other securities laws applicable in municipal securities transactions.

What Is the Role of State Regulators?

State regulators remained relatively inactive in the past with respect to municipal securities. One recent exception is with regard to auction-rate securities, as to which a number of state regulators initiated enforcement actions. You are able to learn more about the role of state securities administrators at their respective websites and also at the website of the North American Securities Administrators Association (NASAA) at www.nasaa.org/.

One beneficial aspect of state regulation that may be helpful to you is your ability to check on the regulatory backgrounds of investment advisers. You are able to do this through the SEC's website at www.adviserinfo.sec.gov/(S(yzx32dpneegy4mkttxjxdes4))/IAPD/Content/Search/iapd_Search.aspx/.

What Changes Were Made by the Dodd-Frank Act?

The Dodd-Frank Wall Street Reform and Consumer Protection Act (the Dodd-Frank Act), H.R. 4173, was signed by the president in July 2010.

The Dodd-Frank Act made important changes in municipal securities regulation. Those extensive changes will require years for the SEC and MSRB to implement, but are certain to have impacts upon the municipal market in ways that benefit investors significantly.

A key change made by the Dodd-Frank Act is the modification of the membership of the MSRB to a majority of public members. The Board's membership must include at least one investor.

Dodd-Frank also provided for the regulation of a new group of formerly unregulated professionals, namely, "municipal advisors" to issuers and borrowers. The term *municipal advisors* includes financial advisors to municipal securities issuers and borrowers, as well as a variety of other advisors. These advisors (who do not advise investors) must register with both the SEC and MSRB, and are to be subject to statutory provisions and a variety of rules to be adopted by the MSRB and enforced by the SEC governing professional standards, a fiduciary duty to issuer and borrower clients, a special antifraud provision, and many other matters. The diversity of municipal advisors appears to be extensive, but as of this writing, remains to be defined fully by the SEC.

A prospective benefit for municipal securities investors is in the potential for requirements that municipal advisors warn issuers and borrowers against participation in poorly-structured and other unwise transactions and that the advisors advise issuer and borrower clients to make sound disclosure to investors.

Dodd-Frank also elevated the importance of the SEC's Office of Municipal Securities and provided for additional staffing of that office.

What Is the Role of Voluntary Disclosure Guidance?

Because the municipal securities market lies outside the typical securities regulation structure for corporate securities, the market is not subject to detailed disclosure requirements imposed by the SEC.

That void is filled in part by creative and growing voluntary disclosure guidance prepared by various groups of market participants.

Despite a wide use in the market of the term *voluntary* disclosure, in fact, federal and state laws provide significant mandates and incentives, echoed in market practices, for municipal issuers and borrowers to provide full and fair disclosure of important information in offerings. Regulations regarding affirmative continuing disclosure are less compelling.

National Federation of Municipal Analysts

The National Federation of Municipal Analysts (NFMA) is one of the key groups that has undertaken to prepare disclosure guidance for the municipal market. The NFMA's membership consists of professional financial analysts from the perspectives of both the investor side (the buy side) of the municipal market and the sell side (e.g., dealers and municipal advisors).

NFMA's disclosure guidance appears in the form of numerous Best Practices in Disclosure and White Papers relating to specific market sectors or issues. Those publications, which are identified in the Appendix, contain detailed discussions of factors that market professionals consider important for municipal securities from different market sectors.

You can access NFMA's Best Practices and White Papers at www.nfma.org/mc/page.do?sitePageId=91110&orgId=nfma/.

Government Finance Officers Association

The Government Finance Officers Association (GFOA) was an early force in improving practices in the municipal securities market.

From the mid-1970s into the early 1990s, GFOA sponsored the preparation of Disclosure Guidelines for State and Local Government Securities. Those Guidelines applied broadly across market sectors in a single publication.

The most recent edition of GFOA's Disclosure Guidelines was published in 1991. Thereafter, at a point in the 1990s, GFOA ceased publication of the Guidelines. In the

1990s, NFMA assumed the role of preparing disclosure guidance segmented by market sector.

The GFOA also publishes Best Practices and advisories for issuers regarding their debt management pro-grams and other aspects of their operations. These can be accessed at www.gfoa.org/index.php?option=com_content&task=view&id=118&Itemid=130/.

CHAPTER 12

Investor Questions and Answers (Q&As)

Investors in municipal securities commonly have many questions regarding their investments. This chapter is intended to anticipate and answer some of those questions.

Many of the questions and answers relate to information regarding securities terminology, provisions, and procedures.

What Are the Primary Forms of Municipal Securities?

The municipal securities market is highly diverse. That is another reason why simplistic generalizations by pundits and media fail to present an accurate picture for investors.

One way in which the market can be dissected is by the variety of credits securing differing municipal securities. Those differentiations are discussed in prior chapters in this book.

This discussion focuses primarily on certain forms of municipal securities structures, rather than credits, although it also points out some areas regarding which you may wish to make closer review.

What Are Bonds?

Bonds are long-term debt securities. Typically bond issues have maturities of up to 20 to 30 years. Some are shorter, such as 10 to 15 years. Occasionally, bonds may have final maturities as short as 4 years or as long as 40 years.

In some cases, different names might be used for long-term obligations, but "bond" is the most common name for long-term structures.

What Are Leases, COPs, and Lease Revenue Bonds?

Leases, certificates of participation (COPs) and lease revenue bonds are discussed earlier in this book in Chapter 4, "General Fund and Other Municipal Securities." As discussed, they represent a different form of obligation from bonds.

What Are Notes?

Notes are municipal debt securities issued for shorter terms, such as one, two, or three years. Sometimes the term *notes* may be applied to longer-term securities. Notes are discussed in greater detail in Chapter 4, "General Fund and Other Municipal Securities," in the section entitled "What Are TRANs, BANs, VRDNs, VRDOs and Other Municipal Notes?"

Notes are issued most commonly for cash flow purposes in anticipation of receipt of future payments or to fund preliminary or construction costs in early stages of a project.

An example of cash flow purposes might be for a city using a June 30 fiscal year that will incur expenditures prior to the receipt of taxes later in the year. An illustration might be property taxes payable in November or December, while the city still must pay for operations beginning in July. The notes would be payable generally upon the receipt of taxes.

Some note issues may serve as bridge financings until more definitive cost estimates can be obtained for a project or to avoid multiple long-term bond issues as

construction proceeds. In that case, after construction of the project has proceeded to a suitable stage, the issuer may issue a larger amount of long-term bonds in a single issue and then will pay off one or more earlier series of notes.

When that is planned to occur, one of your primary initial concerns as a note investor may be the ability of the issuer or borrower to issue the long-term bonds at the later stage. That will depend, among other things, upon the issuer's or borrower's credit. It may be affected by future market interest rate fluctuations, as well.

What Are Variable-Rate Securities?

Variable-rate municipal securities (VRDNs, VRDOs) are long-term securities that often (but not always) are subject to investors' options to *put*, or demand the repurchase of, the securities upon the expiration of a typically brief period. The periods generally are daily or weekly (or sometimes, 7, 14, 28, or 35 days). VRDNs and VRDOs are discussed in greater detail in Chapter 4, "General Fund and Other Municipal Securities," in the section entitled "What Are TRANs, BANs, VRDNs, VRDOs, and Other Municipal Notes?"

The expectation is that those securities that are *put* by previously-owning investors will be remarketed to new investors at new then-prevailing market interest rates.

The securities are supported commonly by a liquidity feature (such as a bank standby purchase agreement) to assure that the issuer or borrower is able to repurchase the securities if the securities cannot be remarketed.

These securities are designed primarily for money market funds, corporate money management, and other institutional purchasers. Except when investing exceptionally large amounts for short-term purposes, you are not likely to see these securities.

A somewhat similar form of security, known as auction-rate securities, was issued in the past, but has fallen into disfavor due to remarketing difficulties after bond insurers enhancing the credits were downgraded. Dealers then stopped supporting the auctions. That froze the market for those securities and caused illiquidity and losses to many investors. Those securities are no longer issued, and you should not see them. If you do, you may wish to exercise considerable investigative care before buying them.

Who Are the Principal Parties in Municipal Securities Offerings?

The principal parties in municipal securities offerings vary from transaction to transaction. The following are the most common parties, and their roles.

Issuers

Municipal securities issuers are state and local governments and their agencies and instrumentalities that borrow money in the municipal securities market in order to obtain funding for their projects and programs.

In securities issues for governmental purposes, the issuers are considered by the Securities and Exchange Commission (SEC) to have primary disclosure responsibilities regarding important information they control.

Private Borrowers

Private borrowers are profit-making and nonprofit entities that obtain tax-exempt funding through the issuance of municipal securities. These borrowers effectively borrow monies from municipal issuers in what are known as *conduit* transactions. In those transactions, the governmental issuers serve as conduits through which funds pass between investors and private borrowers. See the section entitled "What Are Conduit Financings?"

Essentially, however, the private borrowers are the substantive parties who make payments for application to the securities. The governmental issuers pay or assign those payments for the benefit of investors.

In conduit securities offerings, the private borrowers are considered by the SEC to be primarily responsible for disclosure of material information they control.

Underwriters

Underwriters are securities dealers who purchase municipal securities from municipal issuers and resell the securities to investors.

In the municipal market, underwriters are expected to conduct sufficient investigations in order to form a reasonable basis for belief in key representations in official statements. They are also expected to disclose important information they know or should know.

Weighted Cost of Municipal Issuance 2010

State	State Code	Weighted Cost of Issuance/ Underwriter Discount %	Weighted Cost of Issuance/Underwriter Discount per $10 million borrowed
Delaware	DE	0.492	49,200.00
Utah	UT	0.534	53,400.00
North Carolina	NC	0.543	54,300.00
New Hampshire	NH	0.548	54,800.00
New Mexico	NM	0.553	55,300.00
Washington	WA	0.555	55,500.00
New Jersey	NJ	0.561	56,100.00
Alaska	AK	0.565	56,500.00
New York	NY	0.569	56,900.00
Massachusetts	MA	0.570	57,000.00
Minnesota	MN	0.573	57,300.00
Arizona	AZ	0.581	58,100.00
Illinois	IL	0.582	58,200.00
Vermont	VT	0.592	59,200.00
South Carolina	SC	0.602	60,200.00
Virginia	VA	0.603	60,300.00
Oregon	OR	0.608	60,800.00
Florida	FL	0.615	61,500.00
Hawaii	HI	0.617	61,700.00
California	CA	0.629	62,900.00
Michigan	MI	0.631	63,100.00
Oklahoma	OK	0.633	63,300.00
Connecticut	CT	0.638	63,800.00
Wyoming	WY	0.643	64,300.00
Ohio	OH	0.654	65,400.00
Texas	TX	0.660	66,000.00
Louisiana	LA	0.660	66,000.00
Maine	ME	0.661	66,100.00
Rhode Island	RI	0.661	66,100.00
District of Columbia	DC	0.665	66,500.00
Pennsylvania	PA	0.668	66,800.00
Tennessee	TN	0.682	68,200.00
West Virginia	WV	0.688	68,800.00
Colorado	CO	0.707	70,700.00
Virgin Islands	VI	0.710	71,000.00
Kentucky	KY	0.722	72,200.00
Indiana	IN	0.726	72,600.00
Georgia	GA	0.733	73,300.00
Mississippi	MS	0.742	74,200.00
Nevada	NV	0.743	74,300.00
Maryland	MD	0.760	76,000.00
Puerto Rico	PR	0.796	79,600.00
Kansas	KS	0.800	80,000.00
Wisconsin	WI	0.807	80,700.00
Iowa	IA	0.816	81,600.00
Idaho	ID	0.824	82,400.00
Missouri	MO	0.848	84,800.00
North Dakota	ND	0.854	85,400.00
Alabama	AL	0.864	86,400.00
Arkansas	AR	0.866	86,600.00
South Dakota	SD	0.876	87,600.00
Montana	MT	0.896	89,600.00
Nebraska	NE	1.140	114,000.00
Guam	GU	1.268	126,800.00
Entire Muni Market	National	0.643	64,300.00

Exhibit 12.1

Exhibit 12.1 based upon Bloomberg data, presents information regarding interesting variations in underwriter compensation and costs of issuance from state to state in long-term, fixed-rate municipal securities issues sold in 2010 (note that not all issuers break out data on costs of issuance).

Issuers may sell municipal securities to underwriters either through competitive bidding or through direct negotiation with one or more preselected underwriters.

The following graph (Exhibit 12.2), based upon Bloomberg data, presents information regarding the ratios of municipal long-term, fixed rate securities issuances that were sold by issuers and borrowers through negotiated sales versus competitive bids from 2003 through 2010:

Exhibit 12.3 presents Bloomberg data regarding the top 10 underwriters of long-term, fixed-rate municipal securities in each of 2006, 2010, and the first half of 2011. The contrasts between 2006, on one hand, and 2010 to 2011, on the other, demonstrate changes occurring in conjunction with the financial crisis de-emphasizing national underwriters somewhat and allowing greater underwriting participation by regional underwriters.

Certain regional firms are able to participate actively in specific states. This is demonstrated in Exhibit 12.4, which presents Bloomberg data regarding the top three underwriters of long-term, fixed-rate municipal securities by state in the first half of 2011.

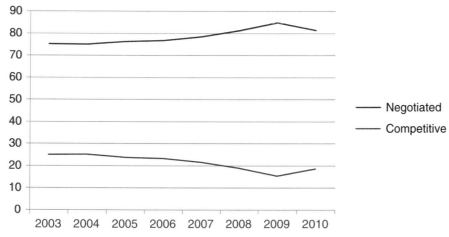

Exhibit 12.2

Long-Term Fixed-Rate Municipal Underwriting (100% Credit to Lead Underwriter)

Lead Underwriter	% Underwritten 2006	Lead Underwriter	% Underwritten 2010	Lead Underwriter	% Underwritten through June 30, 2011
Citigroup	12.4	Citigroup	13.8	Citigroup	12.1
Merrill Lynch	9.1	Banc of America Merrill	12.8	Morgan Stanley	11.2
UBS	8.6	JP Morgan	10.9	Banc of America Merrill	10.2
Goldman	7.7	Morgan Stanley	9.1	JP Morgan	10.1
JP Morgan	6.0	Barclays	7.1	Wells Fargo Bank	5.1
Lehman	5.4	Goldman	5.6	Barclays	4.5
Bear Stearns	4.8	RBC Capital	4.4	RBC Capital	4.4
Morgan Stanley	4.4	Morgan Keegan	3.2	Morgan Keegan	4.3
Banc of America	3.8	Wells Fargo Bank	2.6	Piper Jaffray	3.4
RBC Capital	3.8	Robert W. Baird	2.2	Goldman Sachs	3.4
Other	34.1	Other	28.3	Other	31.5

This is LT Fixed Rate. Does not Include variable rate issuance.
This chart shows how the exit of major firms during financial crises has allowed regional firms to get a larger share of the market.

Exhibit 12.3
Reprinted with permission from Bloomberg L.P. Copyright 2011 Bloomberg L.P. All rights reserved.

Financial Advisors

In municipal market offerings, financial advisors are financial firms that provide advice to municipal issuers or private borrowers in connection with the structuring and sale of municipal securities. In competitively bid offerings, financial advisors may also assist in the bidding process. Financial advisors are not underwriters. These financial advisors do *not* advise investors. These financial advisors are required to be registered as "municipal advisors" with the Securities and Exchange Commission and the Municipal Securities Rulemaking Board, and are subject to regulation by the MSRB. See Chapter 11, "Municipal Securities Regulation," in the section entitled "What Changes Were Made by the Dodd-Frank Act?"

Bond Counsel

Bond counsel are specialized legal firms generally employed by issuers or borrowers. Bond counsel issue legal opinions assuring investors that municipal securities are legal, valid, and enforceable under state law and, except when interest is intended to be taxable (as in the case of Build America Bonds), that the interest payable on the securities is exempt from federal and (where applicable) state income taxation. The opinions are contained in the issuers' official statements.

Bond counsel usually prepare the securities documentation and may or may not undertake to advise the municipal issuers or private borrowers on other matters.

Top Three Underwriters per State 2011 (Jan. 1 through June 30) (100% Credit to Lead Underwriter)

State/Territory	Underwriter	Amount ($Billions)	% Underwritten Within State
New York	Total	12.083	
	Citigroup	1.650	13.656
	Jefferies	1.323	10.949
	Wells Fargo Bank	1.296	10.726
California	Total	9.421	
	Morgan Stanley	2.250	23.883
	Stone & Youngberg	1.448	15.370
	Piper	1.278	13.565
Texas	Total	7.820	
	Citigroup	1.357	17.353
	Morgan Keegan	1.013	12.954
	Banc of America Merrill	0.810	10.358
Illinois	Total	6.820	
	Morgan Stanley	3.736	54.780
	Citigroup	1.056	15.484
	Loop Capital	0.312	4.575
Pennsylvania	Total	3.868	
	RBC Capital	0.883	22.828
	Banc of America Merrill	0.458	11.841
	Morgan Stanley	0.427	11.039
Massachusetts	Total	3.641	
	JP Morgan	1.227	33.700
	Citigroup	0.588	16.149
	Morgan Stanley	0.469	12.881
Florida	Total	3.640	
	Citigroup	0.868	23.846
	Banc of America Merrill	0.830	22.802
	JP Morgan	0.740	20.330
New Jersey	Total	3.303	
	Banc of America Merrill	1.496	45.292
	JP Morgan	0.647	19.588
	Raymond James	0.179	5.419
Washington	Total	2.738	
	Citigroup	1.155	42.184
	JP Morgan	0.457	16.691
	Banc of America Merrill	0.375	13.696
Georgia	Total	2.061	
	Citigroup	0.625	30.325
	Morgan Keegan	0.417	20.233
	Morgan Stanley	0.337	16.351
Virginia	Total	2.034	
	Wells Fargo Bank	0.663	32.596
	JP Morgan	0.540	26.549
	Citigroup	0.196	9.636
Wisconsin	Total	1.873	
	JP Morgan	0.429	22.904
	Robert W. Baird	0.364	19.434
	Citigroup	0.315	16.818
Michigan	Total	1.750	
	Banc of America Merrill	0.378	21.600
	JP Morgan	0.311	17.771
	Stifel Nicholaus	0.266	15.200

State/Territory	Underwriter	Amount ($Billions)	% Underwritten Within State
Oregon	Total	1.736	
	Citigroup	0.460	26.498
	Morgan Stanley	0.321	18.491
	Banc of America Merrill	0.241	13.882
Ohio	Total	1.643	
	Barclays	0.411	25.015
	Siebert Brandford	0.196	11.929
	RBC Capital	0.167	10.164
Maryland	Total	1.623	
	Banc of America Merrill	0.708	43.623
	Citigroup	0.289	17.807
	Siebert Brandford	0.191	11.768
Puerto Rico	Total	1.540	
	Banc of America Merrill	0.650	42.208
	Morgan Stanley	0.442	28.701
	Barclays	0.357	23.182
Arizona	Total	1.535	
	RBC Capital	0.570	37.134
	Stone & Youngberg	0.273	17.785
	Citigroup	0.204	13.290
Minnesota	Total	1.403	
	Barclays	0.335	23.877
	Piper Jaffray	0.215	15.324
	Wells Fargo Bank	0.146	10.406
Missouri	Total	1.376	
	JP Morgan	0.274	19.913
	Oppenheimer	0.221	16.061
	George K. Baum	0.178	12.936
North Carolina	Total	1.372	
	Wells Fargo Bank	0.537	39.140
	Banc of America Merrill	0.190	13.848
	Citigroup	0.180	13.120
Kentucky	Total	1.261	
	JP Morgan	0.408	32.355
	Morgan Keegan	0.211	16.733
	Robert W. Baird	0.123	9.754
South Carolina	Total	1.130	
	JP Morgan	0.510	45.133
	Wells Fargo Bank	0.150	13.274
	Banc of America Merrill	0.110	9.735
Colorado	Total	1.129	
	Goldman Sachs	0.396	35.075
	Citigroup	0.350	31.001
	RBC Capital	0.183	16.209
Indiana	Total	1.060	
	City Securities	0.415	39.151
	JP Morgan	0.122	11.509
	Fifth Third	0.073	6.887
Connecticut	Total	1.028	
	MR Beal	0.252	24.514
	Samuel A Ramirez	0.183	17.802
	RBC Capital	0.100	9.728

This is LT Fixed Rate. Does not include variable rate issuance.
Table shows how the regional nature of muni bonds allows both small and large firms to dominate in certain states

(continued)

State/Territory	Underwriter	Amount ($Billions)	% Underwritten Within State
Iowa	Total	0.978	
	Hutchinson Shockey	0.192	19.632
	Morgan Keegan	0.108	11.043
	Robert W. Baird	0.101	10.327
Tennessee	Total	0.926	
	Morgan Keegan	0.281	30.346
	Banc of America Merrill	0.186	20.086
	JP Morgan	0.160	17.279
Alabama	Total	0.901	
	Merchant Capital	0.278	30.855
	Morgan Keegan	0.199	22.087
	Frazer Lanier	0.123	13.651
Oklahoma	Total	0.875	
	Bosc	0.198	22.629
	Banc of America Merrill	0.143	16.343
	Robert W. Baird	0.102	11.657
Louisiana	Total	0.745	
	Barclays	0.300	40.268
	Morgan Keegan	0.174	23.356
	Citigroup	0.150	20.134
Nebraska	Total	0.699	
	Ameritas	0.309	44.206
	Goldman Sachs	0.143	20.458
	DA Davidson	0.098	14.020
Kansas	Total	0.660	
	George K. Baum	0.096	14.545
	BMO	0.090	13.636
	Robert W. Baird	0.067	10.152
Arkansas	Total	0.657	
	Crews	0.231	35.160
	Prager Sealy	0.136	20.700
	Morgan Keegan	0.130	19.787
Utah	Total	0.629	
	George K. Baum	0.198	31.479
	JP Morgan	0.104	16.534
	Piper Jaffray	0.060	9.539
District of Columbia	Total	0.485	
	Banc of America Merrill	0.290	59.794
	Barclays	0.083	17.113
	PNC	0.045	9.278
Maine	Total	0.483	
	Wells Fargo Bank	0.211	43.685
	JP Morgan	0.069	14.286
	BMO	0.040	8.282
New Mexico	Total	0.460	
	JP Morgan	0.190	41.304
	Robert W. Baird	0.100	21.739
	George K. Baum	0.030	6.522
Alaska	Total	0.326	
	Goldman Sachs	0.105	32.209
	Wells Fargo Bank	0.072	22.086
	Banc of America Merrill	0.062	19.018

State/Territory	Underwriter	Amount ($Billions)	% Underwritten Within State
Mississippi	Total	0.301	
	Morgan Keegan	0.119	39.535
	Duncan-Williams Inc	0.098	32.558
	Crews	0.044	14.618
New Hampshire	Total	0.208	
	Piper Jaffray	0.088	42.308
	George K. Baum	0.050	24.038
	Banc of America Merrill	0.036	17.308
North Dakota	Total	0.200	
	Cain Brothers	0.133	66.500
	UBS Financial	0.025	12.500
	Dougherty	0.024	12.000
Nevada	Total	0.190	
	JP Morgan	0.117	61.579
	Citigroup	0.069	36.316
	Robert W. Baird	0.004	2.105
Rhode Island	Total	0.182	
	Cain Brothers	0.042	23.077
	Barclays	0.040	21.978
	Wells Fargo Bank	0.035	19.231
West Virginia	Total	0.152	
	Raymond James	0.052	34.211
	JP Morgan	0.040	26.316
	Wells Fargo Bank	0.037	24.342
Guam	Total	0.091	
	Samuel A Ramirez	0.091	100.000
Wyoming	Total	0.077	
	George K. Baum	0.053	68.831
	RBC Capital	0.020	25.974
	Zions Bank	0.004	5.195
Montana	Total	0.076	
	Wells Fargo Bank	0.042	55.263
	RBC Capital	0.016	21.053
	DA Davidson	0.014	18.421
South Dakota	Total	0.071	
	Dougherty	0.035	49.296
	DA Davidson	0.016	22.535
	RBC Capital	0.011	15.493
Hawaii	Total	0.070	
	Piper Jaffray	0.066	94.286
	Wedbush	0.004	5.714
Idaho	Total	0.064	
	Morgan Keegan	0.032	50.000
	Seattle-Northwest	0.023	35.938
	Stone & Youngberg	0.004	6.250
Delaware	Total	0.040	
	Raymond James	0.016	40.000
	Morgan Keegan	0.013	32.500
	PNC	0.008	20.000
Vermont	Total	0.020	
	RBC Capital	0.011	55.000
	Citigroup	0.009	45.000

Exhibit 12.4

Issuer Disclosure Counsel

Issuer disclosure counsel advise issuers regarding disclosure issues and assist the issuers in the preparation of official statements. Some issuers do not employ this counsel, and may instead rely upon underwriters and underwriter counsel to prepare the issuers' disclosures. That practice is declining, however, as issuers are finding their disclosure responsibilities becoming greater over time in the face of both private litigation and SEC enforcement actions with increasing penalties for both issuers and issuer officials.

Issuer Local Counsel

Generally, issuer local counsel fill a relatively minor role in municipal securities offerings. These counsel may be city or county attorneys, general counsel to agencies or authorities, or attorneys in private local firms. Among other things, issuer local counsel usually provide legal opinions regarding appropriate conduct of meetings by issuer governing bodies, due adoption or approval of resolutions or ordinances, and other matters relating directly to the issuers.

Underwriter Counsel

Underwriter counsel advise the underwriters in connection with the securities issues. Usually, underwriter counsel advise underwriters as to securities purchase agreements and assist underwriters in the conduct of due diligence investigations.

In some offerings, underwriter counsel may prepare the issuers' or borrowers' official statements. That occurs even though underwriter counsel represent parties adverse to the issuers and borrowers—the underwriters—and even though underwriter counsel do not have contracts with or represent the issuers or borrowers.

Trustees and Paying Agents

Trustees are appointed in many municipal securities transactions, except that trustees are not present in many general obligation securities issues or note issues. The roles of trustees are bifurcated in the sense that, prior to defaults, trustees generally have administrative roles that are carefully defined in specific terms in the securities documents. After defaults, trustees generally have broader responsibilities to investors defined by reference to prudent person standards.

Paying agents serve in certain municipal securities transactions in which the full range of trustee services is not believed to be needed. This may occur in general obligation securities and note transactions. The paying agents serve to distribute payments to investors.

Unlike trustees, paying agents do not enforce securities documentation on behalf of investors. Particularly when there is no trustee, you should consider what enforcement powers you will have as an investor and whether it will be practicable for you and other investors to engage in such activities in court.

Auditors

Auditors provide audit reports regarding issuers' or borrowers' financial statements used in offerings.

> **KEY POINT:**
> Prior to defaults, trustees generally have administrative roles that are carefully defined in specific terms in the securities documents. After defaults, trustees generally have broader responsibilities to investors defined by reference to prudent person standards.

> **KEY POINT:**
> Unlike trustees, paying agents do not enforce securities documentation on behalf of investors.

Sometimes (but not always), especially when audited financial statements may be older or in transactions involving private parties, auditors may be asked to take additional steps or to provide additional information in the due diligence process.

An example of an additional due diligence step is when an issuer, borrower, financial advisor, or underwriter asks an auditor to conduct a subsequent events review regarding the issuer's or borrower's financial information for the period following the most recent audited period. Subsequent events reviews are not as thorough as audits. As a very helpful due diligence step, however, especially when audited financial information may be stale, the reviews involve certain investigation and question asking by auditors about recent issuer or borrower financial developments.

If you do not see an auditor's consent to be named as an expert or to the inclusion of its financial report in an official statement or other disclosure document, it is highly unlikely that the auditors have conducted a subsequent events review.

Regarding auditors, see also Chapter 10, "Understanding Expert Work Products."

Other Experts

Other experts may be asked to provide financial feasibility studies or projections or may conduct appraisals of property associated with a municipal issue. These are discussed further in Chapter 10, "Understanding Expert Work Products."

Developers and Other Private Parties

In addition to direct private borrowers, developers, and other private parties may also be involved in municipal securities offerings in various ways. Some of these are discussed further in Chapter 4, "General Fund and Other Municipal Securities," in the section entitled "Private Involvement," and in "Chapter 6, "Greater Rewards and Greater Risks."

What Are Basic Provisions in Securities Structures?

The following is a brief outline of certain basic information on municipal securities structures.

What Are Serial Securities?

The use of serial structures in municipal securities issues permits you to purchase securities with maturities that you desire at interest rates appropriate for those maturities. This facilitates the buy-and-hold strategy of many municipal securities investors who plan to hold the securities to maturity. The serial securities also permit issuers and borrowers to take advantage of the yield curve and to issue shorter-term securities at lower interest rates or yields.

What Are Term Securities?

Long-term municipal securities structures generally contain term maturities following serial maturities. These securities generally are payable at their principal (par) amounts over periods of 5, 10, or sometimes 15 years, with periodic, usually annual, mandatory redemptions of stated principal amounts. For example, a term security maturing in 2031 may be payable annually in 2022 through 2030 in stated amounts before the final maturity in 2031.

Exhibit 12.5 illustrates a hypothetical $100 million municipal securities issue rated triple-A with 10 years of serial bonds, a 20-year term bond, and a 30-year term bond. The table was calculated using Bloomberg interest rate data for triple-A rated municipal securities (BVAL) from "Bloomberg Brief: Municipal Market" for March 11, 2011.

What Is the Coupon of My Securities?

The stated interest rate or coupon of your securities is simply the interest rate borne by the securities pursuant to their terms. It is an annual percentage applied to the principal amount of the securities.

Historically, municipal bonds were issued in printed form with literal coupons attached for each interest payment. Investors would *clip* their *coupons* when the respective payments were due and would submit them to the trustees for payment, commonly through the banking system.

Today, in the age of electronics, such paper work has been eliminated. Payments are channeled through the Depository Trust Company. Municipal securities no longer are in printed form, but the word "coupon" has survived. See the section entitled "What Is DTC?" following.

What Are Optional Redemption Provisions, and Why Do They Matter?

In addition to the mandatory redemption of term securities described above, most long-term municipal securities issues are subject to early redemption at the option of the issuer or borrower at a price stated as a percentage of the principal (par) amount redeemed, plus interest accrued to the redemption date. Because this is the issuer's or borrower's option, you have no say about it.

The most common first available early redemption date is 10 years after issuance. Sometimes, redemption prices begin at one level and decline to 100% from year to year, such as 102% after 10 years, 101% after 11 years, and 100% after 12 years. At other times, only one optional redemption price—100% of the principal redeemed—is used. See Chapter 7, "Considerations When Buying," in the section entitled "What Are Some of the Factors I Should Consider?"

Pursuant to rules of the Municipal Securities Rulemaking Board, yields on municipal securities are calculated to the lower of the first redemption (call) date or the maturity date.

When you receive the redemption price (principal, premium, if any, and interest), if you are not planning to spend the money, you will have to invest it at then-prevailing interest rates. Generally, those will be lower than the interest rates you had been receiving on the redeemed securities. That is probably why the issuer or borrower will have made a decision to refinance

STEP-BY-STEP

The following is a simplified example of optional redemption provisions:

The Bonds with Maturity Dates on or after December 31, 2021, are subject to optional prepayment by the City prior to their respective Maturity Dates, upon notice as provided in the Trust Indenture, as a whole or in part by lot within each Maturity Date (or in the case of Term Bonds, the same mandatory redemption date) in integral multiples of $5,000 of principal components pro rata on any date on or after December 31, 2020, from any source of available funds. The optional redemption price is the principal amount of the Bonds redeemed plus accrued interest to the date fixed for Redemption.

KEY POINT:

In addition to the mandatory redemption of term securities, most long-term municipal securities issues are subject to early optional redemption. Because this is the issuer's or borrower's option, you have no say about it.

Pursuant to rules of the Municipal Securities Rulemaking Board, yields on municipal securities are calculated to the lower of the first redemption (call) date or the maturity date.

Example of Maturity Structure

Maturity	Serial Bonds		20-Year Term Bonds		30-Year Term Bonds		Annual Principal
	Principal	Yields	Principal	Yields	Principal	Yields	
7/1/2012	$2,025,000	0.410%					$1,990,000
7/1/2013	2,035,000	0.759%					2,005,000
7/1/2014	2,055,000	1.081%					2,025,000
7/1/2015	2,080,000	1.540%	Serial Bonds				2,050,000
7/1/2016	2,115,000	1.783%	(Annual				2,085,000
7/1/2017	2,160,000	2.065%	Maturities)				2,125,000
7/1/2018	2,205,000	2.350%					2,175,000
7/1/2019	2,260,000	2.575%					2,230,000
7/1/2020	2,325,000	2.803%					2,290,000
7/1/2021	2,390,000	2.980%					2,360,000
7/1/2022			$2,480,000	4.315%			2,455,000
7/1/2023			2,590,000	4.315%	Term Bonds		2,570,000
7/1/2024			2,705,000	4.315%			2,685,000
7/1/2025			2,825,000	4.315%	Mandatory		2,810,000
7/1/2026			2,950,000	4.315%	Redemptions		2,940,000
7/1/2027			3,075,000	4.315%	(Single Maturity		3,075,000
7/1/2028			3,215,000	4.315%	In 2031)		3,220,000
7/1/2029			3,355,000	4.315%			3,365,000
7/1/2030			3,505,000	4.315%			3,525,000
7/1/2031			**3,655,000**	**4.315%**	Final Maturity		3,685,000
7/1/2032					$3,830,000	4.810%	3,860,000
7/1/2033					4,015,000	4.810%	4,050,000
7/1/2034					4,215,000	4.810%	4,250,000
7/1/2035				Term Bonds	4,425,000	4.810%	4,455,000
7/1/2036				Mandatory	4,640,000	4.810%	4,675,000
7/1/2037				Redemptions	4,870,000	4.810%	4,905,000
7/1/2038				(Single Maturity	5,110,000	4.810%	5,145,000
7/1/2039				In 2041)	5,360,000	4.810%	5,395,000
7/1/2040					5,625,000	4.810%	5,660,000
7/1/2041				Final Maturity	**5,905,000**	**4.810%**	5,940,000
Totals	**$ 21,650,000**		**$ 30,355,000**		**$ 47,995,000**		**$100,000,000**

The arrow and bracket identify serial securities that, unlike term securities, mature in each year shown.

Exhibit 12.5

(refund)—to pay a lower interest rate after rates declined in the market.

As discussed in Chapter 7, "Considerations When Buying," if you paid a premium for the securities, you may lose money upon a redemption.

What Are Typical Denominations?

Municipal securities generally are issued in $5,000 denominations or multiples thereof.

Sometimes, municipal securities are issued in other denominations. A few may be issued in denominations of $1,000 or multiples thereof. Others may be issued in denominations of $100,000 and multiples thereof or multiples of $5,000 above $100,000. The larger denominations are used for riskier securities as a method of restricting investments in limited offerings.

What Are Debt Service Reserve Funds?

Most long-term municipal securities issues, other than general obligation securities, contain a debt service reserve fund. The reserves usually are in the amount of one year's debt service, and are intended to afford the issuer or borrower a period for working out unexpected problems that may emerge in connection with the securities. The reserves generally are funded from proceeds of sale of the securities.

If an issuer or borrower fails to pay the full amount of principal and interest due on a particular payment date, the reserve for the securities is to be applied by the securities trustee to make up the difference. The issuer or borrower then is obligated to replenish the reserve fund, as well as to continue paying principal of and interest on the securities in a timely manner.

In many, but not all, cases, when reserve fund draws do occur, the issuer or borrower is able to work out its financial issues.

A word of caution: Sometimes, instead of funding debt service reserve funds directly with invested cash borrowed in the securities offering, issuers may purchase security bonds issued by bond insurers or other private companies. That introduces a private risk that you may wish to consider. See the discussion in Chapter 7, "Considerations When Buying," in the section entitled "What Is the Significance to Me of the Bond Insurance Industry's Decline?"

What Is Capitalized Interest?

Capitalized interest is used by the issuer or borrower to pay interest due on the securities during a construction or start-up period for a project or program. That is because the new project or program may be unable to generate revenues to pay the interest until the project or program is functional.

What Are Coverage Requirements?

As described in Chapter 5, "Revenue Securities," the section and subsection entitled "Traditional Revenue Securities, Why Are Traditional Revenue Securities Extremely Safe?, What Are Rate Coverage Requirements?" coverage requirements are a common component of municipal securities payable from user fees. The requirements necessitate user fee increases as needed not only to pay principal of and interest on the municipal securities (usually after first paying operation and maintenance expenses), but also to provide an additional level of protection.

What Are Additional Bonds Tests?

Additional bonds tests are used in municipal securities issues to place restrictions on the issuance of additional securities payable from the same sources as the specific municipal issues. This is also discussed in Chapter 5, "Revenue Securities," the section and subsection entitled "Traditional Revenue Securities, Why Are Traditional Revenue Securities Extremely Safe?, What Restrictions Are Placed on Additional Securities?"

What Are Capital Appreciation Securities?

Capital appreciation securities (CABs) do not pay interest on a periodic, or current, basis. Rather, there is effective accumulation (accretion) of interest periodically until the maturity of the securities. Generally, CABs are not subject to optional redemption.

Other forms of municipal securities that are substantially similar to CABs may be called zero coupon or accretion securities.

If you purchase CABs, you will pay a low price initially, and at maturity, you will receive both the principal and all of the accumulated (accreted) interest. CABs allow you both to avoid the reinvestment of the periodic interest payments and to receive a larger amount at a targeted date.

Investment in CABs can be useful when you are saving for children's education, for retirement, or for other purposes when you wish to receive a large future lump sum payment.

In general, the tax treatment of CABs can be complex, although the goal is for you to receive the interest at maturity on a tax-exempt basis. Premiums and discounts are calculated in relation to the accreted amounts of the CABs. If you are considering CABs, you should review carefully bond counsel's tax opinion regarding the tax treatment of CABs and may wish to consult with your own tax advisor.

What Types of Defaults May Occur?

There are different types of defaults that may occur under municipal securities documentation. Some are of more immediate concern than others.

Payment Defaults

Payment defaults on securities are, of course, especially serious. These payment defaults are not considered in the market to be technical defaults, which are discussed later.

Securities trustees may be required to declare an *event of default* within a short time after payment failures occur. In turn, such a declaration initiates remedial action.

Technical Defaults

When securities structures have debt service reserve funds, those funds may be used at first to make payments directly to investors. That avoids an immediate payment default on the securities, but the occurrence does weaken the securities' structure by reducing the remaining reserves. Some municipal market participants attempt to downplay the significance of draws on reserves funds, calling them technical defaults.

The issuer or borrower is required to replenish the reserves in almost all securities issues, but that will not occur if the issuer or borrower continues to fail to make required payments. In unlimited tax general obligation issues (which typically do not have reserve funds) or generally in traditional revenue issues, issuers are required to raise taxes or user fees in order to remedy payment defaults and to ensure that future payments are made as required. That is why those securities are so sound and strong—a requirement that many pundits and media have ignored.

If, on the other hand, an issuer or borrower continues to fail to make required payments in full, reserve funds will be depleted eventually. Generally, trustees will delay remedial action so long as reserves are not fully depleted.

Since, however, those draws are monetary in nature and are the result of issuers' or borrowers' failures to pay in full amounts due, and since they reduce the reserves, you may wish to take them into account. Unscheduled reserve fund draws, while often called technical defaults, are indicative of the potential for serious financial problems.

Other defaults are, in fact, more technical in nature. They may include, for example, failures to provide documents or certificates to securities trustees. They may involve relatively minor, isolated failures to honor covenants, such as a failure to deliver a required certification that may be remedied easily. Some of those failures, however, may indicate more serious cause for concern, such as failures to honor financial covenants, and it can be especially important when failures to honor those covenants occur repeatedly.

Failures to make timely payments of principal or interest to investors are not technical defaults.

What Is Duration?

Duration is a concept used by professional investors in debt securities. The duration of a debt security is a measure that varies, in general, with maturity or redemption features, but is more complex.

Without becoming overly technical, the volatility of fixed-rate municipal securities prices and their sensitivity to changes in yields prevailing in the market may differ substantially depending upon the securities' durations. In general, the greater a security's duration, the more its price will respond to changes in prevailing market yields.

What Is Fund Accounting?

State and local governments serve many purposes and have many functions. They do not pool all of their monies in a single fund. Rather, they maintain a variety of funds or accounts that are restricted to particular uses. For example, some funds may be used solely for trust purposes, such as administration of grants for libraries in the case of a city or county or of state aid for specific educational programs, such as bilingual education, in the case of a school district.

Municipal securities commonly, although not entirely, are paid from specific funds.

In issuing municipal securities, governments commonly agree to make payments of principal and interest only from designated funds, taxes, or other sources.

For example, a local government would not agree to pay a general obligation bond or general fund securities from water or wastewater system user fees. It would apply the user fees only within the structure of the water or wastewater system enterprise fund. The general obligation securities would be paid from obligated taxes. The government would pay general fund securities from the general fund.

Similarly, unless it agrees to do so (which may occur in "double-barreled" securities issues, discussed in Chapter 3, "General Obligation Securities," in the section entitled "What Are Double-Barreled Securities?"), a local government would not be obligated to pay principal or interest on water or wastewater revenue securities from its general fund or from taxes. (Sometimes, however, to avoid default and preserve their reputations in the market, local governments voluntarily will make such payments, even though not obligated to do so.)

Given the fund accounting aspect of governmental accounting, it is especially important for you to identify and understand the specific source of taxes or revenues that provide the security for municipal securities in which you are interested.

The screen in Exhibit 12.6 from the Bloomberg Terminal provides information regarding the general funds of the State of Tennessee and certain local governments in Tennessee.

What Are Refundings?

In a simplified view, refundings in the municipal securities market are simply refinancings, as you might refinance a home mortgage. Of course, the documentation and tax law application are far more complex.

Most municipal securities refundings are for the purpose of reducing the issuers' or borrowers' interest costs, although the savings at times are modest. A few refundings are for the purpose of restructuring an issuer's or borrower's contractual obligations.

Credit analysis of refunding securities is not usually different from analysis of municipal securities issued for a new project or program.

What Are Prefunded Securities?

When refundings of municipal securities occur, they are issued commonly, although not entirely, in advance of the first permissible optional redemption date for the refunded securities.

```
<HELP> for explanation.                                    EquityMIFA
Edit criteria to start a new search, 90<GO> to save criteria
 96) Output ▾  97) Actions ▾   98) Customize  ▾        Page 1/15  Muni Issuer Screening
Add/Edit Criteria                                                                  ≫
Sectors GO ▾ Types General      ▾ States Tennessee ▾ Issuers All    ▾ Fiscal Years All ▾
 Name                               Field <Select a searchable field> ▾ 9) Displayable Fields
   Selected Screening Criteria                                          Matches
 3) ◎ Fund Type = General and State = Tennessee                           192
```

	Name	Type	Current Fiscal Year	Tot GF Rev	Net Chg Fd Bal	Tot Assets	GF Tot Liab	Total Operating Expenses
21)	State of Tennessee	GEN	2010	17,974.79	120.30	3,564.23	1,697.24	16,862.86
22)	Metropolitan Governm	GEN	2010	751.52	-18.83	548.66	487.76	720.49
23)	City of Memphis TN	GEN	2010	547.98	-22.03	449.31	364.74	582.89
24)	County of Shelby TN	GEN	2010	358.64	2.99	382.31	304.16	346.39
25)	County of Hamilton TN	GEN	2010	206.43	3.85	214.69	126.77	153.61
26)	City of Chattanooga T	GEN	2010	191.62	-2.12	163.78	123.95	174.08
27)	City of Knoxville TN	GEN	2010	167.41	8.32	145.50	84.83	137.60
28)	County of Knox TN	GEN	2010	153.58	-1.48	169.13	117.33	149.54
29)	City of Murfreesboro	GEN	2010	88.90	1.30	86.88	46.98	53.71
30)	City of Johnson City T	GEN	2010	65.50	-1.25	53.59	34.25	50.25
31)	County of Williamson	GEN	2010	64.90	4.02	72.72	35.22	59.99
32)	County of Rutherford	GEN	2010	64.78	6.93	56.75	34.04	62.75
33)	City of Jackson TN	GEN	2010	61.14	6.61	57.03	31.28	57.45

```
 1) Table View (SMUN)  2) Map View (SMUN MAP)              Numbers are in Millions
Australia 61 2 9777 8600 Brazil 5511 3048 4500 Europe 44 20 7330 7500 Germany 49 69 9204 1210 Hong Kong 852 2977 6000
Japan 81 3 3201 8900    Singapore 65 6212 1000      U.S. 1 212 318 2000    Copyright 2011 Bloomberg Finance L.P.
                                            SN 268301 CDT  GMT-5:00 G515-401-2 10-Aug-2011 10:02:03
```

Exhibit 12.6
Reprinted with permission from Bloomberg. Copyright 2011 Bloomberg L.P. All rights reserved.

(continued)

also a useful concept in assessing the reinvestment risk associated with a given portfolio or the interest rate risk associated with matching particular interest-rate-sensitive assets and liabilities. (Municipal Securities Rulemaking Board (MSRB).Glossary of Municipal Securities Terms at www.msrb.org/msrb1/glossary/default.asp.)

KEY POINT:

State and local governments maintain a variety of funds or accounts that are restricted to particular uses.

Municipal securities commonly, although not entirely, are paid from such specific funds.

KEY POINT:

A local government would not agree to pay a general obligation bond from water system user fees.

Similarly, a local government would not be obligated to pay principal or interest on water or wastewater revenue securities from its general fund or from taxes.

Prerefunded securities are those municipal securities that have been refunded prior to the dates on which the securities are subject to redemption. In municipal market terminology, the securities have been advance refunded.

In that case, both municipal securities issues remain in the hands of investors for a time, with the earlier issue being secured by an escrow consisting of U.S. Treasury securities. The refunded securities then will be fully paid on the first permissible redemption date, but not until. The escrow is structured so the interest and principal on the U.S. Treasury securities is scheduled to be paid immediately prior to the time when the monies are needed to pay principal and interest on the prefunded securities.

The prefunded securities are considered to be particularly desirable, as they continue to pay tax-exempt interest at the original interest rates and have security in the form of the U.S. Treasuries in the escrow account.

What Are Pooled Financings, Why Are Pools Used, and What Are Risks?

Often, smaller municipal issuers, or issuers issuing smaller amounts of obligations, consider the costs of public securities issuance for underwriters, lawyers, and financial advisors to be unduly expensive on a proportional basis. Consequently, issuers may choose to participate in coordinated financings through state agencies or, sometimes, other funding agencies consisting of cooperating groups of local governments or specific local governments acting for others (often called joint powers

or interlocal agencies). Local governments acting for others serve as "conduits," as discussed in the later section entitled "What Are Conduit Financings?"

Pools come with a variety of structures. Some are not really pools at all, but rather are simply two or more local governments borrowing at the same time using a common marketing plan and disclosure document. In that case, your risks and review would focus appropriately upon the specific obligations you are considering.

More commonly, pools consist of obligations payable from multiple local obligations. In that context, there are two primary structural forms of pooling. One requires the entire pooled obligation to be paid by all of the pooled local obligations combined. Each obligation may have its own reserve fund. In that structure, you may receive full and timely payment only if all of the pooled obligations are paid in full and on time. Consequently, you may wish to review closely the disclosure information regarding each of the borrowers.

In another structure, there may be at least some degree of mutual credit support among the borrowers. For example, a common reserve fund may provide credit support for each local obligation. The common reserve fund's support would not be allocated proportionately among the borrowers, but would be available in full to support each of them, if needed. If there are no draws on the common reserve fund, or if monies remain in the reserve fund after the pooled obligations are paid in full, then at that time, the local obligors may receive a distribution of their appropriate proportionate share of the reserves. Despite the limited reserve fund support, you still may wish to review closely the disclosure information regarding each of the borrowers.

State agencies may provide their own credit support for pooled financings assisting groups of local governments within the states. In that event, you may wish to consider the state's credit in addition to the local borrower's credit. There also may be implicit, but not legally enforceable, state moral obligation support for pooled local obligations sold by a state agency. See Chapter 4, "General Fund and Other Municipal Securities," in the section entitled "What Are Moral Obligation Securities?"

What Are Conduit Financings?

In municipal market conduit financings, governmental issuers serve as conduits through which funds pass between investors and private or other governmental borrowers (Exhibit 12.7). Apart from state agencies (which may serve in such a role), often these local governments doing so, particularly in Western states, are called joint powers or interlocal agencies. The literal issuers generally do not have liability for repayment of the securities, except from funds payable by the ultimate borrowers. On occasion, however, a local issuer may support the borrower with the issuer's own credit, although the issuer continues to expect that it will be functioning as a conduit. The pure conduit settings are more common.

Most conduit issuers serve merely as facilitators to give the conduit borrowers access to the market and to the benefits of tax-exempt interest rates. The issuers, as opposed to the borrowers, generally are not substantive parties to the securities issues.

The actual issuers of the securities are acting generally as an accommodation for the borrowers. The borrowers may be other governmental entities or may be private parties. In the former case, there may be restrictions or state law idiosyncrasies that motivate the use of the conduit structure.

In the case of private borrowers, there are usually more pervasive reasons for the structure. One important goal usually is to give the private borrowers access, pursuant to federal tax law and regulations, to the tax-exemption of interest paid on the securities. Another important reason is that longer-term securities, up to 30 years, are tolerated in the public municipal securities market. Meanwhile, private borrowers may be restricted by banks or other private lenders to shorter-term maturities, such as 10 years or less, and therefore, may be required by the banks or lenders to pay higher annual debt service that impacts the borrowers' cash flows.

In a pure conduit setting, the funds invested by investors are used directly by the borrowers for the borrowers' projects or programs (although pending expenditure, the monies are likely to be in the custody of a trustee). When the borrowers make payment, the monies are paid directly to the investors (or for the investors, to the trustee). In a pure setting, the actual governmental issuers have no actual or implied liability to investors.

In pure conduit securities offerings, the borrowers are considered by the SEC to be primarily responsible for disclosure of information to investors. The literal issuers generally provide very little information about themselves, and generally accept no responsibility to review the borrowers' disclosures or the borrowers' compliance with securities documentation.

In that setting, the rating agencies rate the securities based upon the credits of the borrowers. When considering those conduit securities, you may wish to focus on information regarding the ultimate borrowers. Of course, if another layer of credit support is added to the borrower's credit, you may wish to consider also the additional credit.

What Is DTC?

From the perspective of issuers and borrowers, municipal securities are not owned any longer in a literal sense by the actual investors in those securities or even by the investors' brokers or dealers.

Instead, municipal securities are owed in electronic form by book-entry through the Depository Trust Company (DTC). DTC is a subsidiary of The Depository Trust and Clearing Corporation (DTCC) (www.dtcc.com/about/subs/dtc.php).

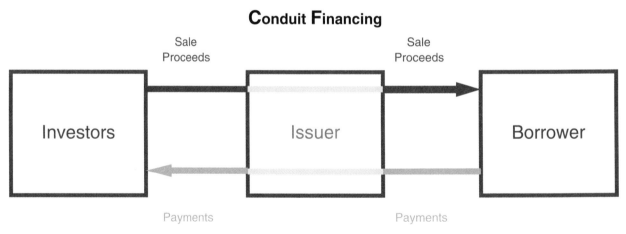

Conduit Financing

Exhibit 12.7

DTC maintains records of brokers and dealers (direct participants) that have accounts with DTC and of the securities and the principal amounts of securities owned by those firms. Those firms, including your own broker or dealer, then maintain their own records regarding your ownership and that of other customers who own municipal securities through the firms. Your broker or dealer likely is a direct or, through another firm, indirect participant in DTC.

DTC receives the payments from the trustees and paying agents for the securities and disburses the payments to the brokers and dealers (direct DTC participants), which then make distributions to you. If your broker or dealer is an indirect participant in DTC, the payments flow from DTC through another firm to your broker or dealer.

While this may seem complicated, it vastly reduces the paperwork involved and associated costs of and errors in the securities industry. The bottom line for you is a more efficient outcome.

What Considerations Relate to Investing in Mutual Funds and ETFs Versus Individual Securities Issues?

Sometimes, the execution costs of investing directly in smaller principal amounts of municipal securities have a negative impact on the yields you receive. This is discussed in Chapter 7, "Considerations When Buying," in the section entitled "How Does the Size of My Purchase Affect the Price?"

You also may wish to have the benefits of greater diversification and professional credit and structural analysis of your municipal securities investments, as well as professional price evaluation and negotiating power.

You have the option of investing either in individual securities issues or in municipal bond funds (or more recently, exchange-traded funds, or ETFs). These differing forms of investments may vary in terms of risks and performance.

Professional Management and Research

Municipal bond mutual funds provide professional management of portfolios based upon professional experience and research. If you wish to utilize this investment approach, then you need to conduct research on mutual funds, their portfolios, their investment practices, and the quality and records of their managers, as well as considering certain features of mutual funds.

Particularly for states with high income tax rates, the mutual fund industry provides state funds that invest in municipal securities issued only in those states and exempt from those respective states' income taxes.

Another consideration is the credit quality of the municipal securities in which a particular mutual fund invests. The securities in the fund's portfolio may be limited to only highly-rated securities. Other funds may invest in high yield municipal securities, with rewards and risks that are typical of those securities. Some funds use leverage through borrowing to increase yields, thus introducing associated risks.

Yet another variation is the duration of securities in a fund. Some may be money market funds investing solely in very short-term municipal securities, while others concentrate in medium- or long-duration securities portfolios. The volatility of the funds' share prices and their sensitivity to inflation risks (and to associated changes in yields prevailing in the market) may differ substantially depending upon the securities' durations. Duration is discussed briefly in the earlier section entitled "What Is Duration?"

Exchange-traded funds (ETFs), which (unlike mutual funds) are traded throughout the trading day, generally do not utilize active management or research, but may consist of relatively stable portfolios. Some municipal securities dealers also sponsor closed-end funds that invest in stable portfolios and introduce leverage rewards and risks through borrowing.

Management Fees

Mutual fund managers do not provide free services. They are paid management fees.

If you invest in mutual funds or exchange-traded funds, management fees (and other fees and costs) are important as they reduce the return on your investment in return for professional management. You may wish to consider the fees charged by funds in which you are interested in relation to the investment policies and the records of the funds and their managements.

Fund fees have been shown to be a key component in funds' level of success over time.

Character of Income

Interest earnings on municipal securities in mutual funds generally are tax-exempt. If you are subject to the alternative minimum tax, you may wish to be aware of any securities in the mutual fund's portfolio that may lead to tax liabilities for you. If you are a social security (or railroad retirement) recipient, you may wish to consult your tax advisor regarding your receipt of tax-exempt interest.

In addition, you may incur capital gains treatment of gains or losses if you sell mutual fund shares or, in some cases, if the fund incurs capital gains or losses upon sales or redemptions of securities in its portfolio. Portfolio sales may occur, for example, if the fund experiences rapid withdrawals that force securities sales in order to pay for share redemptions.

Risk of Mutual Fund Changes in Value

Mutual fund and exchange-traded fund shares rise or fall in value.

As noted, investors in municipal securities mutual funds may choose to withdraw their investments by redeeming their shares when they need liquidity, in response to market conditions, or for other reasons.

Risks associated with mutual funds include risks that the value of fund shares may decline if portfolio securities are sold in response to share redemptions, if the market values of portfolio securities decline in response to interest rate volatility in the market, or if there is a decline in credit strengths of issuers or borrowers (or credit enhancers) of portfolio securities. A fund's leverage (borrowing) may magnify the decline in values.

Although individual municipal securities held in portfolios also rise and fall in value in response to changes in market price levels, buy-and-hold investors often are largely indifferent to day-to-day changes in value because they do not intend to sell their municipal securities. Those investors may focus attention instead principally upon receipt of scheduled interest payments and receipt of principal on predetermined maturity dates.

Those aspects of a buy-and-hold strategy allow you to structure your portfolio for scheduled receipt of cash flows (often called a ladder). That does not protect you, however, any more than mutual fund investments against the negative impacts of inflation upon the cash flows that you receive. In addition, it does not protect you if you must sell securities for cash flow.

Fund Data and Analyses by Broker-Dealers

Many broker-dealers provide website information on municipal bond funds relating to past performance, management and other matters, including in some cases, ratings by private fund analytical services.

Private Mutual Fund and ETF Analytical Services

Private services analyze municipal bond funds (and other funds) in considerable detail and provide ratings of the funds' performance, managements, and other matters. Some of these are identified in the Appendix.

Additional Resources for You

This Appendix directs you to valuable additional resources to use in your consideration of municipal securities.

Every municipal security has its own unique factual setting. Each is different from others, sometimes in major ways and sometimes with only minor variations.

I do not intend to elaborate on all, or even most, of the relevant factors that you might consider for various municipal securities. Instead, when you are serious about making wise investments, the following information directs you to certain information resources that may assist you.

What Are Bloomberg Resources?

Bloomberg offers a number of informative data, news, and other information at its free website at www.Bloomberg.com/. The information also is available for Android-based mobile phones and on I-Phones.

Bloomberg Municipal News

Bloomberg offers free municipal securities market news, information, reports and opinions regarding market events at http://noir.bloomberg.com/news/ markets/muni_bonds.html/ and http://noir.bloomberg.com/markets/rates/munievents.html/.

Bloomberg Bond Data and BVAL

Bloomberg offers free up-to-date interest rate data at http://noir.bloomberg.com/markets/rates/index.html/. Bloomberg's data cover both U.S. Treasury securities and municipal securities.

Bloomberg also offers the Bloomberg Valuation AAA Benchmark Municipal Yields, known as BVAL—interest rate data for triple-A municipal securities—on the Bloomberg Terminal and in "Bloomberg Brief: Municipal Market" as described later. Regarding BVAL, see Chapter 7, "Considerations When Buying," in the section entitled "What Is the Relationship Between Interest Rates (Coupons) and Yields?"

Bloomberg Terminal

For more serious investors who wish to receive complete real-time market data and expansive information for a price, Bloomberg offers the Bloomberg Terminal, which is used by financial professionals across all market sectors.

The screen in Exhibit A1 from the Bloomberg Terminal illustrates graphic data analysis from annual information filed by the State of California on the Electronic

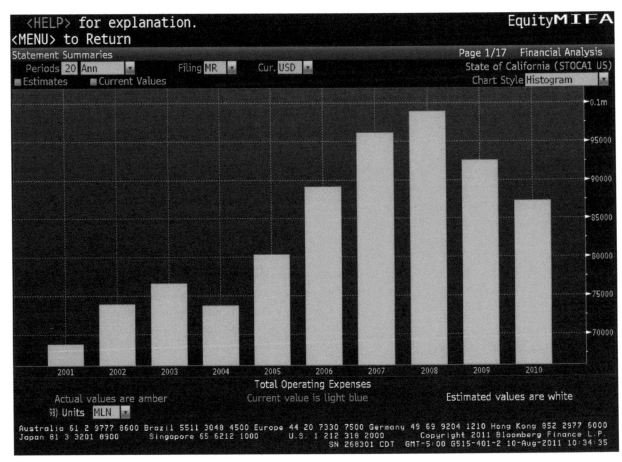

Exhibit A1

Municipal Market Access (EMMA) platform maintained by the Municipal Securities Rulemaking Board (MSRB). In this case, the graph presents California's "Total Operating Expenses" from 2001 through 2010.

Bloomberg Brief: Municipal Market

Bloomberg also publishes a daily news and opinion newsletter entitled "Bloomberg Brief: Municipal Market" to subscribers to the Bloomberg Terminal. You are able to receive the publication by contacting Bloomberg at bbrief@bloomberg.net/.

What Are Issuer/Borrower Information Sources?

The following resources also are discussed in Chapter 2, "Basic Information Resources."

Official Statements

Official statements are the prospectuses (disclosure documents) that municipal securities issuers and private borrowers prepare for investors as a part of the municipal securities issuance process.

You are able to obtain official statements on the MSRB's EMMA website at www.emma.msrb.org/.

Continuing Disclosure Statements

SEC Rule 15c2-12 prohibits underwriters from offering most municipal securities in public offerings unless the issuers or private borrowers agree to provide certain

annual financial and operating information. The agreements are contained in the official statements for the initial offerings of the securities.

In addition, the issuers or borrowers are to agree to provide disclosure of the occurrence of certain events identified by the SEC in Rule 15c2-12.

As discussed in Chapter 2, "Basic Information Resources," securities issued on or after December 1, 2010, are subject to greater continuing disclosure requirements in terms of subject matter and timing for filing reports of event occurrences.

As discussed later, you are able to obtain copies of issuer and borrower annual and event disclosures the on the MSRB's EMMA website at www.emma.msrb.org/.

Issuer/Borrower Websites

Many municipal securities issuers and private borrowers are proactive in terms of providing useful information for investors. Often, the information appears in investor pages on issuer or borrower websites.

What Resources Does the SEC Offer?

The Securities and Exchange Commission's website at www.sec.gov/ provides numerous resources for you.

A link to SEC Rule 15c2-12 can be found on the SEC's website on the page devoted to municipal securities matters, http://sec.gov/info/municipal.shtml/.

On the SEC's home page you can find links to proposed regulations, final regulations, speeches by Commissioners and staff, administrative enforcement actions and litigation releases.

What Resources Does the MSRB Offer?

The Municipal Securities Rulemaking Board (MSRB) maintains a website at www.msrb.org/ that contains significant information intended to assist investors.

MSRB's EMMA

The most outstanding of the tools provided by the MSRB to you as an investor is its EMMA website at http:// emma.msrb.org/. The information available on EMMA is discussed in greater detail in Chapter 2, "Basic Information Resources."

EMMA provides a wealth of information regarding municipal securities issues, issuers, and private borrowers, as well as market information.

Information can be searched on EMMA by using either CUSIP numbers, discussed under Chapter 7, "Considerations When Buying," in the section entitled "How Can I Use CUSIP Numbers?" or by using issuer names.

Disclosure Documents

Both official statements and continuing disclosure reports are available on EMMA for specific municipal securities issues. The information also includes, as a new feature, underwriter submissions of names of issuers or borrowers who agree to provide annual and event reports and the dates by which annual information is due to be filed.

The MSRB also accepts voluntary issuer and borrower submissions of disclosure information, including preliminary official statements, quarterly financial statements, budgets, changes in accounting standards, disclosures on related derivatives transactions, and other disclosures.

Incidentally, some of EMMA's files may be quite large. If you are not technologically savvy, and have difficulty downloading files to your computer, you might try a computer at your local library.

Pricing and Trading Data

EMMA offers you another significant resource in the form of real-time trading and pricing data on municipal securities, including data regarding specific securities. This information allows you to review market prices and trading histories for municipal securities you are considering.

See Chapter 8, "Municipal Securities Pricing and Trading."

Where Are the MSRB's Rules?

On the MSRB's website, you are able to view the MSRB's rules, and interpretations of the rules, governing the activities of municipal securities dealers and municipal advisors. Among the many rules of interest to investors are Rule G-17 (fair dealing), G-19 (suitability), G-30 (prices and commissions), and G-32 (delivery of official statements).

You are able to obtain the MSRB's rules, and interpretations of those rules, at www.msrb.org/Rules-and-Interpretations/MSRB-Rules.aspx/.

What Investor Resources Does the MSRB Offer?

The MSRB provides "Investor Resources" at http://msrb.org/Municipal-Bond-Market/Investor-Resources.aspx/.

The listed resources include information on researching and investing in municipal securities, market facts, and filing complaints.

What Is the MSRB's Glossary?

If you are curious regarding the meaning of technical terminology, you may wish to consult the MSRB's Glossary at http://msrb.org/msrb1/glossary/default.asp/.

What Resources Does FINRA Offer?

What Is FINRA BrokerCheck?

The Financial Industry Regulatory Authority (FINRA) offers on its website a BrokerCheck tool for you to check the regulatory records of, and other information regarding, individual and firm brokers and dealers with whom you conduct business.

FINRA's BrokerCheck tool appears at www.finra.org/Investors/ToolsCalculators/BrokerCheck/.

What Else Does FINRA Offer?

FINRA also offers information to educate and assist investors at www.finra.org/Investors/.

How Can I Check on My Investment Adviser?

One beneficial aspect of state regulation that may be helpful to you is your ability to check on the regulatory backgrounds of investment advisers. You are able to do this through the SEC's website at http://www.adviser-info.sec.gov/(S(yzx32dpneegy4mkttxjxdes4))/IAPD/Content/Search/iapd_Search.aspx/.

You are able to learn more about the role of state securities administrators at their respective websites and also at the website of the North American Securities Administrators Association (NASAA) at www.nasaa.org/.

Can I Get Information from Brokers, Dealers, and Advisors?

You may have established relationships with brokers, dealers, or financial advisors. Those firms or individuals may be additional important sources of information. Many firms offer research, as well.

Where Are NFMA's Best Practices in Disclosure?

Another especially valuable tool for evaluating securities from particular municipal market sectors is available from the National Federation of Municipal Analysts (NFMA).

NFMA's website (www.NFMA.org) provides various Best Practices and White Papers discussing factors that professional municipal securities analysts consider to be important regarding specific market sectors and subjects. These documents are accessible as "Disclosure Guidelines" in a drop down list under "Publications" on NFMA's home page/.

As of this writing, NFMA's Best Practices and White Papers are, as follows:

◼ White Paper on Expert Work Products

◼ White Paper on Disclosure for GASB 45

◼ White Paper on Federal Securities Law Relating to Municipal Securities

◼ White Paper on Project Finance Risk Assessment and Disclosure

◼ Recommended Best Practices in Disclosure for Water and Sewer Transactions

◼ Recommended Term Sheet and Legal Provisions for Hospital Debt Transactions

◼ Recommended Best Practices in Disclosure for Toll Road Financing

◼ Recommended Best Practices in Disclosure for Airport Debt

◼ Recommended Best Practices in Disclosure for the Public Power Sector

◼ White Paper on Disclosure for SWAP Transactions

◼ Recommended Best Practices in Disclosure for Tax Increment Supported Debt

◼ Recommended Best Practices in Disclosure for Variable Rate and Short-Term Securities

◼ Recommended Best Practices in Disclosure for Long-Term Care/Senior Living Debt

◼ Recommended Best Practices in General Obligation and Tax-Supported Debt

◼ Recommended Best Practices in Disclosure for Solid Waste Transactions

◼ Recommended Best Practices in Disclosure for Private College and University Transactions

◼ Recommended Best Practices in Disclosure for Hospital Debt Transactions

◼ Recommended Best Practices in Disclosure for Housing Revenue Bond Issues

◼ Recommended Best Practices in Disclosure for Land Secured Transactions

Where Are Rating Agency Criteria by Bond Market Sector?

Yet another means for you to gain insights into factors that may be significant in evaluating particular categories of municipal securities is to review detailed criteria applied by rating agencies. These public finance criteria are quite helpful in discussing considerations that professional municipal securities analysts view as important for differing categories of municipal securities.

In order to gain access to certain following information, you must register with S&P's, Moody's, and Fitch Ratings' websites. The registrations are free.

S&P

Standard and Poor's (S&P) publishes its criteria for various market sectors. The criteria are available at www.standardandpoors.com/ratings/govs-uspf/en/us. The website also contains S&P's definitions of its ratings.

Moody's

Certain information regarding Moody's rating methodologies can be accessed on Moody's website (www.moodys.com) at a drop down list titled "Research and Ratings." The website also contains Moody's definitions of its ratings.

Fitch

Fitch Ratings publishes public finance criteria at www.fitchratings.com/jsp/general/Research.faces?listingName=criteriaReport/. Choose the link for "U.S. Public Finance." The website also contains Fitch's definitions of its ratings.

How Can I Check Bond Ratings?

Ratings are useful as one tool in considering the credit quality of municipal securities. They are not, however, a substitute for the exercise of your independent judgment, and do not take into account many considerations that may be important to you. Rating agencies emphasize that ratings are not recommendations to buy, sell, or hold any security.

You are able to monitor rating changes for your securities at the MSRB's EMMA website at www.emma.msrb.org/. This is one type of event disclosure that issuers and borrowers are to make pursuant to their continuing disclosure agreements. As of this writing, the MSRB plans also to reflect on EMMA credit ratings provided by S&P and Fitch.

You also can obtain ratings from the rating agencies directly as discussed in the following sections.

S&P

For S&P's public finance ratings, use www.standardandpoors.com/ratings/en/us/. Select the drop down list at "Governments—Public Finance."

S&P also maintains a website at www.understandingratings.com/ that explains ratings and the rating process.

Moody's

Moody's website (www.moodys.com) contains a search box through which ratings can be identified for specific issuers or borrowers.

Fitch

Fitch Ratings' website (www.fitchratings.com) contains a search box through which ratings can be identified for specific issuers or borrowers. My search also directed me to certain rating reports on issuers.

The Bond Buyer

The Bond Buyer is a daily news source for the municipal securities market. It is available in both print and online editions. The online edition (www.bondbuyer.com) provides headlines and generally two free stories per day. For a subscription, the online edition provides additional news, opinion, and market data.

Municipal Market Data (MMD)

Municipal Market Data (MMD) is a service of Thomson Municipal Market Monitor. The service publishes and sells municipal securities interest rate data and other municipal market information. The website is located at www.tm3.com/homepage/homepage.jsf?ur=y/.

Municipal Market Advisors

Municipal market advisors (MMA) prepares and sells detailed in-depth market analyses and issues daily, weekly, and monthly reports containing those analyses, as well as interest rate and other market data. MMA's website is located at www.mma-research.com.

Among other things, MMA publishes "Consensus" municipal market interest rate data.

Delphis-Hanover

Delphis-Hanover Corporation sells online (www.delphishanover.com) tables of daily municipal market securities yields segmented by credit strength and maturity. It also provides certain market information. Some of Delphis-Hanover's data are published in the *Wall Street Journal*.

Fund Services

Private fund services sell extensive information, analytical services, and ratings regarding bond funds and exchange-traded funds. See, for example, www.morningstar.com and www.lipperweb.com.

Bloomberg Functionality Cheat Sheet

Municipals

Press <GO> after each command to run the function

* Denotes a single-security function
** Denotes a multiple-security function

News and Credit Ratings

N Main News page
FIRS Bloomberg First Word briefings
TOP Top BLOOMBERG NEWS® stories
TOP MUN Top Municipal Market News
NH BOB Bond Buyer News Stories
NH MRA Municipal Ratings Changes
STGO State G.O. bond ratings
IMRS Current insured financial strength ratings of municipal bond insurers
LOCR Letter of credit provider ratings

Current Markets

BTMM Treasury and money market rates

WB Monitor world bond markets
WBF World bond futures
WBX World bond spreads
WBMV Sovereign debt movers
ECO Economic releases by country
ECFC Economic forecasts/indicators
BYFC Bond yield forecasts
CG Yield curve
BVMB Municipal benchmark curve transparency
MMMR Municipal money market rates
MUNS Municipal spreads and ratios
MBIX Municipal indices menu
CMMA Municipal Market Advisors, Inc. page
MBIT Muni insurance exposure by state
MSRB MSRB transaction reports

Finding Securities

SRC Generate custom municipal bond searches
SECF Security find on Bloomberg

Public Offerings and Bids Wanted

BOOM Variable rate and municipal CP offerings

PICK Primary/secondary municipal bond offerings

MIOF Post municipal offerings

MCHG Edit your municipal offerings

MBWD (Sellside) Municipal bids wanted view and submit bids

MBWU (Buyside) Post municipal bids wanted

MBWB (Buyside) View bids received

Issuer Analysis

MIFA Municipal State issuer analysis

SMUN Municipal issuer screening tool

ALRT Alerts for pricing, ratings and financial filings

CACT Material events for an issuer or bond

*CUSD Find munis with the same base CUSIP

*SER List municipal bonds by series

Security Analysis

*DES Fundamental background and financial info

*ALLQ Comparative price sources

*BVAL Snapshot of Bloomberg valuation

*TDH Track MSRB trade disclosure history

*RCHG Track bond ratings changes

*SCN Specific municipal bonds news

*CACS Material events for a security or issuer

*CF Search issuer filings

*FA Issuer financial analysis

*YAS Bond prices based on yield curve spreads

*YTC Calculate yields to call

*SF Sinking fund analysis

*OAS1 Option-adjusted spread analysis

*HZ2 Analyze municipal total return horizons

*FTAX Federal taxation calculator

*QTAX Municipal prices used to calculate taxes

New Issues

CDRA Municipal fixed rate calendar

CDRC Municipal competitive calendar

CDRN Municipal negotiated calendar

CNDS Municipal short-term calendar

CNDM Current/historical 14 day short term visible supply

SPLY Current/historical 30 day visible supply

YTDM Current/historical year-to-date issuance

NIRM Compare municipal new issue yields

DEAL Add or access new municipal deals

Essentials

PDF Set personal defaults

EASY Learn ease-of-use tips and shortcuts

BU BLOOMBERG UNIVERSITY®

BLP Start BLOOMBERG LAUNCHPAD™

BBXL Bloomberg calculations in Microsoft® Excel

Communication Tools

MSGM Message related functions menu

IMGR Commingled messages from RUNS and MSG

RUNS Create and send custom run sheets

IB INSTANT BLOOMBERG® messaging

ANY Learn about BLOOMBERG ANYWHERE®

About the Author

Robert Doty is president and owner of AGFS, a private consulting company in Sacramento, California. Mr. Doty served in the municipal securities market for more than three decades as a financial advisor to issuers, bond counsel and investment banker, and in other capacities.

Mr. Doty, a Harvard Law School graduate, has been active since the mid-1970s in advocating improvements in disclosure to municipal securities investors. As early as the mid-1970s, he was an author and co-author of several seminal publications in that field. He has testified in favor of municipal investors, as well as issuers and others.

Mr. Doty served as general counsel to the Government Finance Officers Association (GFOA) and, for almost two decades, as a member of GFOA's Disclosure Task Force; as a member of the Board of Governors, and Chair of a disclosure committee, of the National Federation of Municipal Analysts (NFMA); as chair of the Section on Economic Development, Taxation, and Finance of the International Municipal Lawyers Association (IMLA); as chair of the Southern Municipal Finance Society; as vice president and member of the Board of Directors of the National Association of Independent Public Finance Advisors; and as an officer of committees and subcommittees of the National Association of Bond Lawyers and of the American Bar Association's Section of State and Local Government Law and Section of Business Law. Mr. Doty is a recipient of the NFMA's Municipal Industry Contribution Award and of IMLA's Outstanding Associate Member Award.

Mr. Doty has participated in principal drafting roles for several national and regional municipal disclosure, securities law guidance and related publications, including the GFOA's *Disclosure Guidelines for State and Local Government Securities* and several related market disclosure guidance publications; the first edition of NABL's/ABA's *Disclosure Roles of Counsel in State and Local Government Securities Offerings*; the exposure draft of IMLA's "Financing Procedures Checklists"; the NFMA's "White Paper on Expert Work Products"; and the California Debt and Investment Advisory Commission's "Guidelines for Leases and Certificates of Participation."

Mr. Doty is the author or co-author of half a dozen books and over 80 articles on finance. He served as a member of a U.S. delegation on municipal finance to the People's Republic of China sponsored by the Smithsonian Institution's Woodrow Wilson International Center for Scholars and by the National Committee on United States-China Relations. Mr. Doty has served as consultant to and as expert witness for legal counsel in connection with certain municipal securities litigation.

Mr. Doty's website is located at www.agfs.com/.

INDEX